SON OF HEAVEN

IMPERIAL ARTS OF CHINA

SON OF HEAVEN

IMPERIAL ARTS OF CHINA

Robert L. Thorp

Introductory Essay by Yang Xiaoneng

Organized by the **Chinese Overseas Archaeological Exhibition Corporation**

Beijing

Published by **Son of Heaven Press**

Text copyright © 1988 by Robert L. Thorp
Translation of Chinese texts by Robert L. Thorp

Curatorial research by Yang Xiaoneng, Xu Bingkun
and Chen Lie

Library of Congress Catalog Card number:
88-070439

ISBN 0-929209-00-1
ISBN 0-929209-01-X (pbk.)

Art Direction and Graphic Design by
Douglas Wadden
Production Assistant: Brian Boram

Edited by Lynn Caddey Schweber and
Mitsu A. Sundvall

Photography by Don Hamilton

Typography by Thomas and Kennedy, Seattle

Printed and bound by Nissha Printing Co. Ltd.
in Kyoto, Japan

The official publication of the exhibition
Son of Heaven: Imperial Arts of China

Seattle
July-December, 1988

Columbus, Ohio
March-August, 1989

The cover and jacket are a detail of the Emperor's
Outer Robe, No. 13 (see p. 76)

The first page of the book shows the Chinese char-
acters 天 (tian), "heaven," and 子 (zi), "son."
Detail of the "The Stone Terrace Classic of Filial
Piety, No. 49 (see p. 110).

The frontispiece and front matter details are from
"The Emperor's Honor Guard in Procession," No. 25
(see p. 88).

Foreword

中國古代艺术展览是

中美两国文化交流長藤

上结出的新的花果。

谨祝这个展览获得

巨大成功!

　　　　张德勤

　　　　八八年

　　　　六月十日

为进一步展出所做的努力!

为進一步展出所做的努力!

了解和友谊，萬感谢美国友人

出，希望中美两国人民增进相互

祝贺中国古代艺术展览在美展

We hope that "Son of Heaven: Imperial Arts of China" will promote greater understanding and friendship between the people of China and America. We are deeply grateful to our American friends for the extraordinary efforts they have made on behalf of this exhibition.

Wang Meng
Minister
Ministry of Culture

This exhibition—"Son of Heaven: Imperial Arts of China"—opens a new chapter in cultural exchange between China and America. We hope that "Son of Heaven: Imperial Arts of China" achieves great success.

Zhang Deqin
Director
State Administrative Bureau of Museums and Archaeological Data

Preface

On behalf of the Son of Heaven National Committee, and in cooperation with the Chinese State Administrative Bureau of Museums and Archaeological Data, it is an honor to share with you the story of China's emperors and their feudal predecessors, and of the China they ruled from the 7th century B.C. until the last emperor of 1911.

This catalogue documents an exhibition organized by a dedicated group of Chinese and Americans. "Son of Heaven: Imperial Arts of China" represents 26 centuries of China's past, during which China's artists produced treasures of unequaled beauty and drama. The very finest of these were reserved for China's feudal rulers, the "Sons of Heaven." Due to the considerable efforts in China of museum directors, curators, conservators, art historians and archaeologists, over 200 of the most significant of these treasures have been gathered from eight provinces and Beijing to represent China's imperial institution. You now have an opportunity, through these ancient art objects, to gain a true glimpse into the life of the "Son of Heaven"; how he ruled, lived, worshiped and prepared for his afterlife.

Each object in this exhibition was selected for its historical significance and for the creative genius that has characterized China's artists for millennia. The discovery and preservation of these objects is the result of the extensive archaeological efforts currently underway in China and of China's long tradition of caring for cultural relics.

The years of planning for "Son of Heaven" have required the collective efforts and support of hundreds of individuals and numerous organizations in China and America. It is a great pleasure to acknowledge the following organizations and senior leaders for the major contributions each has made to the exhibition: The Honorable Han Xu, Ambassador Extraordinary and Plenipotentiary of the People's Republic of China to the United States of America; The Honorable Wang Meng, Minister of the Ministry of Culture; Mr. Zhang Deqin, Director and Mr. Lu Jimin, former Director of the State Administrative Bureau of Museums and Archaeological Data; Mr. Xie Chensheng, Senior Advisor, State Administrative Bureau of Museums and Archaeological Data; Mr. Zhang Yong, Manager of the Chinese Overseas Archaeological Exhibition Corporation; Mr. Rich Walsh, President and Executive Director of the Resource Center for the Handicapped

and member of the Son of Heaven National Committee; Mr. Lawrence Childs, President of the Son of Heaven National Committee; Messrs. Graham Dorland, Bruno Strauss, Robert Skare, Robert Brorby, Albert Howell, and Robert Cummings, members of the Son of Heaven National Committee; Mr. Harvey West, Executive Director of the "Son of Heaven" Exhibition; Mr. David Baker, Director of the Ohio State Department of Development; Mr. Jay Wright, Special Consultant to the Ohio State Department of Development; and Mr. Raymond Hanley, Executive Director of the Son of Heaven Ohio Exhibition Committee.

"Son of Heaven" brings China's imperial past to life. In this respect, our purpose is to help the exhibition visitor and you, the reader, better understand China's present-day society. "Son of Heaven" also represents the future. By working together to create the exhibition and related programs a unique bond of friendship, trust and understanding has developed between the Chinese and American "Son of Heaven" organizers. Through this bond, the foundation has been laid for continuing cultural exchanges between China and America.

Elling Halvorson
Chairman
Son of Heaven National Committee

Acknowledgements

In early 1985, in a meeting at the Forbidden City, representatives of the Chinese Overseas Archaeological Exhibition Corporation (COAEC) and the Son of Heaven National Committee agreed to work together to create an extraordinary Chinese art exhibition expressly for America. Our commitment then, as now, was based on mutual respect, friendship and professional enthusiasm for the potential good that would be generated by such a project. The result, after three and one-half years of planning and work by both organizations, is "Son of Heaven: Imperial Arts of China."

The Chinese Overseas Archaeological Exhibition Corporation (COAEC) is the central government agency responsible for organizing all international Chinese art exhibitions in association with foreign organizations throughout the world. Prior to "Son of Heaven," COAEC organized three exhibitions which came to America: "The Chinese Exhibition" (1974-1975), "The Great Bronze Age of China" (1980-1981), and "The Quest for Eternity" (1987-1988).

The Son of Heaven National Committee has administered the organization of "Son of Heaven" in America, with the ultimate goal of expanding cultural understanding and friendship between the people of China and America. The American art professionals, led by Harvey West, have managed the American curatorial duties, exhibition display, art care services, visitor education programs, publishing and administration for the American tour of "Son of Heaven," on behalf of COAEC and the Son of Heaven National Committee. These art management efforts were complemented by extensive governmental support in China and America and corporate support in America.

In developing the "Son of Heaven" program, our first objective was to create an art exhibition befitting the grandeur and scale of the art produced for China's imperial institution, complemented by a comparable exhibition catalogue to serve as a permanent record of the event. For both we turned to Mr. Yang Xiaoneng and Dr. Robert Thorp. The "Son of Heaven" host organizing committees in each state agreed to educate and serve the exhibition visitor on a scale and with imagination not seen before in their respective regions. The hosting encompassed a comprehensive visitor education program, which included a dramatic installation, audio tour and orientation theaters. All aspects of the program were conceived to inform and fascinate a wide range of interests and ages.

To accomplish all of this, many talented and dedicated people in both countries have contributed to "Son of Heaven" in significant ways. Unfortunately, space does not permit each to be acknowledged individually. We would, however, like to recognize certain special members of the international "Son of Heaven" team who have contributed to the success of the exhibition and the catalogue in a major way during the pre-exhibition planning. We extend our gratitude to Mr. Rich Walsh, Mr. Elling Halvorson, Mr. Robert Cummings, Mr. Lawrence Childs, Mr. Graham Dorland, Mr. David Baker, Mr. Jay Wright, and Mr. Raymond Hanley.

One very special person became the bridge between China and America—Ms. Xiaobo Yao, Director of China Affairs for the Son of Heaven National Committee. She had the challenging task of understanding both our cultures and communicating for a common purpose. The result of her specialized effort is best represented by the friendship and understanding underlying the "Son of Heaven" project.

Harvey West

Harvey West
Executive Director
Son of Heaven: Imperial Arts of China Exhibition

護軍校 護軍參領 護軍九

侍衛一百六十員

親軍五

護軍校 護軍參領 護軍九

Acknowledgements

"Son of Heaven" is the result of a long period of close cooperation between Chinese and American scholars. Organized around the theme of the imperial institution and the arts, this exhibition has been created largely from the archaeological discoveries and research that have taken place in China since 1949. In selecting exhibits for "Son of Heaven," we were concerned both with their connections to the theme and their intrinsic merit. Largely untouched by modern scholars, a comprehensive study of all aspects of the imperial arts of China will require many decades of further cooperative scholarship. We hope this exhibition will introduce the American people to the beauty of China's imperial art, and at the same time encourage more study of this important theme.

In late 1985 and early 1986, Mr. Yang Xiaoneng and I respectively began our curatorial duties and have worked as close associates in all aspects of the planning for "Son of Heaven." In particular, during the object negotiations in spring 1986, Mr. Yang consistently improved the list of exhibition objects and refined its thematic organization. The creative give-and-take that has characterized our curatorial relationship is a source of lasting pleasure for each of us. Mr. Xu Bingkun, Director of the Liaoning Provincial Museum, was responsible for the selection of Ming and Qing paintings and wrote notes for the paintings that appear in the text.

We are enormously indebted to the curators of the 21 museums and institutions from eight provinces and Beijing that have contributed objects to the exhibition. We also wish to acknowledge the essential contributions of the lending institutions to the exhibition catalogue. We would especially like to thank the staffs of the Henan Cultural Relics Research Institute, Henan Provincial Museum, Luoyang Cultural Relics Work Team, Liaoning Provincial Museum, Shenyang Palace Museum, Nanjing City Museum and Nanjing Museum, Shanxi Archaeology Research Institute and the Shanxi Provincial Museum for hosting the eight-member American "Son of Heaven" team during May and June, 1986. In facilitating this curatorial and project planning trip, the Beijing staff of COAEC was invaluable.

The discussions of the objects are an amalgam of texts prepared by myself and Mr. Yang, with the assistance of Mr. Chen Lie. We gratefully acknowledge the critical readings of Mr. Yang Hong, Research Associate of the Institute of Archaeology, Beijing, and Mr. Yu Weichao, Director of the Museum of History, Beijing. They reviewed the entire Chinese manuscript for accuracy and made important suggestions for improving the text. We would like to thank several readers who reviewed all or part of the English manuscript: Ms. Virginia L. Bower, Dr. Karen L. Brock and Dr. Robert Harrist. Dr. Chu-tsing Li and Mr. C.C. Wang provided advice on the selection of Ming and Qing paintings.

The design, editing and production of the catalogue benefited immeasurably from the creativity and dedication of Douglas Wadden, Mitsu Sundvall and Lynn Schweber. Ms. Sundvall edited the English manuscript and prepared it for typesetting. Mr. Wadden and his assistants brought such intensity and inspiration to the design process that it is difficult, if not impossible, to summarize their contributions. Ms. Schweber ably saw the manuscript through its crucial final stages. Mr. Robert Lewis provided tireless editorial assistance. The objects in "Son of Heaven" have been brought to life by photographer Don Hamilton and his associates. The catalogue publishing project was also aided by members of the COAEC staff, especially Mr. Wang Yugui, Ms. Fan Shenyan, Mr. Xu Dong, Ms. Shen Jingxia, Ms. Ma Eryun, and Mr. Zhang Mingshan of the Design and Photography Section.

Finally, we would like to thank our associates in the Ministry of Culture, the State Administrative Bureau of Museums and Archaeological Data, the Overseas Archaeological Exhibition Corporation, the Son of Heaven Exhibition Committees of Washington and Ohio and the Department of Art History and Archaeology at Washington University in St. Louis for their active support throughout this long and challenging project.

Robert L. Thorp
Chief American Curator and Associate Professor of Art History, Washington University in St. Louis

Table of Contents

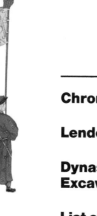

1 THE ALTAR
Rituals of the Early Periods — **49**

2 THE OUTER COURT
The Last Dynasty — **67**

3 THE TEMPLE
The Emperor and the Three Teachings

4 THE INNER COURT
Life in the Palace

5 THE TOMB
Imperial Burials

Chronology of Dynasties

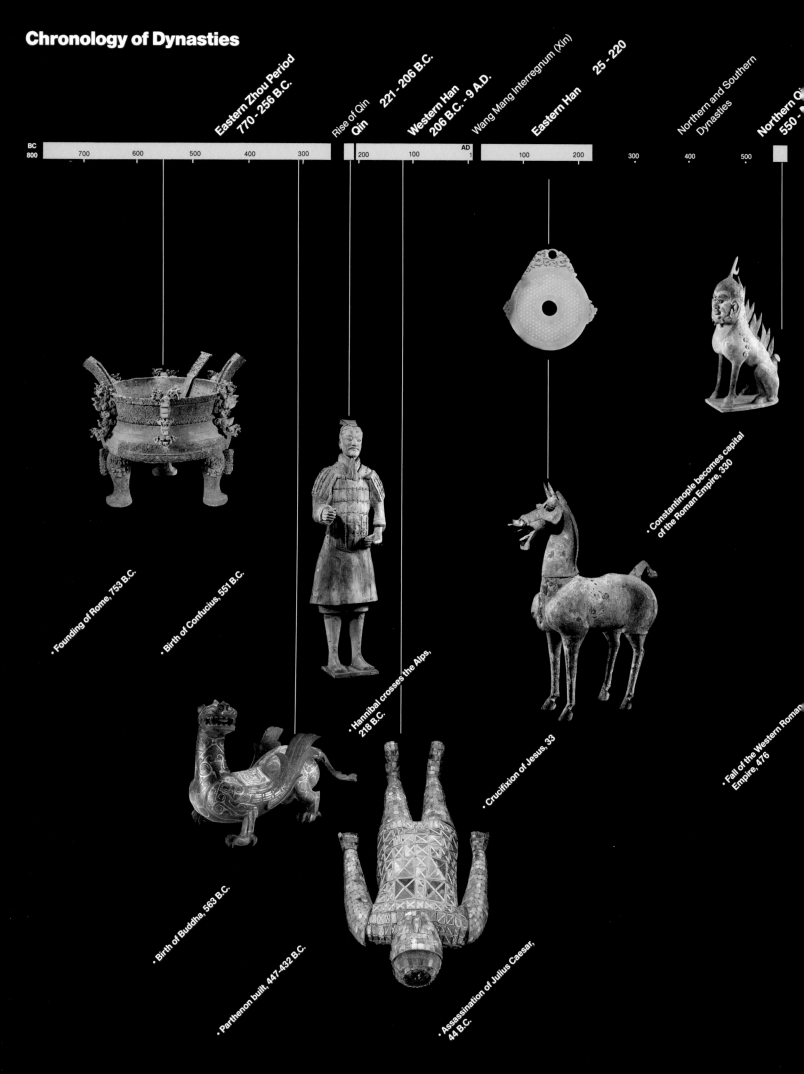

Eastern Zhou Period
770 - 256 B.C.

Rise of Qin
Qin **221 - 206 B.C.**

Western Han
206 B.C. - 9 A.D.

Wang Mang Interregnum (Xin)

Eastern Han **25 - 220**

Northern and Southern
Dynasties

Northern Qi
550 -

| BC 800 | 700 | 600 | 500 | 400 | 300 | 200 | 100 | AD 1 | 100 | 200 | 300 | 400 | 500 | |

• Founding of Rome, 753 B.C.

• Birth of Confucius, 551 B.C.

• Hannibal crosses the Alps, 218 B.C.

• Crucifixion of Jesus, 33

• Constantinople becomes capital of the Roman Empire, 330

• Fall of the Western Roman Empire, 476

• Birth of Buddha, 563 B.C.

• Parthenon built, 447-432 B.C.

• Assassination of Julius Caesar, 44 B.C.

Sui

Tang   618 - 906

Five Dynasties

Northern Song
960 -1126

Southern Song
1127 - 1279

Yuan (Mongol)
1279 - 1367

Ming   1368 - 1644

Qing (Manchu)
1644 - 1912

| 700 | 800 | 900 | 1000 | 1100 | 1200 | 1300 | 1400 | 1500 | 1600 | 1700 | 1800 | 1900 | AD 2000 |

• Birth of Mohammed, 570

• Charlemagne crowned first Holy
Roman Emperor, 800

• Chinese invent gunpowder, 1000

• Genghis Khan founds the
Mongol Empire, 1206

• Magna Carta, 1215

• Marco Polo's journey to China,
1271-92

• Gutenberg invents movable
type, 1453

• Columbus discovers the New
World, 1492

• Leonardo paints the *Mona Lisa*,
1503

• *Mayflower* reaches America,
1620

• Declaration of Independence,
1776

• French Revolution, 1789

• Marx writes the *Communist
Manifesto*, 1848

Lenders to the Exhibition and Map of China

Baoding District Cultural Relics
Administration, Baoding

Beijing Palace Museum, Beijing

Dingzhou City Museum, Dingzhou

Hebei Cultural Relics Research
Institute, Shijiazhuang

Hebei Provincial Museum, Shijiazhuang

Henan Cultural Relics Research
Institute, Zhengzhou

Henan Provincial Museum, Zhengzhou

Hunan Provincial Museum, Changsha

Liaoning Provincial Museum, Shenyang

Luoyang Cultural Relics Work Team,
Luoyang

Luoyang Guanlin Stone Sculpture
Museum, Luoyang

Nanjing City Museum, Nanjing

Nanjing Museum, Nanjing

Museum of Qin Figures, Lintong

Overseas Archaeological Exhibition
Corporation, Beijing

Ruicheng County Museum, Ruicheng

Shandong Provincial Museum, Jinan

Shanxi Archaeology Institute, Taiyuan

Shanxi Provincial Museum, Taiyuan

Shenyang Palace Museum, Shenyang

Xinyang District Cultural Relics
Administration, Xinyang

Zhenjiang Museum, Zhenjiang

miles
0   200

Dynastic Capitals and Location of Excavation Sites

▲ Numbered triangles indicate location of excavation sites.

1. **Baoding**
2. **Changge**
3. **Changsha**
4. **Changzhi**
5. **Dantu**
6. **Dingzhou**
7. **Guangshan**
8. **Jiyuan**
9. **Jurong**
10. **Lintong**
11. **Linzi**
12. **Luoyang**
13. **Mancheng**
14. **Nanjing**
15. **Pingshan**
16. **Ruicheng**
17. **Taigu**
18. **Taiyuan**
19. **Xichuan**

Capital	Dynasty
Beijing	Yuan Ming Qing
Hangzhou	Southern Song
Kaifeng	Northern Song
Linzhang	Northern Qi
Luoyang	Eastern Zhou Eastern Han Tang
Nanjing	Eastern Jin Southern Dynasties Ming
Xianyang	Qin
Xi'an	Western Han Tang

miles
0   200

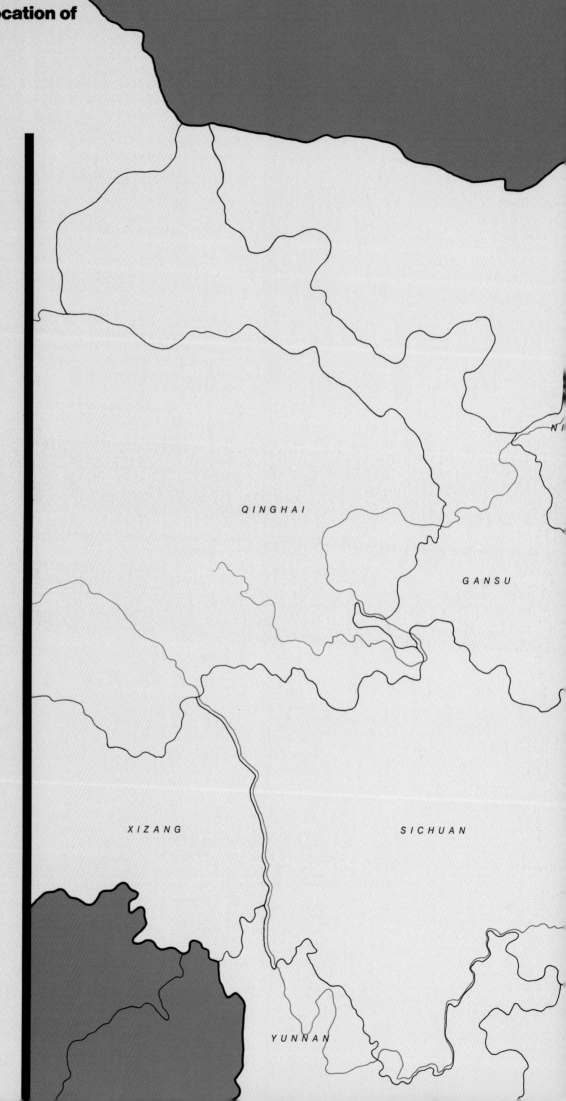

QINGHAI

GANSU

N

XIZANG

SICHUAN

YUNNAN

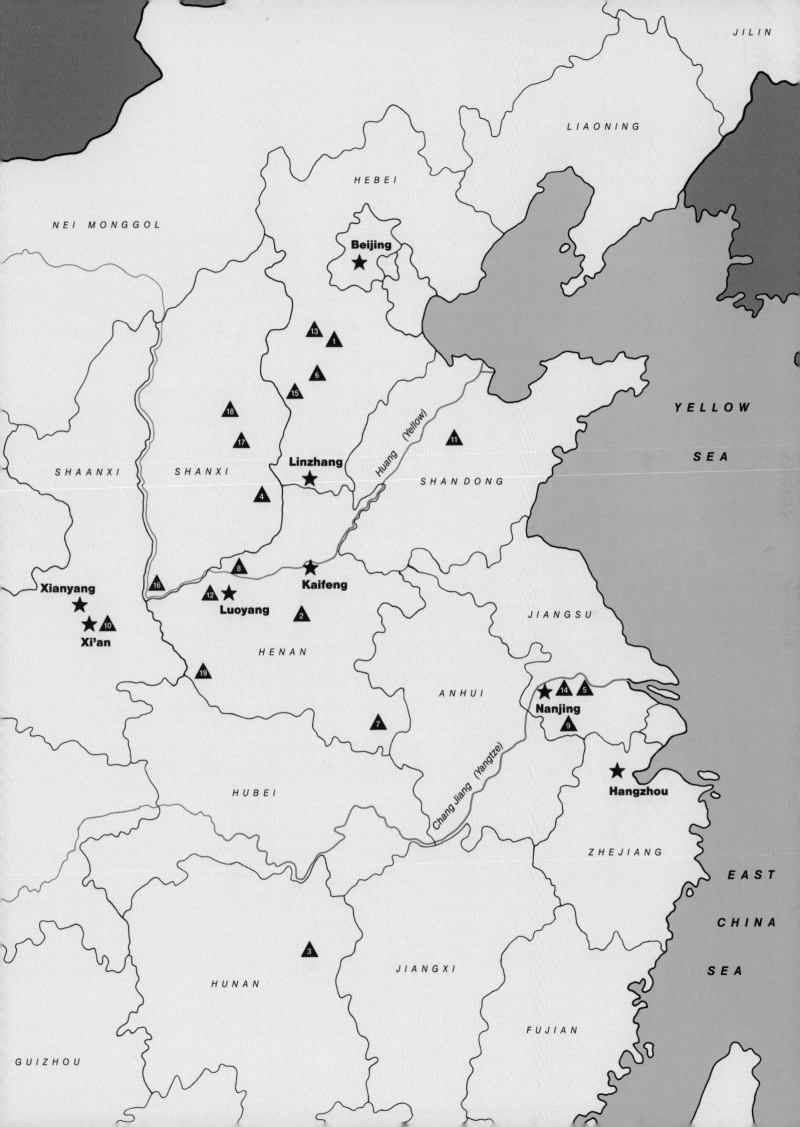

List of Illustrations

Objects in lighter type are not illustrated.

Note on Chinese Pronunciation

The Pinyin spelling employed in this catalogue represents the sounds of the modern standard dialect (called Mandarin or "common speech"). For English speakers, several initial consonants require explanation. The Wade-Giles system, once standard in English publications, is given for reference.

Pinyin	Wade-Giles	Sound Value
q	ch'	*ch* sound in cheat
x	hs	*sh* sound in she
zh	ch	*j* in job
z	ts	*dz* sound in adze
c	ts'	*ts* sound in its

Exploring the Imperial Arts of China

One naturally associates China with such images as the winding Great Wall and the resplendent Forbidden City, with soaring dragons and elegant phoenixes. All are manifestations of the industry and wisdom of the Chinese people and each had a direct connection with the rulers of ancient China. So, one ponders many questions about the emperors and kings of ancient China. When did imperial rule begin? How long did the imperial dynasties continue in Chinese history? How did the emperors and kings of China rule and live? How were they different from the rulers of other countries? What kinds of art were created for their palaces? With these questions in mind, let us look at the imperial arts of China.

Detail of Bronze Horse, No. **115** (see p. 184)

Introduction

The people of ancient China entered a stage of high civilization marked by the appearance of the state and its rulers by at least 2000 B.C. For 4,000 years after, dynasties controlled all or parts of China: the Xia, Shang, Zhou, Qin, Han, Three Kingdoms, Jin, Southern and Northern Dynasties, Sui, Tang, Five Dynasties, Song, Liao, Jin, Yuan, Ming, and finally the Qing, which was overthrown in 1911 (see Timeline). The longest of these dynasties survived several hundred years and the shortest lasted only a few years. During this time, there were more than 300 rulers, representing the Han-Chinese, Xiongnu, Jie, Xianbi, Di, Qiang, Qidan, Nuzhen (or Manchu), and Mongol peoples. If one then adds the many princes and lords who controlled portions of these states, the number of rulers is too numerous to mention. All were men, with the exception of Empress Lu of the Han (early 2nd c. B.C.) and Wu Zetian of the Tang (7th c.). The royal and imperial systems were manifestations of traditional Chinese patriarchy.

In life these emperors and kings were all-powerful; after death the majority of them were forgotten, actors who quickly strode across the stage of history. They were all remembered by later historians, however; some were praised and used as models, others were cursed and used as negative examples.

In retrospect, the history of the rulers of China can be divided into three successive and continuous developmental stages: the Primitive Society and the Huang and Di rulers of legend, the Slave Society and its kings *(wang)*, and the Feudal Society and its emperors *(huangdi)*.

Primitive Society. The first period comprises the rule of the "Three Huang and Five Di" of myth and traditional history who supposedly existed before the Xia Dynasty. The actual dates of these rulers are unknown, but this period is certainly prior to 2000 B.C. Their names were Fu Xi, Shen Nong, Yan Di, Huang Di, Zhuan Xu, Di Ku, Yao, and Shun, and whether or not they actually existed remains a riddle.

The most prominent traits of this late period in Primitive Society are the increasing frequency of warfare, the changes in social relations, and the expanded scope of sacrificial rites. Early stages of the later system of emperors and kings already appear among the traces of this transitional period between primitive and advanced societies. As sacrifice and other ritual activities were standardized, implements made of jade became more important. Examples of this stage include

the temple and altar sites, tombs, and jade dragons of the late Hongshan culture of modern Liaoning Province; the jade *cong* tubes, *bi* disks and animal mask decor of the Liangzhu culture of the areas of Shanghai and Hangzhou; and the ceramic and wooden ritual and musical equipment and painted coffins of the Taosi Longshan culture of Shanxi Province. All these examples reflect the concentration of power and elevated social status of an elite few. Many were related to rituals or were special emblems used in the worship of spirits. They are the precursors of the ritual system and symbols of the emperors and kings. They also signify the dawn of Chinese civilization.

None of these artifacts were things that could be owned by ordinary people. They were reserved for the exclusive use of the elite. For example, at the Longshan culture site at Taosi (Xiangfen County, Shanxi Province), most of the more than 1,000 tombs excavated are small with no coffins or furnishings. Less than one percent are large tombs with artifacts such as a painted ceramic *pan* vessel with a coiled-dragon motif, wooden drums with crocodile drumheads, stone chimes, and other important ritual and musical gear. In addition, there are sets of ceramic, wooden, jade, and stone artifacts, plus evidence of offerings of whole pigs. There are as many as 100 to 200 objects per large tomb. Such tombs also contained painted wooden coffins, which were always for the burials of males. The great disparities in the burial furnishings reflect distinctions in wealth and status. The persons buried in these large tombs probably were leaders of tribes, the rulers who held sway over the people. In reality, 5,000 years ago China had already moved to the threshhold of an advanced civilization. The primitive clan system was disintegrating, and rulers called *bo* or *da ren* had appeared. The state—the social product of class distinction—was about to be born.

Slave Society. The second stage, approximately 2000 B.C. to 200 B.C., consists of the Xia, Shang, and Zhou dynasties of kings and extends to the time that the Qin king, named Zheng, unified China and proclaimed himself *huangdi* (emperor). It is generally believed that the stage from Xia through the first half of Eastern Zhou, the Spring and Autumn period, constitutes the Bronze Age, while the Iron Age began in China with the Warring States Period.

Deep and systematic changes appeared in Chinese society beginning with the Xia Dynasty. First, a system of royal accession replaced "democratic" selection by the people themselves. The system of abdicating the position of ruler to the most worthy was now thoroughly demolished. Succession by the legitimate son replaced succession by the most worthy. Lineal descent of the proper wife's son became firmly established from the late Shang period, and this became the standard practice for changing rulers thereafter. The state system in this historical stage consisted of a king as ruler with an elite in control of fiefs. Qi, the son of Yu, hypothetical founder of the Xia, first adopted the term *hou* to represent his status as the highest ruler. Thereafter, the rulers of the Xia took the title *wang* (king) to symbolize the absolute power and military might of the ruler. This term was employed until the Qin unification throughout this second stage of the history of Chinese rulers.

A second profound change in Chinese society followed. Each king called himself "Son of Heaven" *(Tian Zi),* descendant of the High God *(Shang Di).* His power was a manifestation of the will of the High God and was bestowed by his ancestors. Deceased rulers were deified and thought to reside with the High God, transcending the local character of tribal and clan protective spirits. Their sons and grandsons, the later kings, were believed to be inherently different from ordinary men, possessing some of the power of the High God. The ideology that the lord's power came from the spirit world was easily accepted. The rule of kings became absolute.

The third significant change was the appearance of the structure of state power. It is believed that in the Xia Dynasty there were already palaces and fortified cities, as well as appropriate officials, military forces, prisons, punishments, and laws. Of the greatest significance was a system of religion and rituals that maintained the king's power and the royal succession. This system (described below) appeared in the Xia and Shang and became stricter in the Western Zhou.

Only the middle and lower reaches of the Yellow River and the middle reaches of the Yangtze River shared this advanced civilization. Other regions in the vast area of China were most probably still at a stage of clan (pre-state) society. Regions of this advanced society had superior natural geographical conditions for agricultural production, such as the first state, the Xia, which originated in the middle reaches of the Yellow River (modern Shanxi and Henan provinces). In historic times this area, called the Central Plains, was the focal point of royal struggles in successive dynasties, and many blood lineages of different areas mingled here. An advanced culture crystallized, and the Central Plains truly became the center of Chinese civilization, the crucible and cradle of the Han-Chinese people. With their strong tendency to absorb and fuse valuable elements from other less-advanced peoples around them, the "great family" of the modern Chinese people was created.

Archaeology has been able to progressively verify and supplement the history of the Shang and Zhou kings, whereas the Xia kings and Xia culture are still difficult to trace. The Erlitou culture (first discovered at Erlitou, Yanshi County, Henan Province) stands between the late local Henan Longshan culture and the Shang culture and is still the object of debate: Is this culture a part of the Xia, a part of the Shang, or are the earlier stages Xia and the later ones Shang? The Xia culture has become one of the major topics in contemporary Chinese archaeology. Archaeological research has already proven that the main features of an advanced civilization, such as cities and palaces, writing, and cast bronzes, had appeared by the Shang period. Bronze-casting had already reached an unprecedented level by that time. With the distinctively Chinese tradition of jade carving (also present in Meso-American civilizations), bone and ivory carving, incised white pottery, proto-porcelains, and the chariot, the magnificent Shang and Zhou cultures took shape.

Feudal Society. The third historical stage, extending from 221 B.C. to A.D. 1911, is the period from the establishment of the Qin empire to the collapse of the Qing Dynasty. When King Zheng of the Qin destroyed the six rival states, he ended the long period of feudal divisions, unifying China and laying the first foundations of the multi-ethnic, unified, feudal imperial institution. King Zheng took for himself the term *huangdi* (from the mythical "Three Huang and Five Di") and styled himself the First Emperor. This signified that his merit surpassed that of the "Three Huang," his virtue exceeded that of the "Five Di," and his sons and grandsons would succeed him in generation after generation for ten thousand years.

It was decreed that all affairs of the world, small or large, were to be decided by the emperor. All authority, which included legislation, administration, law, the censorate, and the military, was concentrated in the hands of the emperor. The old system of divided feudal authority was replaced by a completely centralized organization with commanderies and counties for local administration and the "Three Worthies and Nine Ministers" for central administration. All officials were appointed and all officials were dismissed by authority of the emperor. These measures greatly strengthened control over the people and increased the efficiency of administration. At the same time, the Qin implemented unified systems of law, weights and measures, coinage, and script. Private land ownership was also instituted.

The Qin Dynasty's autocratic system of centralized power, although flawed, had great vitality. It had a profound influence on the Feudal Society of China for a period of about 2,000 years. Each successive dynasty, however different its governmental structure or officials' titles, continued and further developed the centralized Qin system.

As a result of Qin unification, China became a centralized, autocratic feudal empire with a vast territory and a multi-ethnic population numbering tens of millions. The economy of Feudal Society advanced rapidly, and for more than 2,000 years it created and developed Chinese culture through fusing and distilling disparate elements from the many places and peoples within the empire. Thus, Han-Chinese culture gradually took shape. The imperial institution originated earlier and developed more completely than other similar governing systems in the world. In the Shang and Zhou dynasties, China had become a strong state. From the Qin onward, with the exception of the last centuries, China became even more powerful, with a highly developed economy, a flourishing culture, and advanced science and technology that was in the forefront of the world's civilizations.

The changes that resulted from China's entry into a feudal system are obviously different from those that occurred in Europe. In the early stages of European feudalism, cities withered, commerce deteriorated, transportation and communication were cut off, and self-sufficient estates or manors had very little contact with each other. The power of the king was weakened, and the church took this opportunity to bolster its power. The church had great influence in government, economy, and culture, and the politics, law, philosophy, and literature became the servants of theology.

Assemblies made up of nobles and common people played a role in the development of European monarchies. These power structures supported the king and served a certain purpose for the monarch.

China never has had such institutions of theological power or legislative assembly. The monarchy loomed over everything, and in fact royal power increased. All officials were servants of the emperor. The concept of one-man dictatorship with power concentrated in the hands of the emperor reached its fullest manifestation in the Chinese imperial system. Except for the emperor, there were no other independent power structures. All officials, institutions, and religions were the docile tools of the emperor.

The Role of Ritual in State Government

Upon entering the exhibition galleries, among the most striking objects are the gigantic bronze tripods, the awesome chime of 26 musical bells, the precious jade *bi* disk with carved dragons, and an unusual set of five ritual vessels (Nos. **1-11**). Solemn, quiet, and mysterious, these objects transport the viewer into the midst of the coiling smoke of a sacrifice or banquet. These objects were created during the second stage in the history of Chinese rulership as tools of ritual to maintain the power of the kings and the existing social order. They represent elements of the original full system of ritual and music.

Ritual *(li)* was applied to every aspect of social ethics of the Zhou and subsequent dynasties. The idea of ritual originated with the state, was firmly established at its altars, imposed order on the people, and benefited posterity. Essential to ritual was the system of names used to differentiate social levels within the elite. Ritual outlined respectful nomenclature and conduct between a lord and his ministers, fathers and sons, older and younger brothers, husbands and wives, and between friends. The rites did not extend down to the common people. At the state level, ritual was a part of political, economic, cultural, and diplomatic relations. On a day-to-day basis, it affected dress, food, social conduct, marriages, and funerals. The power, duties, and expected treatment of each rank within the ruling elite were strictly correlated with social station. One was not allowed to overstep one's authority, and distinctions were made in wealth, age, dress, residences, servants, funerals, and sacrifices.

The arts were used in ritual to influence and edify the ruling class. Without music, the rites were regarded as incomplete and ineffective. Music added a refinement and elegance that made rituals easier to promote in this intrinsically harsh system. For this reason, music was closely linked to the rites from the beginning. The emperor regulated the system of rites and music, and its strict observance was the most important indicator of the stability of the government. For the ruling class, to abrogate the rites was in effect to violate a law, and the punishments for such transgressions were extremely strict and could even include death. For example, when a feudal lord did not extend the welcoming rites to the Son of Heaven, he could lose his rank and fief and incur military punishment. A concrete example occurred in the Spring and Autumn Period when the Earl of Zheng did not pay court to the Zhou king, who thereupon summoned his armies of the royal house to punish this earl.

The rites of Zhou were consistently perpetuated and promoted as models throughout Chinese history. Those rites, traditionally regarded as products of the Western Zhou period (11th-8th c. B.C.), can be divided into five categories: (1) auspicious rites, for sacrifices addressed to the spirits; (2) inauspicious rites, for matters of grief and sorrow, primarily funerals and burials; (3) rites for guests, referring to the conduct of meetings, mostly court gatherings; (4) rites of warfare, for sending out an army to punish an adversary; (5) celebratory rites, for the conduct of marriage banquets, capping ceremonies, and other joyous occasions. From birth to death, in human affairs and in sacrifices, in daily life and in governmental activities, each member of the elite lived within a world informed by ritual appropriate to rank and with privileges according to rank.

Implementation of the rites lay in the lineage system, which determined distinctions in name and rank for the elite within Shang and Zhou society. The lineage system itself originated in clan societies in which blood relations were the basis of political organization, based on succession of the oldest son of the principal wife.

The Shang and Zhou systems divided society into five levels: the Son of Heaven, the feudal lords, the high ministers, the grandees, and the gentry. Common people, artisans, and merchants were excluded. The Zhou Son of Heaven was the owner of all the land and its inhabitants, as well as being the political ruler and head of the Great Lineage. His royal position was the result of the succession of

oldest sons within the Great Lineage. The younger brothers of the Son of Heaven received fiefs as feudal lords or high ministers and grandees; in relation to the Zhou king, they comprised the Lesser Lineages. Within their own fiefs, however, the feudal lords constituted the Great Lineage, and their succession also followed lineal descent. The younger brothers of the lords in turn were enfeoffed as high ministers and grandees and became Lesser Lineages within each state. In the Qin period (3rd c. B.C.) the system broke down somewhat, but its remnants survived into later ages. It became the foundation of rank distinctions in Feudal Society and was used in later times in those families whose members held military and bureaucratic positions in generation after generation. This lineage system was inseparable from the system of rites and music.

During the second stage of Chinese rulership, the archaeological evidence of the system of rites and music consists primarily of bronze ritual vessels. Ritual vessels were important to discriminate rank and status in Shang and Zhou society. They were used on all ritual occasions, principally sacrifices and banquets. They include food, wine (actually alcoholic spirits made from grains) and water vessels, musical instruments, and weapons. They are extremely varied in form, and some of their names are not known with certainty. The earliest bronze ritual vessels have been found in Erlitou culture sites at a date equivalent to the Xia Dynasty (first half of the 2nd millenium B.C.). At present, however, only the *jue* pouring-cup type is known from this period. In the Shang period (16th-11th c. B.C.), the number and variety of ritual vessels greatly expanded, and wine types became the most important. The most basic grouping consisted of the *jue* pouring cup, the *jia* warming vessel, and the *gu* goblet. The importance given to these types substantiates those textual references indicating that the Shang rulers indulged to excess in alcohol. With the Shang as a negative example, the Zhou strictly forbade excessive drinking, and by the middle of the Western Zhou period the number of wine vessels had decreased markedly. Food vessels accordingly increased in importance.

6. Tripod with Ladle, bronze
H: 26.5 in. (67.4 cm.); D: 26 in. (66 cm.);
Wt: 243.4 lbs. (110.4 kgs.)
Eastern Zhou (6th c. B.C., before 552-548 B.C.)
Tomb 2 at Xiasi
Xichuan County, Henan Province
Excavated 1979
Henan Cultural Relics Research Institute

24

The most important of the ritual vessels was the *ding*, a tripod vessel (compare Nos. **1** and **6-8**) used for cooking meat, which came to symbolize the king. This symbolism had already appeared during the Shang period. The largest ritual vessel known is the Si Mu Wu *fang ding* (a *ding* vessel of rectangular cross-section) of the Late Shang period, weighing more than three-quarters of a ton (875 kgs.). This vessel is from the royal cemetery at Anyang, where the only unlooted tomb excavated (that of Fu Hao) had more than 30 *ding* vessels. Both these examples make clear the importance of the *ding*. Unfortunately, however, neither textual nor archaeological information makes it possible to understand clearly the ritual system by which the Shang used *ding* vessels, perhaps because in this period the system was not yet well-formulated. These sets of *ding* were similar in form, decor, and inscriptions, progressively decreasing in size and for the service of different meat courses in a sacrifice or banquet. In the Western Zhou period, following further developments in the lineage system, sets of *ding* vessels appeared as tokens of rank. The higher the rank, the greater the number of *ding*. As a consequence, the number of meat courses increased. Excavated *ding* vessels are usually odd-numbered sets, which correlates with historical texts stating that the Son of Heaven used nine *ding* in sacrifices, the feudal lords used seven, the grandees used five, and the gentry used three. However, in the Eastern Zhou period, ritual and music fell into decline, and both superiors and inferiors exceeded the number of their perquisites and their authority. Many examples of excess *ding* vessels in sets are known from burials so that in the Eastern Zhou period both the Son of Heaven and the feudal lords might use nine *ding*, the high ministers seven, the grandees five, and the gentry either three or one.

Some scholars question the generally accepted description of the use of sets of *ding* vessels given above. From a text in the *Rites of Zhou*, which mentions twelve *ding* used by the Son of Heaven, they infer that twelve was the proper number for the king, nine for the feudal lords, seven for the high ministers, etc. However, as the set of *ding* in this exhibition (Nos. **6-8**) shows, seven were made for the Chu prince Zi Wu, although later they were given to another person named Sun Zhi Peng. Both these men were Chief Military Commander of the state of Chu, which correlates with the rank of high minister and adds support to the seven *ding* of the previously stated theory.

Gui grain-service vessels and chimes of musical bells often are found with sets of *ding* vessels. The difference between the *gui* sets and *ding* is that the former are found in even numbers. According to textual sources, the Son of Heaven had eight *gui*, the feudal lords six, the grandees four, and the gentry either two or one, and archaeological finds verify these numbers. The number of bells was seven groups in a chime for the Son of Heaven, three groups for the feudal lords, two for the grandees, and one for the gentry. As with other ritual vessels during the Eastern Zhou, excavations reveal that the number of chimes of bells were not always consistent with these prescriptions. In general, tombs with sets of nine *ding* vessels have four groups of bells per chime, tombs with sets of seven *ding* have two or three groups per chime (No. **9**), and tombs with five *ding* have two groups; tombs with three *ding* generally lack a chime of musical bells. In addition to the bronze bells, there were also sets of stone musical chimes.

After the inception of the imperial age, these vessels declined in ritual significance. *Ding*, for example, were used as everyday cooking pots or as measures for grain. Nonetheless, the influence of the Zhou rites described previously proved durable, according to the *Qing Hui Dian*, the compendium that describes the rites of the last dynasty. In the Qing system, auspicious rites were for sacrifices; celebratory rites for accession ceremonies, court events, enfeoffments, marriages, banquets, and the like; military rites for great reviews, the beginnings of imperial campaigns, the dispatch of generals, their triumphant returns, and the presentation of war captives; rites for receiving guests were for both foreign emissaries and the reception and dispatch of officials; inauspicious rites were for mourning for the Son of Heaven and the gentry and commoner classes. If one compares the rites of each dynasty with those of the Zhou, in substance they did not change.

Engineering feats such as the Great Wall and the Grand Canal are testimony to the third, imperial stage in the history of Chinese rulers. Because of wars and natural disasters, well-preserved material remains are limited almost entirely to sites and objects of the Qing Dynasty. The best are the Forbidden City in modern Beijing, which was the center of government as well as the court and palace, and the imperial palace created by the Qing before their conquest of China at Shenyang in Liaoning Province. Court paintings are the best evidence reflecting the solemnity, majesty, and florid style of Qing rituals. They depict the Son of Heaven's administration of the many affairs of state, the large scale of military drills, imperial tours of inspection, hunts, and the like. Imperial portraits and the costumes of the Son of Heaven and empress also survive, along with their seals and the furnishings of throne rooms and studies, as do the myriad objects, treasures, and miscellanea of the palaces. For this exhibition, we have selected a small part of this wealth to convey something of the life of the Son of Heaven.

The Emperor and the Three Teachings
Religion played an important and useful role in the political life of the rulers of China (see Ch. 3). Although the character, forms, and uses of religion varied in each of the three developmental stages of Chinese rulership, this exhibition emphasizes only the Three Teachings of the third, imperial stage. During this stage, three living religious or ethical traditions developed in China: Confucianism, Taoism, and Buddhism, each of which underwent a complete life cycle. Both Confucianism and Taoism were native to China, while Buddhism was transmitted from India.

Confucianism. Confucianism did not receive great attention from the lords of the Spring and Autumn and Warring States periods. It was regarded merely as one of three major teachings, along with Taoism and Mohism. In the Western Han period, Dong Zhongshu and other Confucians absorbed the theories of the Yin and Yang and "Five Elements" school and embedded their new Confucian theories into the foundations of Feudal Society. At this time, Confucianism began to serve the imperial state. From the time of Emperor Wu of the Western Han (r. 141-87 B.C.), Confucianism came to occupy the position of state orthodoxy and became even more entrenched after the Song and Yuan (10th-14th c.) when officials adopted the ideas of Neo-Confucianism. Confucianism preached the Great Unity in

12. Emperor's Summer Court Attire, silk
H: 54.25 in. (138 cm.); W (hem): 31 in. (79 cm.)
Qing (18th c.)
Shenyang, Liaoning Province
Shenyang Palace Museum

which the fundamental political idea was "virtuous rule," or the "way of the King." He who could practice virtuous rule would receive the Mandate of Heaven as "Son of Heaven," and this became the theoretical basis of the orthodox succession of dynasties. Confucian ethics were derived from the basic ideas of loyalty and filial piety, the highest norms of life and conduct, which were to be directed to the emperor. Because of this, Confucian thinking and teachings could serve the needs of each dynasty in the feudal period. No matter how much the central position of Confucianism may have fallen in certain periods, the rulers never rejected it altogether. Confucian ideas always remained the orthodoxy of Feudal Society.

Theories derived from Confucianism undoubtedly made up the substance of Chinese culture during Feudal Society. Representative Confucian works—the so-called *Four Books, Five Classics,* and *Thirteen Classics*—were canonized as the classics of Chinese literature by the emperors of each period. Ideological concepts and psychological attitudes of Han-Chinese culture reflected in Confucian thinking also influenced other ethnic and cultural groups, and thus Confucianism served as a bridge spanning different cultures. But Confucianism was different from other religious systems. Although Confucius was the founder of this school and was later regarded as a sage, he never became a deity or a prophet, and as a result he lacked the powers of a deity. His teachings chiefly affected the conduct of life and human affairs, not matters of death or the afterlife. Confucianism took a respectful but disengaged attitude toward ghosts and spirits and thus perpetuated superstitious attitudes toward spirits and the weak psychological aspects of Chinese religious belief. Confucianism would be supplemented by other co-existing religions; in Feudal Society no one religion was totally embraced and none were entirely rejected. There was no single all-powerful deity. Thus, China never experienced the kind of religious warfare that characterized European feudalism and Islamic civilization.

The character of Confucianism differed from both Taoism and Buddhism. It lacked a rigorous formal organization and it did not have priests or clergy. In fact, whether or not Confucianism should be classified as a religion is still debated.

Taoism. Like Confucianism, Taoism also emerged from Chinese soil and Han-Chinese culture. Its origins derive from the ancient reverence for spirits, the "shamanism" of the Xia, Shang, and Zhou periods, and the techniques of adepts at immortality during the Qin and Han periods. Sects of Taoism began to appear from approximately the middle of the Eastern Han period. In the middle and lower reaches of the Yellow River, there was Taiping Taoism (The Way of Great Peace), while in Sichuan and Shaanxi there was a sect established by Zhang Daoling called the "Five Pecks of Rice." These sects claimed Lao Zi, who lived some 700 years before, as their founder and canonized him as Taishang Lao Jun. Subsequently, Lao Zi became deified as one of three spirits in the Taoist pantheon. Early Taoism had many popular aspects and was often a banner rallying peasants to revolt. Taoism became an official creed with the support of dynasties from the Six Dynasties period through the Song and was controlled to differing degrees by the imperial state. In its formative development, Taoism accepted the Confucian hierarchical order as well as the techniques of the adepts of long life. It added some aspects of Buddhist belief as well as ancient shamanism and other esoteric practices. It also appropriated and adapted certain aspects of Buddhist organization and terminology to establish Taoist temples and Taoist images, making it more complete both in theory and in form. The basic tenet of Taoism was belief in The Way, recognizing that the cosmos, *yin* and *yang,* and all things were all creations of The Way. The highest deities were three anthropomorphic transformations of The Way. Taoism also appropriated the worship of Shang Di, who became the emperor of the realm of the immortals who controlled The Heavenly Way. Shang Di was given many names, of which the Jade Emperor was the most widely revered. The classics of Taoism were collected as the *Taoist Patrology.*

Buddhism. Buddhism is one of the world's three largest religions. It was transmitted from India across Central Asia in the Han period. As a foreign religion, it initially spread among China's royal houses and elite but had little influence at this time. The son of Emperor Guangwu of the Eastern Han, Liu Ying the prince of Chu, chanted the words of Huang and Lao and worshipped the shrine of the Buddha. At this time, Huang-Lao, a branch of Taoism, was equated with Buddhism, but Buddhism itself was resisted and rejected by Confucianism. Only after it absorbed traits of Chinese culture did a sinified form of Buddhism meet the needs of the people, and its political position rose as a consequence. With the support and cultivation of the elite, this Chinese Buddhism gradually became an important component in Chinese society. Thereafter, it began to have a strong influence in politics, thought, economics, and the arts. Following establishment of the Sui and Tang dynasties, Buddhism entered a golden age and began to merge with Confucianism. At this time, the Buddhist temples prospered and different Buddhist sects, each with their own organization, arose throughout China. Lamaism, which was later to flourish in Tibet, Qinghai, and Inner Mongolia, also appeared. The sinification of Buddhism was complete and it was exported abroad. Buddhism adapted to Chinese conditions and came to terms with both Confucianism and Taoism. It entered a stage of independence and service to Feudal Society and added fresh blood to Chinese culture. But this advantageous situation could not persist and, after the Tang, Buddhism began to stagnate and increasingly to decline.

Among the world's three largest religions, Christianity and Islam are monotheistic, while Buddhism believes in a higher spirit, Sakyamuni Buddha, under whom there are different ranks of Buddhas, bodhisattvas, and arhats. This is comparable to the Chinese imperial system with its emperor and hierarchy of many officials, which is one reason why, of these three religions, Buddhism alone had any great influence in China.

Influence of the Three Teachings in Chinese Culture

Confucianism, Taoism, and Buddhism existed in Chinese Feudal Society for almost 2,000 years. From the start, the rulers decreed the primacy of Confucianism, and the culture of Feudal Society was encompassed within the tenets of Confucianism. Although there were many religions introduced into China which flourished for a time or in one region, none was able to achieve a position of supremacy. The main oppositional force came from Confucian theories. From the Six Dynasties through the Qing period, there was internal conflict among the Three Teachings from time to time, as well as mutual growth and decline and mutual learning and borrowing, with Confucianism the strongest and Taoism the weakest. Only in the Sui and Tang periods did the Three Teachings approach equal footing, but the other two were never able to dislodge Confucianism from its favored position. Thereafter, the three tended to merge as parts of Chinese culture. Buddhist and Taoist thought were absorbed by Confucianism, and Chinese thought entered the age of Neo-Confucianism.

The attitude of the emperors toward the Three Teachings was clear. The emperor was above religion, which was regarded as his tool and dependent on him. When the rulers needed these religions, the emperor became their head, but there could be absolutely no figure or even deity higher than the emperor. The emperors of China not only ruled over human society, they were higher than the gods. For example, the bodhisattva Avalokitesvara was first known in Chinese as Guanshiyin. Because the name of the Tang emperor Taizong was Li Shimin, the character *shi* shared by the two names was banned and the deity became known thereafter simply as Guanyin.

In general, the emperors regarded the Three Teachings as useful, and so they pursued policies that treated the three as compatible. Because of differences in the Three Teachings themselves, however, their use by the imperial institution differed. Confucianism was focused on duties to Heaven, the ancestors, and human relations, while Taoism was oriented toward longevity and Buddhism was concerned with escape from this world. The emperors took what they needed from each, using them to supplement each other. Emperor Xiaozong of the Southern Song (r. 1162-1189) said: "Buddhism for control of the mind, Taoism for control of the body, and Confucianism for control of the world." These imperial attitudes largely determined the fate of religions in Chinese history. The three great persecutions of Buddhism ordered by imperial decree are examples.

The Three Teachings have left us a rich artistic heritage of architecture, sculpture, painting, and calligraphy. Three notable trends were manifest in the development of the arts of these religions.

One is the sinification of Buddhist art. Early styles from Gandhara and Central Asia were gradually modified by absorbing or copying Han-Chinese elements, subjects, and forms to produce the classic Chinese Buddhist styles. This process was accomplished by the Tang period. For example, the faces of Buddhas and other deities changed: the noses were gradually lowered, the ears became larger, the face changed from a long to a more rounded shape taking on the features of the Chinese people. The costume changed from an Indian, half-clothed type covering one or both shoulders to one similar to Chinese court dress. These changes in Buddhist images are well illustrated at the three great cave-chapel complexes at Yungang, Longmen, and Dunhuang.

Detail of Arched Door Frame, No. **51** (see p. 114)

The architecture of these cave chapels also copied timber-frame Chinese architecture representing a joining of these two traditions. The foreign architecture of the pagoda, under the influence of traditional Chinese culture and architectural styles, became a new architectural type. Other subtypes within the Chinese tradition of pagodas are the famous Large and Small Goose Pagodas in Xi'an from the Tang period; the wooden pagoda at Ying Xian County, Shanxi Province, from the Liao period; and the pagoda at Bao'en Temple in Nanjing, from which there are several glazed tiles (No. **51**) in this exhibit. In accommodating Chinese ways of thinking and customs, Buddhist art generally diluted foreign influences. In architecture, sculpture, costume, activities, and thought, Buddhist art became increasingly Chinese. Conversely, Buddhist art had a deep impact on Chinese art, opening up new possibilities in subject matter and representation.

The second trend in religious art was increasing secularization and an ever stronger stress on political content. As the Buddha became less exotic and mysterious, its stern and awesome aspects became softer and more peaceful. It embodied a kinder expression, and people of the real world entered the world of the Buddhas. It is said that in the Northern Wei period the proportions of Buddhist images were modeled after the Emperor Wencheng, and his physical blemishes were copied onto the faces and bodies of these images. In paintings illustrating the Life of the Buddha in Cave 290 of the Northern Zhou period at Dunhuang, the father of Sakyamuni Buddha is depicted as a Chinese emperor, and his mother wears the kind of costume appropriate to an empress of the Han or Jin periods. The emperors not only prayed to the Buddha for stability of the reign, they also embraced the concept that they were embodiments of the Buddha themselves, as well as Son of Heaven, so that the depiction of the deity became more and more a graphic reflection of the emperors. A Buddhist cave chapel, temple, or Taoist temple came to represent imperial rule in which its principal images symbolized the emperor and lesser deities symbolized the court ministers. The power and benevolence of the deities reflected the majesty and charity of the emperor; the piety of bodhisattvas and donors reflected the filial piety of ministers and sons. The happiness of the celestial attendants and dwarves in Buddhist compositions was likened to the happiness of the people of the realm.

The cave chapels at both Yungang and Longmen were products of the patronage of the imperial houses. The Binyang Caves at Longmen were built at the command of Emperor Xuanwu (r. 499-515) as a pious act in honor of his mother. The stone images and steles (Nos. **42-50**) included in the exhibition—the "Preface to the Holy Teachings," the "Inscription for the Jin Shrine," and the "Stone Terrace Classic of Filial Piety"—are visual expressions of the Tang emperors' benevolent attitudes toward the Three Teachings and their parity at this time.

The third trend in later Chinese religious art is its increasing homogenization. Perhaps the earliest example of the Three Teachings depicted together within a single composition is the representation of Confucius with an immortal (Taoist) and a figure on a white elephant (Buddhist) found in the wall paintings of the Eastern Han tomb at Holingol, Inner Mongolia. Somewhat later, figures from Chinese myths such as the Queen Mother of the West, and such embodiments of Confucianism as filial sons and chaste women, appear in Buddhist wall paintings. In the Song period cave chapels at Dazu in Sichuan, the patriarchs of the Three Teachings—Buddha, Confucius, and Lao Zi—are often depicted together. The Ming Buddhist paintings made on imperial order for the Baoning Temple in Shanxi Province for use in a "Land and Water Assembly" (Nos. **52-56**) are a compendium of all the gods and spirits, human actors, and denizens of the full Chinese pantheon. Thus, the artistic boundaries among the Three Teachings became less and less distinct.

Life and Art in the Inner Palace

The true goal of managing the affairs of state, implementing ritual, and utilizing religion was the security of the state and the perpetuation of rule. Maintaining the security of the state so that they could enjoy their position was also an aim of the emperors. How, then, did they live? Many accounts of court life were heard, but rarely was it witnessed by outsiders. There were many traditional accounts of the "dragon and phoenix" pavilions, the clever architectural projects, the thousands of palace ladies, the excesses of music and dance, the indulgence in wine and food, and of "spending money like water." But reality was always veiled by a screen to create an air of mystery.

The strong continuity of a long history and extravagant burials has meant that many objects reflecting life in the imperial palaces are well preserved. Moreover, new information is continually emerging through archaeological work. Inner palace life embraced all kinds of sites and objects: main palaces, pleasure parks, and detached palaces; the gardens,

stages, private chambers, studies, and courtyards where great events took place within the palaces; the ritual paraphernalia and treasures presented as tribute; the poetry, music, calligraphy, and painting of the emperors; their collections and seals; the spoons, chopsticks, knives, and forks used for eating; their snuff bottles, spittoons, clothing, and jewelry that comprised everyday necessities and other objects used for various entertainments. The materials include earthenware and porcelain, gold and silver, bronze and iron, jade and other stones, bone and ivory, lacquer and wood, silk and other textiles, glass, crystal and agate, and paper. The techniques comprise weaving, embroidery, dyeing, pottery, cloisonne, casting, sculpting, painting, architecture, and related arts. The topics range from the fine and literary arts to fine cuisine. From a cultural standpoint, the topic of life in the palace becomes the history of the development of all the arts.

A few traits characterize this vast history of imperial and palace arts. First, the settings of this life and all that was required by it were chiefly made by artisans and painters who worked exclusively for the palace. These craftsmen and artists were either selected from society or cultivated within the palace. In each case, they were superior at their trade. In a concrete way, they manifested the creativity of the Chinese people, in command of the newest techniques as well as the best of traditional and newly imported ideas. Art objects used for life within the palace show both a strong Chinese character and obvious period style.

In different periods, the tastes and preferences of the emperors and empresses were diverged widely. In the Xia, Shang, and Zhou periods, bronze vessels and jade stones were the finest works of art. In the Qin and Han periods, textiles, lacquers, and gilded bronzes were the strongest. During the Six Dynasties, glazed green wares became more important, while in the Sui and Tang, gold, silver, and three-color wares were most famous. In the Song, Yuan, Ming, and Qing periods, porcelains and painting were beyond compare. Of these many arts, ceramics, silk, and lacquer each had a history of almost 4,000 years of development. Palace wall painting, carvings, architectural pottery, and gardens continued to flourish through generations and became important artistic traditions.

Detail of Bronze Altar Table, No. **10** (see pp. 58-59)

Each of these arts had its peak of creativity and greatest refinement when it was reserved for the use of the emperors and their courts. In the Spring and Autumn and Warring States periods, techniques for inlaying gold, silver, and copper, engraved designs, and gilding were all quickly developed in large scale by the palace. The five major kilns of the Song period— the Ru, Guan, Ge, Jun, and Ding—were largely imperial kilns. A Ming text records that the palace was already collecting such famous porcelain by the Xuande era (early 15th c.). During the Ming and Qing periods, the kilns at Jingde Zhen in Jiangxi Province reached the peak of their production and they, too, became the largest suppliers of porcelain for the palace. Of course, imperial art was not limited to those objects made for imperial use. On great occasions, such as tours of inspection, marriages, and birthdays, officials and gentry would confiscate strange and rare objects from the people and give them to the emperor to ingratiate themselves with the sovereign.

There was a close connection between the activities of the palace and the government. All stressed the power of the emperor and respect for him. All normal stages in a human life—marriages, birthdays, and funerals of the emperors—were also important components of government. Daily life in the palace also reflected changes in the politics and economy of each period, as well as differences in custom and aesthetics. On the bronze altar table (No. **10**) and *ding* tripods (Nos. **6-8**) from the Spring and Autumn period, animals climb onto the vessels, roaring and extending their long tongues, while others, such as those at the neck of the *hu* (No. **2**), kneel with their heads turned back as if preparing to spring from their crouch and attack. These animals are full of the breath of life and reflect the temperament of their society. They are depicted not as peaceful, but as full of movement and ferocity. They are creatures of myth that have leapt into the real world. From such artistic forms, one can sense changes taking place in the society of the Spring and Autumn and Warring States periods: the struggle among the feudal lords for supremacy, the contending schools of thought, and the turbulence in the minds of men. Similarly, the winged animals inlaid with silver from the tombs of the kings of Zhongshan (Pingshan County, Hebei Province) (No. **63**), are also a reflection of palace aesthetics.

A third trait of palace arts is the concept of the emperor-artist. It is true that a number of emperors indulged themselves lavishly at the expense of the people, oppressing the population without remorse and damaging the state in the process. Consider the Qin First Emperor's construction of the Ebang Palace, Emperor Yang of the Sui's indulgence in pleasures for years on end, the Song emperor Huizong's quest for fantastic rocks for his garden, and Empress Cixi's squandering on herself of money for national defense. But a number of emperors were cultivated in such arts as writing, music, calligraphy, and painting. Collecting and appreciating works of calligraphy and painting were very common, and some emperors became well-known writers and artists. The *History of the Three Kingdoms* relates that Emperor Wu of the Wei, Cao Cao, whenever he ascended a height would compose a poem and accompany it with music. Some of Cao Cao's poetry indicates he understood and sympathized with the plight of the common people. Others of his poems are brimming with heroism and are well-known and widely praised to this day.

The Tang Emperor Taizong (r. 626-649) loved the works of the Eastern Jin calligrapher Wang Xizhi. He sent for the famous "Lanting Preface" to be obtained by any means. He loved this work so much that it is said he placed it in an iron box and had it buried with him. The Song emperor Huizong (r. 1100-1125) was a talented calligrapher and painter with considerable accomplishments in the arts and is the most widely renowned painter-emperor in the history of Chinese art. His calligraphic style was called "slender gold" and frequently was combined with works of painting, for which he received great praise. The emperor was also an art educator who cultivated the imperial painting academy and advanced court painting to a high point. The Qing Qianlong Emperor (r. 1735-1796) loved calligraphy and collected especially rare specimens by Wang Xizhi, Wang Xianzhi, and Wang Xun. These he kept in the Forbidden City in the western chamber of the Palace of Mental Cultivation, which he then renamed the Hall of the Three Rarities. He also ordered one of his court ministers to produce a compendium of all the calligraphy held in the imperial palace named for this hall. Calligraphy by the emperors of the Tang, Song, Ming, and Qing, especially that of the three Qing emperors Kangxi, Yongzheng, and Qianlong, can be found throughout China. The paintings that we exhibit by the Ming emperors Xuanzong and Wuzong, although not extremely well-known, are nonetheless of high quality. The "Ten-Thousand-Year-Old Pine" by Xuanzong (r. 1426-1435) (No. **90**) is an unusual and creative composition, with strong brush work.

90. "Ten Thousand-Year-Old Pine," by Emperor Xuanzong (r. 1426-1435),
hand scroll (section)
H: 13 in. (33.2 cm.); L: 14 ft. 10 in. (453.1 cm.)
Ming (dated 1431)
Shenyang, Liaoning Province
Liaoning Provincial Museum

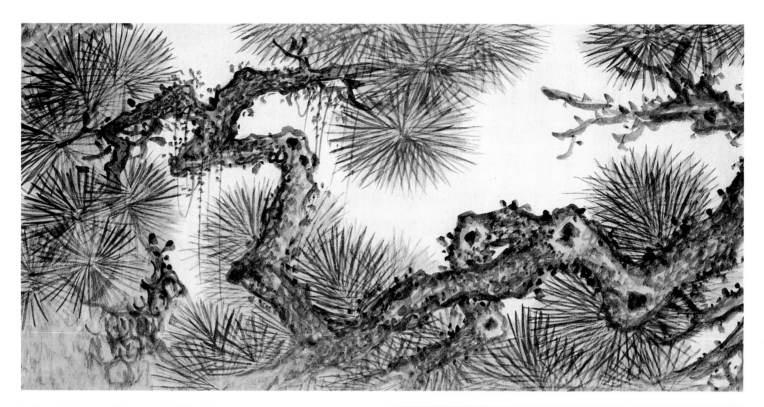

In the sixth year of his reign (1431), this was the young emperor's gift to his mother, the Empress Dowager. Monochrome ink on paper is augmented by light color. Although Xuanzong was trained by respected court artists, the emperor's own style emerges in this long composition of twisting branches glimpsed through the narrow aperture of a hand scroll.

Detail of "Ten Thousand-Year-Old Pine," No. **90**

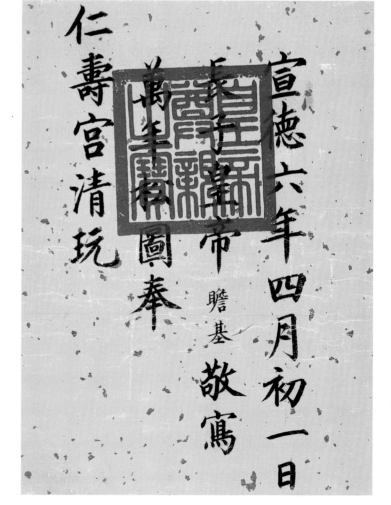

104. Armored Warrior, terra cotta
H: 6 ft. 3 in. (190 cm.)
Qin (ca. 210 B.C.)
Tomb of the First Emperor
Lishan, Lintong County, Shaanxi Province
Excavated 1974-1979
Museum of Qin Figures

Imperial Burials

The splendor and wealth of the emperors, although squandered in a lifestyle of luxury and extravagance, produced an artistic world that was a feast for the eyes. Many emperors sought ways to prolong this lifestyle, even with elixirs of immortality, so that they could enjoy such pleasures for eternity. Some of the most outstanding Chinese rulers, such as the Qin First Emperor, Emperor Wu of the Western Han, and Taizong of the Tang, were mired in such pursuits, wasting great wealth and energy without results.

If long life could not be obtained, there was consolation in the traditional concept of "treating the dead like the living." The concept of the soul and the practice of "rich burials" sought to transport the dead into another world where they could continue to rule, enjoy the pleasures of their status, and in a sense become "immortals." For this reason, the emperors of China placed everything from their life into their tombs. Such a burial became their greatest aspiration. In time, figurines replaced real people within the tombs, and "spirit objects" replaced some actual objects and sacrificial offerings. Burial practices changed as society and government evolved. Still, the custom of rich burials persisted, becoming in itself a complete burial ritual. The system of imperial tombs and the sacrifices conducted at them were important means to promote the power of the emperor and to maintain the social hierarchy.

As Chinese historical writing matured, attention given to the burials of the emperors increased from the Qin onward, and we have a much clearer understanding of the burial system of the feudal stage than the earlier two stages. There are often relatively detailed records, from the construction, funeral, and sacrifices to the robbery and destruction of the same tombs. Because of the extensive development of above-ground architecture and the widespread use of spirit-path sculpture, many examples of these features at imperial tombs of the Qin and later periods have survived to the present and most can be closely correlated with historical records. In addition, there has been considerable archaeological work, such as the excavation of the Yonggu Ling of the Northern Wei at modern Datong (Shanxi Province), the two Southern Tang tombs near Nanjing (Jiangsu Province), the Yongling of the Former Shu at Chengdu (Sichuan Province), and the Dingling of the Ming near Beijing, plus the many accompanying burials of the Qin, Han, Six Dynasties, Tang, and Ming.

The Qin Dynasty. The Qin First Emperor took advantage of several thousand years of experience in building royal burials, and especially the achievements of the feudal lords of the Warring States period, to establish a foundation for the burial system and funerary parks of the imperial era. The necropolis of the First Emperor was created on an economic foundation of unparalleled strength. From his accession to its completion, about 40 years (including the reign of the Second Emperor) were spent on the tomb. This project utilized the energy of several hundred thousand workers and all the resources of the state.

From archaeological work and textual sources, it appears the tomb site of the First Emperor consisted of a double-walled rectangular compound with gates on four sides. The burial mound was situated inside the inner wall in the shape of a truncated four-sided pyramid, originally about 400 feet (120 m.) tall. It was planted with trees and grasses to appear like a mountain. A chamber was built on the north flank for the spirit of the emperor, staffed by many palace women. There were other buildings and staff to provide services for the site. The necropolis may have faced east, with that approach comparable to the spirit path of later imperial tombs. About 17 tombs of imperial relations and officials who had been put to death were found to the south of this eastern approach. Close by to the east were nearly 100 horse pits with real horses and ceramic attendant figurines. About two-thirds of a mile (l km.) further east were three large trenches for the so-called underground army of terra cotta warriors. This discovery augments lost historical records, and as a representation of artistic achievement known the world over, we display some of the warriors here (Nos. **103-108**). To the west, within the funerary park, was an underground menagerie with pits for exotic animals and ceramic figurines. Near the west ramp was a chariot pit containing wooden chariots with canopies and painted bronze chariots and charioteers, of which two have already been excavated. These masterworks represent Qin style at its best.

It is said that the tomb of the First Emperor was robbed and destroyed, but because the site has not yet been excavated its actual condition is not clear. However, the scale of the tomb, the extravagance of its appointments, the richness of its furnishings, and the completeness of its security measures were recorded as early as the *Historical Records* of Sima Qian (ca. 100 B.C.). Sima Qian also reports that upon the death of the First Emperor, the Second Emperor ordered the tomb burial of women of the palace who did not have sons. In addition, to prevent disclosure of information about the tomb, the laborers and artisans were also buried alive inside the chamber. Thus, the First Emperor's tomb perpetuated the evil practices of Slave Society. However, it is also certain that a large number of figurines as well as other surrogate objects for burial were used, a practice that was perpetuated thereafter. The interior design and furnishings of the tomb also strongly influenced later periods, as seen in the painted celestial ceilings that one finds subsequently in large tombs of the Han, Northern Wei, Tang, Song, and Liao periods. The topographic model of the world, including its rivers and lakes, also finds a parallel in the southern Tang tombs at Nanjing.

The Han Dynasty. The Han followed the Qin burial system but also contributed some important developments:

Mountain tombs. At the same time that four-sided pyramidal mounds were the norm for imperial burials, tombs were also being placed inside mountains. The Baling of Emperor Wen of the Western Han (r. 180-157 B.C.) was the first example of such an imperial mountain tomb.

Mausoleum towns. The noble families of the realm were moved to the capital and ensconced at the imperial tombs in "mausoleum towns." This increased central control over these families and strengthened the security of the central government. These towns were in place for 150 years, until the reign of Emperor Yuan (48-33 B.C.).

Commemorative monuments. Accompanying burials were created near the imperial tombs as a form of favorable treatment for worthy officials and nobles after death. In certain cases, special arrangements were made for their burials. For example, the burial mound of General Huo Qubing (d. 116 B.C.) located near the Maoling, the tomb of Emperor Wu, was a simulation of the Qilian Mountain Range in Gansu Province where the general had achieved his victories. Stones carved in the form of animals and men were placed among other stones on top of this mound. This transformed the burial into a kind of large-scale commemorative architecture.

Surrogate burial objects. In addition to placing the most valuable possessions of the deceased in the tomb, more attention was paid to surrogate objects that reflected real life. Ceramic figurines became more common, and human victims were seen less and less. Real horses and chariots consigned to the tomb were replaced from late Western Han times onward with wooden, ceramic, or bronze horses and chariots. The old system of ritual vessels based on sets of graded *ding* tripods also disappeared.

Jade burial shrouds. In hopes of preventing the decay of their bodies after death, the emperors of the Han used jade burial shrouds in place of the many layers of clothing worn in the Shang and Zhou periods. These jade shrouds were sewn with gold, silver, and bronze thread, depending on the rank of the deceased. These distinctions were strictly followed in the Eastern Han with the emperor using gold thread, the princes silver, and others bronze. The use of jade shrouds was limited to the Han, and the practice was prohibited under the Wei emperors (3rd c. A.D.).

Tomb construction. From excavations as well as textual sources, it appears that the imperial tombs and many princely tombs were large-scale wooden chambers with special coffins, a central chamber, and the *huang chang ti zou* method of stacked timber for the walls. Multiple-chamber brick and stone tombs, which appeared in the Eastern Han, were designed to imitate above-ground palaces. Stacked timbers were now replaced by large square stones, such as those found at a Han prince's tomb at Ding County, Hebei Province. The replacement of the wooden chambers by stone and brick was accompanied from the end of the Eastern Han onward by special "couches" for the wooden coffin. The multiple layers of coffins in the Zhou system disappeared.

Other Han features. There were many new developments in Eastern Han (1st-2nd c.) imperial tombs, although they are still poorly explored by archaeologists and we must rely in many cases on textual sources. A "spirit path" was created as the approach to the tomb, lined with stone columns and stone sculptures of protective guardians and auspicious animals. This is the beginning of a trend that was to continue throughout the imperial period. Also, a sacrificial chamber was built in front of the burial mound for ceremonies at the site. The offering halls of the Tang, Song, and later periods originated from these innovations. In this same period steles were erected before the tomb recording the biography of the deceased. The influence of Buddhism was also seen in temples established near the tombs. All these new features were further developed by later dynasties. From the many examples of Han painted tombs and engraved stones that depict the life of the deceased and other subjects, it is likely that the imperial tombs had similar interior decoration.

The Six Dynasties. The political and social disorder that accompanied the fall of the Han badly weakened the economy. In the early Six Dynasties period (3rd-6th c.), the rulers favored frugal burials. The rich burials of the Han age disappeared, and the Qin-Han system was weakened. The Wei and Western Jin (3rd-4th c.) emperors placed their tombs in mountainous regions without man-made earthen mounds over them. They did not establish mausoleum towns, spirit paths, or offering halls. As a result, few if any traces of their tombs can now be found above ground. The rulers of the so-called Sixteen Kingdoms who controlled the North after the early 4th century were mostly non-Han peoples and used other means of burial that left no visible traces. The Eastern Jin and Southern Dynasties (4th-6th c.) monarchs also placed their tombs on mountainous ground, but these are merely single-chamber tombs with designs impressed in bricks decorating the interiors. Their spirit paths had pairs of animals, pillars, and steles that followed the slope of the mountain. Special techniques, including geomancy, were used to site the tomb, so the orientation of these tomb paths was not regular.

The Qin-Han necropolis plan was revived in the Northern Wei period (5th-6th c.). The influence of Buddhism on imperial burials and Chinese art was becoming stronger and stronger. Lotus designs found on the stone carvings of the Southern Dynasties tombs are also widely seen in the north among imperial tombs and Buddhist temples alike. Bronzes and lacquers became less common as tomb furnishings, but glazed stoneware increased. Surrogate "spirit articles" were fairly crude at this time, with an emphasis on certain types of figurines (Nos. **117-123**). The placement of the epitaph inside the tomb became quite common and was a fixed feature by the Sui and Tang periods. The ruling elite during the Six Dynasties normally rode in ox-drawn carts, and so pottery models of these carts are commonly found in tomb furnishings. The carts are featured in groups of figurines and paintings of processions, replacing the earlier horse-and-chariot processions of the Han.

118. Guardian Warrior, painted earthenware
H: 25 in. (63.5 cm.)
Northern Qi (ca. 570)
Tomb of Lou Rui, Prince of Dong'an Commandery
Wangguo Village, Taiyuan, Shanxi Province
Excavated 1981
Shanxi Archaeology Institute

The Tang Dynasty. The Tang Dynasty was the golden age of Chinese Feudal Society. The imperial tombs were created on an unprecedented scale that expressed the heroic spirit of this age. The Tang tombs were of two types: those placed inside mountains and those with man-made earthen mounds. The former were the most common and extremely impressive. The tomb sites included impressive architecture, broad spirit paths, and consummately carved stone figures and animals, including emissaries from the subject peoples of the greater empire. Accompanying burials near the imperial tombs also had mounds, and the sites were oriented along a north-south axis. The paintings covering the walls of these tombs, some of which have been excavated, were recreations of the palaces. Judging from the furnishings of these accompanying tombs, imperial grave goods were more sumptuous than ever before and comprised large amounts of gold, silver, and glazed stoneware as well as glass, agate, foreign coinage, and other rarities. Three-color ware and figurines were at their peak during this time and are justly famous for their color and fine sculpture. It is believed that the Qianling, the joint burial of Tang Gaozong (r. 649-683) and Empress Wu, is the only unrobbed Tang imperial tomb. From its scale, and the reputation of Empress Wu, it may be one of the richest imperial tombs. The most important change in the Tang burial system was the separation of the offering hall for sacrifices and the retiring hall where the spirit of the deceased was maintained. The latter was moved to a lower position on the mountain and hence called the Lower Palace. The offering hall became known as the Upper Palace in the Song period.

The Song Dynasty. The Northern Song (10th-11th c.) built imperial tombs that were still four-sided pyramidal earthen mounds, and it was the last dynasty to maintain this feature. In the Han-Tang system, tombs were built in advance of the emperor's death, which afforded ample time to build on a grand scale. The Song emperors, on the other hand, changed the Han-Tang system and did not begin tomb construction until the death of the emperor. In addition, it was decreed that the emperor must be buried within seven months, which meant there was less time for elaborate construction. Thus, the scale of the Song tombs fell far short of that of the Han and Tang. The Song revived the Han system in which only the empress was buried within the necropolis. All these tombs are located together within a relatively small area in modern Gong Xian County, Henan Province. In the Southern Song (12th-13th c.), the emperors were buried in shallow graves without above-ground stone carvings or the like, with the expectation that they would be reburied with their ancestors after the North was reconquered. The Mongol rulers of the following Yuan Dynasty (13th-14th c.) practiced a secret burial rite without elaborate tombs. The sites of their burials remain uncertain.

The Ming Dynasty. When Zhu Yuanzhang (r. 1368-1398) established the Ming Dynasty, he revived the system of building imperial tombs prior to the ruler's death. He also carried out major reforms in the burial system and implemented new features that dominated the Ming and Qing periods. With the Xiaoling (near Nanjing) of the first Ming emperor himself, the mounds changed from square to round and were called *bao ding*. A large brick wall called the *bao cheng* surrounded the mound. A square tower was erected in front of the mound and wall, with an open pavilion for the emperor's stele. The Lower Palace compound of Tang and Song was abolished, and the system of palace women in attendance at the spirit's quarters was also eliminated. The offering hall compound was enlarged to emphasize the importance of such rites. Each necropolis became rectangular rather than square and consisted of three courtyards aligned on an axis. (The third courtyard was actually the walled mound.) The Ming revisions also enhanced the beauty and solemnity of the site.

Thereafter, the Song system was further elaborated, starting with the Changling of the Yongle emperor (r. 1402-1424) near Beijing. All the tombs were clustered in one area, the Ming Valley, and a common approach was created on the south with formal gate, stele pavilion, and stone sculpture. Each individual tomb was actually an independent unit that consisted only of three courtyards, including the sacrificial hall and mound. The East and West Tombs of the Qing emperors outside Beijing basically followed this same system. At the beginning of the Ming, the emperor ordered many palace ladies put to death at this funeral, but this practice was abolished under Emperor Xuanzong (r. 1426-1435). This period saw the end of the use of tomb figurines, but both ceramic and wooden types are still found in Ming princely tombs. Many extremely valuable objects came from the excavation of the Dingling, the tomb of the Wanli Emperor (r. 1570-1620), but they do not approach the lavishness of rich Han and Tang burials. The system of imperial burials would soon withdraw from the stage of history.

The many changes in the system of imperial burials reflect the strengths and weaknesses of each period. Each tomb is a treasury of art that brings together architecture, arts and crafts, sculpture, painting, and calligraphy. Many of the exhibits are of excavated objects taken from such underground treasuries distributed over the broad expanse of China. They are a true mirror of their age.

130. Guardian Animal, glazed earthenware
H: 40.25 in. (102.5 cm.)
Tang (ca. 709)
Tomb of An Pu, Dingyuan General
Longmen, Luoyang, Henan Province
Excavated 1981
Luoyang Cultural Relics Work Team

Conclusion

The imperial artists of China gathered together lengthy historical traditions and added realism and imagination as well as foreign influences to develop a varied and complete world of art. These arts expressed their society. They capture the most refined aspects of each age and, while building onto the past, never failed to be creative. Each stage in the history of the rulers of China was distinctive both in style and in content.

The first stage, the age of the legendary Huang and Di, began to reveal the contours of these artistic traditions. The works of art vary by region in content and in style. Works of pottery and of jade and hardstone carving epitomize this age, which preceded the first truly historic dynasties.

During the second stage, the age of kings, artistic styles became more unified. The art of cast-bronze ritual vessels in particular progressed at a stately rhythm, developing great power that conveyed the life force of real and imaginary animals. Even comparatively realistic jade carvings of animals were still cloaked in mystery. Styles characterized by power, quiet, and strangeness emerged. By the Spring and Autumn and Warring States periods, there were significant changes in artistic styles, especially toward more realism. While pointing to another world of a mysterious past, these new stylistic trends also opened up the real world. The most important artistic traditions of the period—cast bronzes with gold and silver inlay, painted lacquerware, textiles, and jade carvings—stand between the archaic styles of the past and the new world of the imperial age.

The third stage, the age of the emperors, was characterized by styles that were heroic, realistic, and full of life. These styles created classic forms that are evident in all the arts of such great ages as the Han and Tang.

Each age had its own strong achievements in both content and artistic representation: the Forbidden City, the Great Wall, the underground army of terra cotta warriors, the stone sculptures of the Han and Tang periods, the palaces, costumes, furnishings, paintings, and calligraphies of later epochs. All expressed artistic traits that ranged from the broad, serious, realistic and noble to the elegant, refined, and romantic.

In this introduction for "Son of Heaven: Imperial Arts of China," we have taken a brief look at the life and death of the rulers of China from ancient times through the Qing Dynasty. We hope that their legacy, as represented in this exhibit and this catalogue, will help the viewer and reader to understand the arts of the rulers of China, some unique aspects of Chinese culture, and the inexhaustible creativity and imagination of the people of China and their important contributions to human culture.

Yang Xiaoneng
Assistant Chief, Conservation and Exhibition Section,
Chinese Overseas Archaeological Exhibition Corporation

The Imperial Institution and the Arts

All the objects displayed in this exhibition are in some fashion related to the Chinese imperial institution. What does that mean, and why does it matter? What was the "imperial institution," and why is its relation to the arts the central theme of "Son of Heaven: Imperial Arts of China"?

33, 34. One of a Pair of Auspicious Animals,
gilt bronze (34 not shown)
H: 17 in. (43 cm.); L: 12.5 in. (32 cm.)
Qing (18th c.)
Shenyang, Liaoning Province
Shenyang Palace Museum

The First Chinese Emperor

China's imperial era dawned in the late 3rd century B.C. when the ruler of a state named Qin succeeded after some decades in exterminating his last rivals.[1] This new order was established by the Qin ruler, self-styled the "First August Sovereign," and was, of course, not new at all. It was simply a broader territorial extension of the rigorously organized state apparatus he and his court ministers had already created before unification. In this system, the central state governed all aspects of political, economic, and social life with the primary aim of creating a stronger and more centralized regime. The Qin empire took possession of almost all of China proper and thus inherited the material and human resources of an entire continent. To maintain its imperial position, the Qin state also aggrandized the position of its August Sovereign or emperor as the Son of Heaven.

In theory, the Son of Heaven did not earn his title and position, nor were they created by any human agency. Rather, the concept of a "Son of Heaven" was based on a belief in Heaven as an all-powerful, impersonal force or deity that regulated the workings of the universe. Heaven selected a human agent to assume the role of Son of Heaven so that human society could be properly linked to the universe. The position was bestowed according to the moral virtue of the human being in question, not by reason of his social rank or any other individual traits. If that moral rectitude were abandoned, Heaven would withdraw its mandate of imperial rule. Indeed, Confucian thinkers of the pre-imperial era declared that rebellion against an unvirtuous ruler was a moral act approved by Heaven, in effect advocating a doctrine of revolution that one does not usually find in any official orthodoxy.[2]

"Son of Heaven" is a literal translation of the Chinese *Tian Zi*. By custom, we refer to the Chinese ruler as an "emperor" and to his state as an "empire." Although these terms are common usage, they do not actually convey the manifold implications of the Son of Heaven concept or the roles of the Chinese ruler. Some Western scholars prefer to use such terms as "sovereign" or "thearch" to express the dimensions of the role of Son of Heaven that the term "emperor" does not readily imply. There was no real distinction between the state purse and the emperor's, between public works projects and court projects. All power was concentrated in the hands of the emperor and his high ministers, and all wealth was at his disposal.

In the Qin imperial system, economic production was organized to benefit the emperor, his court, and the capital (near modern Xianyang City in Shaanxi Province). Every new discovery around the Qin capital reveals a grandeur and lavishness unrivaled at any earlier time in Chinese history.[3] Rather than being confined by the walls of a fortified city, a network of connected palaces spread over the whole area "within the passes." Life at court was a sojourn among objects of unprecedented luxury: fine silks, precious jades, gilt bronzes, exquisite lacquerware. Objects of art and craft poured into the palaces from workshops expressly established to sustain the new extravagant lifestyle of the imperial court. The First Emperor could command the production of any ostentatious or frivolous thing his fancy dictated, whatever the cost in human suffering or waste.

The First Emperor stood astride a great historical divide. His reign (246-210 B.C.) encompassed the culmination of China's Bronze Age culture when widespread economic and agricultural revolutions fueled rapid development. Qin's strongest rivals, which were the states of Qi (in modern Shandong Province) and Chu (in modern Anhui-Hubei-Hunan provinces), were themselves militarily powerful and economically advanced. They were renowned for their own artistic traditions, luxury products, and advanced court cultures. It was through military force that the Qin inherited or, more correctly, appropriated the rich cultures of these rival states. Under the First Emperor, various regional traditions, styles, and expertise were unified in the great crucible of the imperial capital. Political unification created a fusion of new traditions and styles from which the material and artistic culture of the imperial era emerged. The reign of the Qin First Emperor was therefore the first chapter in the long history of imperial China, a state system that was to endure until the second decade of the 20th century.

The legacy of the First Emperor was profound. Although his son, the ill-fated Second Emperor, soon died at the hands of a eunuch, the institutions created around the person of the emperor lived on. The new Han ruler, Liu Bang, was a man of commoner stock. He took over in large measure the administrative and economic measures of his predecessor. Taxes were reduced and the harsh legal system was moderated, but the basic machinery of state remained intact. The Han imperial capital (northwest of modern Xi'an, Shaanxi Province) did not surpass the egocentric designs of the First Emperor, but it was literally built on Qin foundations. Following many of the Qin designs and customs, Han Chang'an emerged as a functional prototype of later Chinese imperial cities. Once again, the arts served the imperial court for all ritual, ceremonial, and practical ends. Some of the production was organized under the direct supervision of the palace. Other goods, such as lacquerware, were manufactured at state-run factories outside the capital. The imperial family, including the distaff relatives and the burgeoning number of imperial princes and their offspring, shared a luxurious lifestyle that must have been regarded by a commoner with a combination of awe and contempt. There was no greater contrast than the standard of living enjoyed by the palace and that of the general population (nearly 60 million in Han times).

Objects for Imperial Use
Roughly half of the exhibits in "Son of Heaven" were objects made for imperial or royal use. The ritual vessels (Nos. **1-5**) from the 7th century B.C. were made expressly for the consort of the lord of the state of Huang (in modern Henan Province). The jade shroud and other luxury objects (Nos. **109-114**) taken from the tombs at Mancheng in Hebei Province were crafted for a Han imperial prince in the 2nd century B.C. The court robes and palace furnishings (Nos. **12-40**) from the former Qing Palace at Shenyang (Liaoning Province) have never left the abode of their intended users, the Manchu imperial family, since they were created in the 18th century. In each case, these are objects actually used by a royal or imperial person. They represent, in the truest sense, "imperial arts of China," or their direct predecessors in the case of pre-Qin exhibits. They embody the highest standards of craftsmanship, the finest materials, and the prevailing court taste of their day.

About two-thirds of the exhibits in "Son of Heaven" are the products of palace workshops. This category includes items actually intended for imperial use, as mentioned above, and in addition a number of objects that were given by the court to persons outside the palace. Both the Northern Qi and Tang figurines (Nos. **117-125, 126-137**) were probably made in workshops that prepared funeral accessories for the imperial house. In each instance, these objects were then bestowed on a relative, in the case of Lou Rui, or on a worthy military official of non-Chinese extraction, in the case of An Pu.

Imperial gift-giving was common and transferred modest amounts of arts and crafts from the palace into private hands. Several of the objects from the Mancheng tombs (for example, No. **112**) were made for use in the Han imperial palace but then were presented to an imperial son or daughter. The gold and jade belt from Nanjing (No. **87**) may have been bestowed by the first Ming emperor (late 14th c.) on Wang Xingzu, a high-ranking courtier. The Ming gold filigree hairpins (No. **88**) probably also came from a palace workshop.

However, palace artisans were not the only makers of art objects for the imperial institution. At least from Western Han times (2nd c. B.C.) onward, state factories were established outside the capital to manufacture all kinds of goods demanded by the court and the state.[4] In the arts, the most important industries were those devoted to lacquerware and silks (Nos. **66-71**) in the Han, and porcelains and other fine ceramics in the Song and Yuan (10th-14th c.) (Nos. **78-86**) and later dynasties. Here the combined identity of state and court dictated that the best production be channeled to the court for its exclusive use, while lesser quality wares were distributed to other segments of society. Records of imperial Han lacquer production indicate that thousands of cups and dishes were sent to the palace, and archaeological discoveries have unearthed a wealth of comparable objects from sub-imperial tombs throughout China. The volume of porcelain production in the Song was even more astounding.

Imperial Patronage and Collections
Other works of art were created at the behest of an imperial patron, not for his personal use but as an act of merit. The most impressive examples of such patronage are often works commissioned for a temple of one of the "Three Teachings," Buddhism, Confucianism, or Taoism. Patronage started with the establishment or refurbishing of the temple proper. New halls would be raised and old ones restored before the sculptural images or paintings (Nos. **53-57**) were installed. In Buddhist teachings, such patronage earned religious merit for the donor throughout his lifetime, hastening an eternal repose in paradise. The imperial institution also had more practical reasons to patronize any establishment of the "Three Teachings." Supporting a temple or shrine showed imperial benevolence for the particular region. The economic impact of such projects and their functioning was similar to that of public works in our own society. At the same time, the emperor earned the esteem of his court and its historians as a paragon of virtue by sustaining the moral and religious institutions of his realm (see the "Classic of Filial Piety" stele, No. **49**). Like objects made for his use, works produced under imperial patronage were of the best available materials and workmanship. No Chinese emperor ever entered half-heartedly into an imperial commission.

The court also acquired objects from outside the palace and capital. Some precious objects presented to the Son of Heaven were tribute from non-Chinese subject peoples or bounty from the happy subjects of the realm. Exotica, fine produce, luxury goods, and all kinds of crafts, including Western clocks presented by European envoys in later centuries, were continually offered up to the throne. In the Tang period, fine works of silver (Nos. **72-77**) were presented at court by officials in the provinces. It is very possible that some of the luxury goods from the pre-imperial era exhibited here were similar donations to a royal palace.

From an early date, the throne also took an active interest in collecting, which enhanced the emperor's role as a cultural and moral leader.[5] Fine calligraphy and painting were already amassed in staggering quantities during the Six Dynasties (3rd-6th c.) and Tang. The Tang emperor Taizong (r. 626-649), infatuated with the calligraphy of one master, the Calligrapher Sage Wang Xizhi (307-365), scoured the empire for every trace of his works and reportedly took the originals to the grave with him (No. **47**). (A similar monomania

66. Pan Vessel, lacquer
D: 19.25 in. (49 cm.); H: 1.5 in. (3.6 cm.)
Western Han (ca. 186-168 B.C.)
Tombs of the Family of the Marquis of Dai
Mawangdui, Changsha, Hunan Province
Excavated 1972-1973
Hunan Provincial Museum

43

85. Octagonal Vase with Lid, blue-and-white
porcelain
H: 20.25 in. (51.5 cm.); D: 5.75 in. (14.5 cm.)
Yuan (13th-14th c.)
Baoding City, Hebei Province
Excavated 1964
Hebei Provincial Museum

seems to have beset the late Northern Song sovereign, Huizong, but in this case the quarry was bizarre rocks for the imperial garden.[6]) Imperial collecting included antiquities such as archaic bronzes and jades, as well as calligraphy and painting, porcelains, and silk tapestry. Collecting led to connoisseurship, catalogues, and inevitably forgery; it also led to wholesale destruction when a palace was burned or sacked.

The history of the imperial collections through the centuries presents a remarkable story. A number of the finest paintings first assembled in the Northern Song palace (at modern Kaifeng, Henan Province) in the 11th and 12th centuries still survive today, and most have passed through several later imperial collections. These works, which are now treasured in collections throughout the world, moved in and out of imperial hands as one dynasty succeeded another. When the central government and palace were strong and headed by an art-loving emperor, great works gravitated to the capital. At times of dynastic crisis and military turmoil, such objects left the palace, either for safe-keeping or as booty, and then moved through the art marketplace from one proud private collector to another. Our 20th-century sense of the history of Chinese painting—its major masters and monuments—has been irrevocably shaped by the patterns of imperial collecting.

The Ming and Qing paintings (Nos. **90-102**) in this exhibit are from the Old Palace collection that forms the core of the Liaoning Provincial Museum. Two are actually products of the "imperial brush," works by accomplished Ming emperors (Nos. **90, 97**). However, many of the artists represented did not work at court but instead became esteemed by connoisseurs and collectors whose tastes influenced the Qing emperors. The Ming artist Shen Zhou (No. **98**), for example, is notable for the determination with which he stayed away from court circles.

Other artists represented here worked at court, often at the beck and call of the emperor. A team of 18th-century Qing court artists is represented by "The Emperor's Honor Guard in Procession" (No. **25**). Painting was a functional tool of the court in an age before photography to capture likenesses, properly record decorum, and dutifully document great events. Dong Bangda and Wang Yuanqi (Nos. **101-102**) also served in the 18th-century Qing palace, although under different social circumstances from the actual court artists. No mere artisan painters, Dong and Wang were cultivated court officials who also painted, scholar-artists in government service.

55. "Former Taoist Sages," silk hanging scroll
H: 46.75 (119 cm.); W: 24 in. (61 cm.)
Ming (ca. 1460)
Baoning Temple, Youyu County, Shanxi Province
Shanxi Provincial Museum

74. Lobed Box with Parrot Design, gilt silver
H: 3 in. (7.5 cm.); D: 3.75 in. (9.5 cm.)
Tang (8th c.)
Dingmao Bridge, Dantu County, Jiangsu Province
Excavated 1982
Zhenjiang City Museum

Imperial Art and Chinese Art History

The Chinese imperial institution played a crucial, multi-faceted role in the history of Chinese art. As supreme patron and collector, the emperor often gathered together the finest artists of his day and assembled a personal collection of the greatest works of all times. But those roles pale in importance next to the myriad ways in which all artistic production could be affected by the palace and its requirements.

The impact of the palace lifestyle was felt by all craftsmen and workshops supplying goods to the court (Ch. 4). The solemn purposes of state ritual (Ch. 1) and court ceremony (Ch. 2) could not be fulfilled without the proper regalia. This required an industry located away from the capital near the centers of silk production that produced the robes and other textiles. In the Ming and Qing eras, the large-scale production of other furnishings and porcelains also was centered far from Beijing.

Imperial involvement in moral teaching and spiritual guidance led to patronage of the Three Teachings (Ch. 3). Temples throughout the land might be sustained or improved at imperial decree, bringing the highest level of quality and style into the heartland of the realm. Such monuments, like stones tossed into a pond, had a ripple effect as artisans in each locality mimicked the new styles and subjects that were introduced to their area by an imperial donation. Finally, funeral rites, which passed the imperial corpus on to the other world, were themselves a major impetus for artistic production (Ch. 5). In the capitals this resulted in grand establishments to commemorate the imperial house. In the provinces the result was the transmission of new styles and customs into local regions far beyond the imperial court.

The imperial institution had the power to influence the forms and styles of art in every medium and for every purpose throughout the empire. Much of the history of Chinese art can be read through the institutional activities of the Son of Heaven. No other actor within Chinese society had so much disposable wealth, so many sanctified purposes, or so many practical ways to affect the arts. The time span of the imperial institution encompasses the rise and fall of Buddhist art, the gradual decline of the tradition of rich burials, and the burgeoning wealth of key regions and their elites in later times. This exhibition addresses some of the important questions this theme raises.

The Role of Archaeology

Objects made expressly for the emperor and his court are not available from all times and places in the long pageant of Chinese history. Although recent archaeology has unearthed many impressive objects of every description, relatively little can be directly linked to actual imperial persons.[7] Many finds attest to the wealth and burial practices of the metropolitan and local elites rather than royal or imperial lines. This gap in the archaeological record is due to several factors that affect archaeology in China today.

First, many recent Chinese discoveries have been in the nature of "salvage archaeology," excavations carried out as the result of a discovery made during a construction project, for example. When excavators are called in after a discovery or before bulldozers start to work at a site, they recover and document as much as possible, but because it is a chance discovery they have not themselves chosen the site or had an opportunity to survey the locality before deciding where to dig. The incredible success of Chinese archaeology in the last three decades is evidence of China's efforts to concentrate on building a new society more than of a program of planned excavations. Many of these finds reflect, directly or indirectly, the influence of the imperial institution on the arts, the length of time that institution survived, and its pervasive penetration into Chinese society.

Second, very few imperial sites have been surveyed and excavated. The Qin and Han capitals and the Tang capital nearby have all been the object of careful surface surveys and selective excavations. Several Tang (7th-9th c.) imperial palaces are reported, and in a few cases architectural reconstructions have been attempted, but the results have not yet drawn an adequate picture of the splendors of the Tang court in its prime.[8] The old Yuan (13th-14th c.) capital that lies beneath parts of modern Beijing has also come to light, although only selectively as the Ming walls were torn down in 1965-1975. But most capitals, their palace precincts and other establishments, remain largely untouched by modern archaeologists. In several cases, the major impediment to further archaeological exploration is the position of modern cities atop ancient ones. A thorough investigation of the Yuan capital, for example, would require the dismantling of major edifices in Beijing.

Third, very few proper imperial tombs have actually been opened. It sometimes seems that Chinese archaeologists are continually unlocking burial chambers and their riches, but these have not been imperial tombs. The finds near the Qin First Emperor's tomb are among the most spectacular made to date, but no Han imperial tomb has been excavated and only a few later imperial tombs are reported. The earliest bona fide imperial burials that have been opened are located near Nanjing and date from the period of division between Han and Tang (3rd-6th c.).[9] In every case, the tombs were almost entirely bereft of proper furnishings, and their correct attribution to specific emperors is difficult. Imperial tombs of the 10th century near Nanjing and Chengdu belong to rulers who controlled only a fraction of China proper. The 17th century is the earliest period for which evidence for a grand imperial burial from a strong, unified period is available.[10]

As a consequence, the great majority of actual imperial objects that now exist in the world have been passed down through collections over the centuries, or are the fruits of unscientific digging (looting) before 1949. We still await the opening of a great early imperial burial, or the systematic excavation of a well-preserved imperial palace site. Most art collections, both in China and elsewhere, have some examples of imperial arts, especially porcelains and paintings from the later dynasties, but this is a small representation of a great variety of arts produced for imperial consumers and patrons. "Son of Heaven" is the first exhibition to examine the full range of artistic production created on behalf of the imperial institution.

Robert L. Thorp
Associate Professor of Art History and Archaeology,
Washington University in St. Louis

1. On the rise of Qin, see *The Cambridge History of China,* Vol. 1, *The Ch'in and Han Empires, 221 B.C.-A.D. 220,* ed. D. Twitchett and M. Loewe, Cambridge, 1986.

2. For more on this ideology and its implications, see Wm. Theodore deBary *et al., Sources of Chinese Tradition,* 2 Vols., New York, 1960, and Kung-chuan Hsiao, *A History of Chinese Political Thought,* trans. F.W. Mote, Vol. 1, Princeton, 1979.

3. For a survey of Qin archaeology, see Li Xueqin, *Eastern Zhou and Qin Civilizations,* New Haven, 1985, pp. 222-262. A recent treatment of the capital proper is Wang Xueli, *Qin du Xianyang* [The Qin Capital Xianyang], Xi'an, 1985. A popular but less reliable account will be found in Arthur Cotterell, *The First Emperor of China: The Greatest Archaeological Find of Our Time,* New York, 1981.

4. The Han system is discussed in Wang Zhongshu, *Han Civilization,* New Haven, 1982, Ch. 4-6.

5. Lothar Ledderose, "Some Observations on the Imperial Art Collection in China," *Transactions of the Oriental Ceramic Society* 43(1978-79):33-46.

6. John Hay, *Kernels of Energy, Bones of Earth: The Rock in Chinese Art,* New York, 1986, pp. 25-39.

7. An authoritative introduction is Institute of Archaeology, *Xin Zhongguo de kaogu faxian he yanjiu* [Archaeological Discoveries and Research in New China], Beijing, 1984.

8. *Tang Chang'an Daming gong* [The Daming Palace of Tang Chang'an], Beijing, 1959. A convenient English introduction is Nancy S. Steinhardt, "Hanyuan Hall," in *Chinese Traditional Architecture,* ed. N. Steinhardt, New York, 1984, pp. 92-99.

9. See Robert L. Thorp, "The Qin and Han Imperial Tombs and the Development of Mortuary Architecture," in *The Quest for Eternity: Chinese Ceramic Sculptures from the People's Republic of China,* Los Angeles, 1987, pp. 17-37.

10. The Dingling of the Ming Wanli emperor near Beijing. A monograph is to be published shortly.

1 THE ALTAR

Rituals of the Early Periods

Notes to Chapter 1 are on p. 65.

11. Ritual Disk, jade
H: 11.75 in. (30 cm.); D: 9.5 in. (24.2 cm.)
Eastern Han (2nd c.)
Tomb 43
Beilingtou Village, Dingzhou City, Hebei Province
Excavated 1969
Dingzhou City Museum

The Son of Heaven was more than a secular, temporal head of state or reigning monarch. He was the unique link between the human, terrestial world on the one hand, and the primal force that governed the universe on the other. Only through his faithful and diligent attention to all aspects of his ritual obligations could the world be maintained in proper working order. If the Son of Heaven were lax in performing the necessary annual calendar of sacrifices, for example, Heaven would send omens to display its displeasure. If an evil man ascended the throne and performed heinous deeds, Heaven, through natural calamities and human intervention, would assure his demise. Thus, each new dynasty claimed its founder was responding to Heaven's mandate by taking the throne away from its predecessor and assuming the position of emperor. Not to do so would itself be an immoral act, but it was customary to decline the charge a few times before finally accepting the great task.

The ritual dimensions of the Chinese ruler have been accorded great attention in Chinese writings. Specialists in ritual matters were always in demand at court, and debates over proper ritual are a recurring theme in the dynastic histories. The three canonical books on ritual—the *Book of Rites, Ceremonial,* and *Institutes* of Zhou—generated elaborate commentaries and competing schools of interpretation. Knowledge of the rites was fundamental to traditional learning and necessary for success in the examination system during certain periods. Although these books have been translated into Western languages, ritual has been somewhat neglected by modern scholars.[1]

The Rites

The term "rites" is but one possible rendering of the Chinese concept *"li."* *Li* embraces both the formal rituals of an elaborate court ceremony (see Ch. 2) and daily social interaction. *Li* are especially elaborate for such key events as funerals (see Ch. 5), but they are no less important as forms of human behavior at every level and at all times. Decorum, etiquette, protocol, ceremony, and ritual are all integrated within the Chinese notion of *li*. A Son of Heaven was required to perform numerous rites throughout each day, year, and lifetime. The external forms had to be mastered by the young man and the etiquette and its rationale internalized before he assumed the throne.

Between this detached, intellectual understanding of the Son of Heaven and the reality of that role lies a great gap. What was it like to awake each day knowing that the most austere and demanding responsibilities lay on your shoulders and required your total concentration? What was it like to wear the robes of the Son of Heaven (Nos. **12-14**) and believe with the deepest conviction that the symbols on your costume truly were representations of your role in the universe? What were the psychological and emotional costs of being an emperor? Few men and women in world history have been asked to take on such challenges.[2]

The Altars

The most solemn rites performed by the Son of Heaven took place at altars. This portion of the exhibition brings together important examples of the ritual equipment used with an altar, the paraphernalia needed to carry out sacrifices under the ritual system that maintained the position of the Son of Heaven.

With the exception of the jade disk (No. **11**), none of the exhibits dates from the imperial era (late 3rd c. B.C. and later). Instead, they are relics unearthed through recent archaeology that were created and used during the declining Zhou Son of Heaven's reign. The Zhou ruler was styled a king *(wang),* and the lords who ruled the many states and polities outside the royal domain in theory owed him a kind of allegiance akin to European feudal obligations. Both sets of ritual vessels were produced for feudal lords, the ruler of the state of Huang and a prince of the state of Chu (Nos. **1-5** and **6-10**). While the former observed the niceties of ritual protocol, the latter may have claimed for himself a complement of tripods which by its number challenged the unique status of the Son of Heaven. These objects were physical manifestations of the ideological underpinning for the imperial era. They became prototypes for later ritual vessels and musical instruments.

Ritual equipment of all kinds continued to be used throughout the long span of imperial history. The neglect of later examples here is partially justified by the inclusion of important pre-imperial artifacts, but fundamentally it is an admission that our taste and historical judgment simply do not accord later vessels and bells the significance we grant to their Bronze Age prototypes. It would be possible to assemble ritual equipment from the last, Qing dynasty (vessels, bells, stone chimes, and so on), but it would be more difficult to find authentic imperial ritual paraphernalia from earlier periods. With some exceptions, most imperial ritual equipment seems to have been lost or perhaps still awaits the archaeologist's spade.

Ritual sites have not fared much better for most periods. Even though the Bronze Age witnessed a great flourishing of all kinds of ritual, few sites of altars, temples, or ceremonial courtyards have been discovered through modern archaeology. A few early examples of courtyards are now known, and in their plan they substantiate reasonably well the existence of the kind of "theatre" described in ritual texts in which a Shang or Zhou king would have discharged his ritual duties.[3] The basic courtyard plan served equally well for ritual and court functions and is the foundation for the later continuous development of the Chinese architectural tradition (see Ch. 2). Several sites have also been explored where covenants and oaths between feudal lords were sanctified by sacrifice and the burial of jades on which were written the texts of the compacts. But the look and precise description of a Bronze Age altar remain illusive. The presentation of the tripod vessels, altar table, and chime (Nos. **6-10**) from the tomb at Xiasi in Henan Province can only vaguely suggest the kind of setting where they were originally displayed and used.

The archaeological situation is not much improved for sites of imperial times. The foundations of the Mingtang, or "Hall of Brightness," built at the Western Han capital (near modern Xi'an) early in the 1st century A.D., was rescued from bulldozers in the 1950s and we can guess something of its structure and appearance from the archaeological remains.[4] The plan and functions of this site and its components have been hotly debated since the 1st century A.D. No comparable ritual sites survive from most later dynasties. Only in the Ming and Qing periods (15th-20th c.) do we have detailed plans or renderings of the ritual precincts.

Ming and Qing Dynasty Altars
The one period for which a reasonably complete complement of imperial altars survives is the Qing Dynasty (1644-1911). All are located in modern Beijing, although only a few retain their original look or their intended ambience. In all cases, these altars have been converted into public parks so that today a visit to them can be a surrealistic journey in which children's bumper cars wind their way through groves of ancient cypress, or the music of a carousel can be heard.

The Temple of Heaven. The Temple of Heaven (Tian Tan) is the largest of the Qing ritual precincts *(Fig. 1)*.[5] The immense scale of the site (twice the size of the Forbidden City) and the completeness of its halls make this site the best introduction to this architectural type. The vast expanse of land and many ancient trees evoke its original appearance and character. However, unlike the other altars at Beijing, the Temple of Heaven is divided into several ritual components designed for different sacrifices within the emperor's annual cycle of responsibilities. The most important were the offerings conducted for the winter solstice on the triple-tier Circular Mound at the south end of the precinct and the invocations for a good harvest performed at the triple-eave, conical-roofed Hall of Prayer for a Bountiful Harvest. The latter was rebuilt as recently as the 1890s, but its design and architectural symbolism follow canonical standards developed during the Ming period.

The Altar of the Earth. The Altar of the Earth (Fangze Tan) is north of Beijing outside what were the walls of the Tartar (or Inner) City. This large park is almost unaffected by any recent construction or adaptive uses, and the quiet of the spot is in keeping with the original ambience. The altar is a three-tier square platform faced with stone and yellow-glazed tiles within a pair of walls. Marble gates permit entry from each cardinal direction, but here there was no other competing ritual activity, only supplemental buildings such as the compound where the emperor would purify himself before the solemn event. Today the altar is bereft of its proper fittings. Only a few marble stands and sockets in the stone terraces remain to suggest the canopies and regalia used in a proper sacrifice. (A full array of Qing altar equipment can be seen, however, in the former Confucian Temple, now the Capital Museum.)

The Altar of Soil and Grain. In front of the Forbidden City, within Zhongshan Park, lies the Altar of Soil and Grain (Sheji Tan), the location of annual rites for spirits that were first presented cult offerings in the Zhou period (11th-3rd c. B.C.) when the royal line believed itself to be descended from a deity called Lord Millet. The altar is a small, three-tiered platform and, unlike the others described above, has five colors of earth within its stone facing. Central yellow is flanked by green earth for the east, red earth for the south, white earth for the west, and black earth for the north. This site has lost much of its original identity because of the construction of a playground and theatre nearby, but the sacrificial hall located behind the altar is an early Ming structure (15th c.), a rarity in Beijing today.

The Ancestral Temple. The Ancestral Temple (Tai Miao) lies at the southeast corner of the Forbidden City and is now surrounded by the Workers' Cultural Palace. Its front worship hall, which has been remodeled, is used for exhibitions. However, the front gate and front and middle halls are all Ming structures built during the mid-16th century.

Each of these altar sites had its equivalent in periods prior to the Ming and Qing. The surviving renditions in Beijing were the subject of long scholarly debate and architectural attempts to link the pre-imperial era to the pre-modern age. Although the solemn rites that once took place in these precincts will never be performed again, except perhaps as public theatre or spectacle for tourists, the grand purposes to which each site was dedicated are still evoked by the architecture itself.

Fig. 1 Aerial view of Temple of Heaven, Beijing.

Nos. 1-5 Ritual Vessels
Eastern Zhou (7th c. B.C., before 648 B.C.)
Tomb of Lady Meng Ji
Baoxiangsi, Guangshan County,
Henan Province
Excavated 1983
Xinyang District Cultural Relics
Administration

The Tomb of Lady Meng Ji

During the Spring and Autumn period (8th-5th c. B.C.), arranged marriages strengthened the bonds of loyalty between local lords and the Zhou king and the political alliances made by local lords among themselves. Young women who moved to the fiefs of their new husbands naturally brought with them a dowry, including ritual vessels for use in the ancestral temple. In some cases these objects were later interred in the tomb, as with this selection of ritual vessels. These five vessels were taken from the tomb of the consort of the Lord of Huang, a state located in modern Henan Province.

The consort of the Lord of Huang was called Meng Ji. Her lineage, Ji, is the same as that of the royal Zhou house, although she was actually a native of a small enfeoffed state called Zeng. Her husband, the Lord of Huang, was a member of the lesser-ranking Ying lineage whose ancestors had also been enfeoffed by the Zhou king. As a result of her higher birth, Lady Ji's burial was equivalent to that of the lord of a state.

Her tomb *(Fig. 2)* was excavated in the spring of 1983 following the accidental discovery of an adjoining tomb by workers at a brick factory.[6] After the workers had removed many of the objects from that burial, which we now know was the tomb of the Lord of Huang himself, archaeologists were called to the scene to take charge of the excavation. The consort's well-preserved tomb and its contents were then properly excavated. The coffin containing the Lady's remains was in excellent condition, its brightly painted red and black lacquer decor substantially intact. It is believed that Lady Ji was a woman of about 40. About 100 small jade carvings were found under the Lady's head and elsewhere near her body (Nos. **58-61**).

2. Hu Vessel, bronze
H: 12 in. (30.7 cm.); D: 6.75-9 in. (17-22.5 cm.)
Eastern Zhou (7th c. B.C., before 648 B.C.)
Tomb of Lady Meng Ji
Baoxiangsi, Guangshan County, Henan Province
Excavated 1983
Xinyang District Cultural Relics Administration

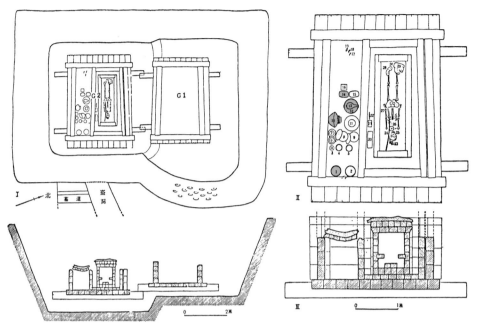

Fig. 2 Plan of tombs at Baoxiangsi, Henan Province.

Fig. 3 Rubbing of inscription on hu vessel (No. 2).

Fig. 4 Rubbing of dragon motifs from hu vessel (No. 2).

Ritual Vessels. Most impressive among the contents of Lady Ji's tomb were the 16 bronze ritual vessels bearing inscriptions naming her as their owner (Fig. 3). Her vessels are similar but superior in quality to vessels from the tomb of the Lord of Huang. Since the vessels actually name the "consort of Huang" as the owner, they must have been made after her marriage was arranged. It is possible they were produced in a Zeng foundry and then sent to Huang with Lady Ji or after she took up her new life. The vessels made for the Lord are consistent in style with those of Lady Ji but were given less attention, especially in their decoration. Whoever ordered these sets of ritual vessels therefore made it clear that Lady Ji was to receive bronzes of the highest quality, while those made for her spouse were executed at a lesser standard.

These bronze vessels survive today unblemished by the corrosion that produces the blue and green patinas common to most ancient bronzes.[7] The purple color is the result of their alloy composition, the percentages of copper, tin and lead used to make them, but why they did not develop a heavy patina after burial is less certain.[8] Although the shapes of these vessels are rather typical for their time and place, they bear exceptionally handsome relief ornament and inscriptions. They have few peers among objects of the same period.

It is clear from their shapes that these vessels are products of the state of Huang or its neighbors. The *hu* (No. **2**) has a pair of tigers with turned heads placed on the shoulder as handles. The vessel is oval in cross-section and carries a lid with a ring in the center. The *ling* wine vessel (No. **3**) is especially unusual because it has a flat lid not previously seen. This vessel type developed in the late Western Zhou period (9th-8th c.), but there are few examples. The *pan* basin and the *yi* ewer, or pouring vessel (Nos. **4** and **5**), form a pair; these types became popular in the Spring and Autumn period. Ancient texts tell us that the ewer was used to pour water into the basin for ritual washing of the hands. In many other discoveries, *yi* have been found placed onto the *pan* itself.

The main motif is a much-simplified dragon (Fig. 4), identifiable only by rudimentary eyes and a snub nose, in the form of a convoluted band which appears to pass over and under itself. Both the stylized dragons and the meanders found on these vessels are descended from the zoomorphic animal mask and dragon decor of earlier periods. In spite of the simplicity of this interlace decor, produced by repeatedly impressing an intaglio stamp into the clay casting molds, the total effect of many stylized dragons generates a pleasant rhythm within the densely packed fields. Similar motifs are in evidence on the lacquer-painted coffin and can be found among the Huang jades as well. Decor of this kind is associated with one of the major bronze finds of the early 20th century, a tomb near the city of Xinzheng (Henan Province) looted in 1923.[9] The dense interlace of simplified dragons seen on many of the vessels from that find is called the "Xinzheng style" by Western art historians. The term is misleading because the style was not created first in the Xinzheng region, nor was it limited to that area. This kind of ornament was one of several used during the Spring and Autumn period by both royal and non-royal foundries and has been found in a number of related discoveries in southern Henan Province, many of which can be associated with the state of Huang by their inscriptions.[10]

These vessels bear cast-in inscriptions and some, like those on the *hu* and *ling* (Nos. **2** and **3**), are placed on the exterior surface. This habit is rarely seen prior to the Spring and Autumn period. The basic intent of the inscription texts is an auspicious wish for the user: "Long life." A number of the characters are miswritten or are variant forms, another typical trait of this period.

1. Ding Vessel, bronze
H: 9.5 in. (24.2 cm.); D: 10 in. (25.3 cm.)
Eastern Zhou (7th c. B.C., before 648 B.C.)
Tomb of Lady Meng Ji
Baoxiangsi, Guangshan County, Henan Province
Excavated 1983
Xinyang District Cultural Relics Administration

3. Ling Vessel, bronze
H: 10.75 in. (27 cm.); D: 12.5 in. (31.4 cm.)
Eastern Zhou (7th c. B.C., before 648 B.C.)
Tomb of Lady Meng Ji
Baoxiangsi, Guangshan County, Henan Province
Excavated 1983
Xinyang District Cultural Relics Administration

5. Yi Vessel, bronze
H: 6.75 in. (16.8 cm.); L: 12.5 in. (31.3 cm.)
Eastern Zhou (7th c. B.C., before 648 B.C.)
Tomb of Lady Meng Ji
Baoxiangsi, Guangshan County, Henan Province
Excavated 1983
Xinyang District Cultural Relics Administration

4. Pan Vessel, bronze
H: 4.75 in. (12.2 cm.); D: 13.5 in. (34.5 cm.)
Eastern Zhou (7th c. B.C., before 648 B.C.)
Tomb of Lady Meng Ji
Baoxiangsi, Guangshan County, Henan Province
Excavated 1983
Xinyang District Cultural Relics Administration

6, 7, 8. Tripod with Ladle, bronze
(One of three, 7 and 8 not shown)
H: 26.5 in. (67.4 cm.); D: 26 in. (66 cm.);
Wt: 243.4 lbs. (110.4 kgs.)
Eastern Zhou (6th c. B.C., before 552-548 B.C.)
Tomb 2 at Xiasi
Xichuan County, Henan Province
Excavated 1979
Henan Cultural Relics Research Institute

Nos. 6-10 Royal Tripods, Altar Table, and Bells

Eastern Zhou
(6th c. B.C., before 552-548 B.C.)
Tomb 2 at Xiasi
Xichuan County, Henan Province
Excavated 1979
Henan Cultural Relics Research Institute

Fig. 5 Rubbing of inscription on sheng ding *vessel (No. 6).*

Tomb 2 at Xiasi

As the Danjiang Reservoir in southern Henan Province filled in 1976, its waters started to inundate and then erode the shore, revealing a concentration of ancient tombs on the west bank near Xiasi. Excavations began in the summer of 1978 to rescue the site. These tripods, bells, and altar table come from Tomb 2, the richest of the 25 burials unearthed. This tomb stands at the center of a cluster of three other medium-sized tombs, 16 small graves, and a chariot pit.[11] The person interred in Tomb 2 was accompanied in death by several persons of some status, at least 16 retainers or servants, and 6 chariots drawn by 19 horses. This discovery is one of the best examples of the full range of perquisites taken to the afterlife by a high-ranking noble in the pre-imperial period.

Many of the bronze artifacts were inscribed naming the "Royal Prince Wu" *(Fig. 5).*[12] The texts describe how he would use the vessels in solemn sacrifices to the Chu ancestors or to sanctify a covenant between feudal lords. These texts also praise the Prince for his fearlessness, strength, and the virtuousness of his rule. According to the early Chinese historical record, the *Zuo Commentary,* Prince Wu was the son of King Zhuang of Chu.[13] Under his brother, King Gong, he served as Marshall of Cavalry and was later elevated to the rank of Chief Military Commander. He died in 552 B.C. at age 49. Artifacts associated with the Chu royal house are not common, but these finds raise a particularly baffling question. Why would a royal prince be buried so far from the Chu capital of Ying (located at modern Jiangling, Hubei Province)?

Some scholars believe that Tomb 2 was not the burial of Prince Wu but that of another high-ranking person. The tripods (Nos. **6-8**) also bear incised inscriptions naming a certain "Chu Shu zhi Sun Peng," and in the case of the bells portions of the original inscriptions have been effaced. Thus, although all these vessels would have been made for Prince Wu, it seems they were later in the possession of one Sun Peng who succeeded Prince Wu as Marshall of Cavalry. Sun Peng died in 548, and it appears possible that he was buried at the Xiasi site after his decease.[14]

Ritual Tripods. The three tripods (Nos. **6-8**) were among seven found in Tomb 2 *(Fig. 6).* Tripods were potent political symbols that came as sets of different numbers according to social rank. In principle, only the Son of Heaven was entitled to the full complement of nine tripods.[15] A set of seven was reserved for nobility a step below the Zhou king. Further distinctions down the social ladder were marked by sets of five, three, and, finally by solitary tripods. By the Spring and Autumn period, these distinctions had eroded in the face of political reality. The kings of Chu and many other states had claimed for themselves the privilege of a nine-tripod set so that a royal Chu prince (or Chief Military Commander) was then entitled to a complement of seven, as found in Tomb 2.

These tripods are a variety peculiar to Chu and its neighboring border states.[16] *Sheng ding,* as they are called in their own inscriptions, are characterized by a flat base, constricted waist, and loop handles that flare outward at an extreme angle. The tripods bear cast-relief decor, including stylized dragons, meanders, and cloud-like patterns. Six dragons climb the sides of these tripods, their jaws engaging the lip of the vessels; other fantastic animals emanate from their heads and tails. The Xiasi *sheng ding* tripods are the most impressive ever discovered. Earlier sets from the tomb of the Marquis Yi (Sui Xian County, Hubei Province),[17] or the Marquis of Cai (Shou Xian County, Anhui)[18] pale by comparison. For example, the Sui Xian vessels are much smaller than the Xiasi tripods, which weigh more than four times as much. There is no doubt that these tripods truly were made for a royal patron.

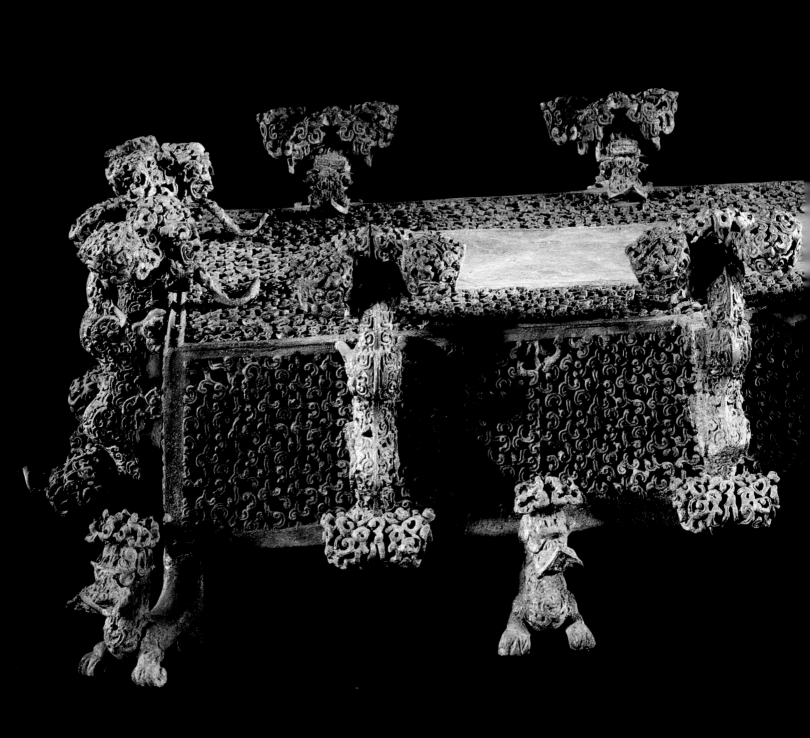

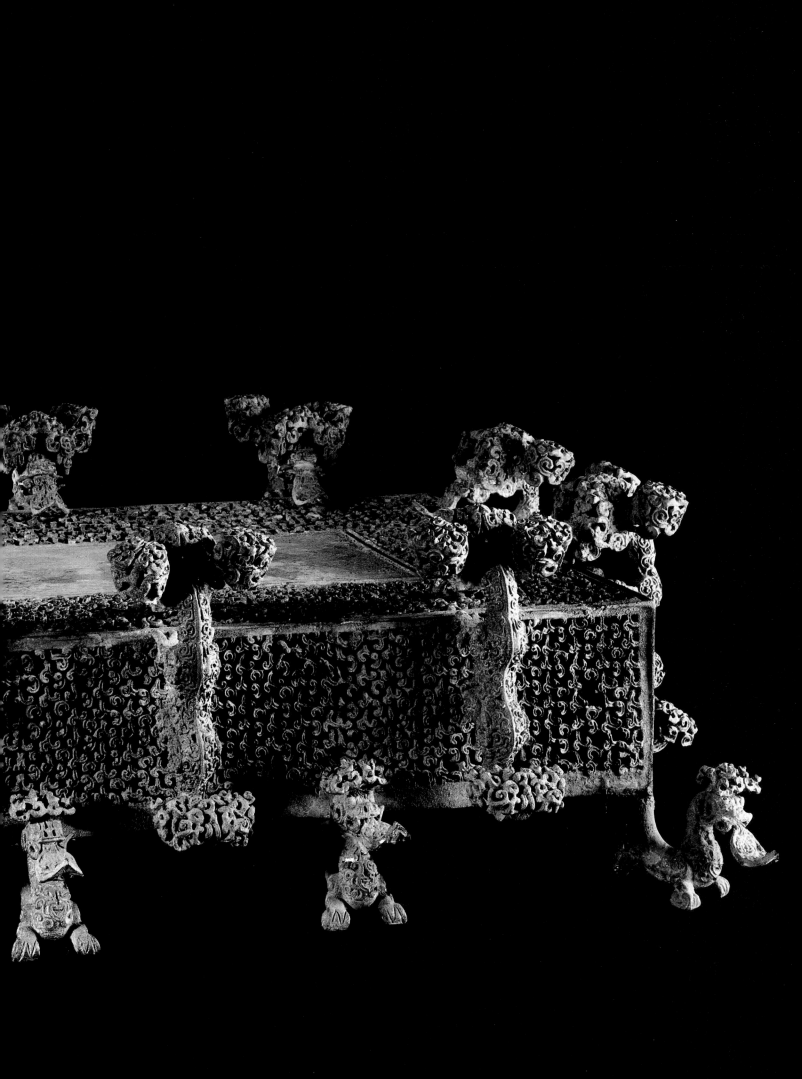

On the preceding pages,

10. Altar Table, bronze
H: 11.5 in. (28.8 cm.); L: 51.5 in. (131 cm.);
W: 26.5 in. (67.6 cm.); Wt: 207.8 lbs. (94.2 kgs.)
Eastern Zhou (6th c. B.C., before 552-548 B.C.)
Tomb 2 at Xiasi
Xichuan County, Henan Province
Excavated 1979
Henan Cultural Relics Research Institute

Bronze Bell from No. 9 (see p. 62)

The Altar Table. Quantity and size are not the only distinguishing features of the Xiasi vessels. The bronze altar table (No. **10**) is, at present, unique. Although a few earlier examples are known from the Western Zhou period,[19] there has been little evidence for the further manufacture of such ritual altar equipment. The table presumably was meant to carry several ritual vessels on its central top panel and would have been a part of a full ritual ensemble including the tripods. The foundry that created this altar table took the opportunity to realize a bizarre and daring design: 10 dragon-like animals support the table itself as legs, while 12 other animals climb the sides, peering over the top edge. The sides and skirting margins of the top were crafted as intricate, three-dimensional inter- lace panels held together by internal struts. These dragons and panels are among the earliest examples of the "lost-wax" process in ancient China.[20]

The usual technique for working bronze throughout the pre-imperial period was a ceramic "piece-mold" method in which a clay core was surrounded by several clay outer molds that received the molten alloy (as in Nos. **1-5**). This system had many virtues. It allowed the foundry artisan to work directly on the inner surfaces of the outer molds when creating the surface decor. The piece-mold method also allowed the use of models and stamps so that multiple versions of a single design could be turned out by a foundry. In the case of the vessels made for the consort of the Lord of Huang, a few master stamps were sufficient to create all the decoration and could be reused. The system also had its limitations. It was impossible to create complex three-dimensional elements using sectional clay molds.

The frothy curls and interlacery of the Xiasi altar table are the result of the new lost-wax technique. To create such effects, the artisans used filaments of wax or a similar material which could be sculpted into shape, however convoluted. When the wax positive was surrounded by clay, a complex mold was created. Upon firing, the wax was melted out, leaving hollow channels within for the molten alloy. Until the discovery of the Xiasi vessels, the earliest verified examples of the lost-wax method in China came from the Sui Xian tomb of Marquis Yi with its vessels dated around 433 B.C.[21] The Xiasi vessels push back the history of the lost-wax method to the 6th century.

The Chime of 26 Bells

This tomb also has another distinctive feature: its imposing chime of 26 bronze bells (No. **9**). At the time of excavation, the bells were found along the south wall of the chamber *(Fig. 6)* apparently removed from their wooden stand before burial. For display, we have reconstructed a stand based on a similar chime found in Tomb 2 at Sui Xian County, Hubei.[22] The bronze fittings of that stand were adequate for a two-tier frame with long horizontal wooden beams. Bronze links locked around the beams allowed the bells to be suspended by hooks inserted through rings on the collars of the shanks. Our reconstruction is hypothetical in some respects. The placement of all of the smaller bells on the upper register and the choice of a straight-line design cannot be verified.

This chime consists of 18 small bells and 8 larger ones. All have cylindrical shanks covered with relief ornament. The surfaces of the bells proper are also decorated with various dragon motifs in relief, but portions of the surfaces are reserved for inscriptions, the longest consisting of 108 characters *(Fig. 7)*. The texts praise the fine quality of the chime and its value in serving the Chu king and entertaining guests of state. From the bells, stone chimes, and wind instruments found in this tomb, it is evident that music was already highly advanced in the ancient state of Chu.

Fig. 6 Tomb 2 at Xiasi under excavation, Xichuan County, Henan Province.

*Fig. 7 Rubbing of inscription on bronze bell (No. **9**).*

Chimes of bronze bells were an integral part of the ritual of a Zhou lord. The bells were played both as the accompaniment to solemn ceremonies and as musical entertainment at court banquets. A large chime like this one probably required several musicians kneeling or standing before the bells, striking the outer lips with wooden mallets. Because Chinese bells are pointed ovals in cross-section, they can produce two different musical notes depending on whether they are struck at the center of the lip or at a point equidistant between center and edge. Thus, a chime of 26 bells could actually produce many more notes. Chimes are relatively common in tombs of Zhou nobility but usually in smaller sets of 9 to 14 bells. Only two larger chimes are known: the 65 and 36 bells of Sui Xian Tombs 1 and 2, respectively. Until a royal tomb from a northern state is excavated, it will not be known if such large chimes were peculiar to the south or were another index of social rank and material wealth common throughout China in this period.

9. Chime of 26 Bells, bronze
H: 9.25 - 47.5 in. (23.6 - 120.4 cm.)(smallest-largest)
W: 5.75 - 23.5 in. (14.8 - 59.7 cm.)(at lower lip)
Wt: 6.2 - 336.9 lbs. (2.8 - 152.8 kgs.)(smallest-largest)
Wooden frame (reproduction), L: 19 ft. (580 cm.);
Ht: 7.5 ft. (230 cm.)
Eastern Zhou (6th c. B.C., before 552-548 B.C.)
Tomb 2 at Xiasi
Xichuan County, Henan Province
Excavated 1979
Henan Cultural Relics Research Institute

No. 11 Ritual Disk
Eastern Han (2nd c.)
Tomb 43
Beilingtou Village, Dingzhou City,
Hebei Province
Excavated 1969
Dingzhou City Museum

Jade Disk Symbolism

Among the responsibilities of the first Western Han emperor's court ministers was the creation of a revised court ritual and etiquette. In producing this new body of practice, they were attuned both to old and new concepts, seeking to blend ideas where possible and in the process enhance the position of the emperor as Son of Heaven. Among the objects hallowed by tradition that could be employed in royal or imperial rituals were "auspicious jades." These objects were of distinctive shape and, according to the ritual specialists of the day, had been created in high antiquity as potent symbols of Heaven, Earth, and the four cardinal directions. The shape of Heaven, for example, was manifest in the circular form of the *bi* jade disk (No. **11**). In the ritual texts, these jades were also correlated with the colors associated with each direction: blue for Heaven, yellow for Earth, green for the East, red for South, white for West, and black for North. The symbolism extended even further: the colors and directions were also related to the "five agents," a cycle of forces that in effect propelled the functioning of the natural order. The seasons, natural materials, times, directions, and colors were all therefore linked by a common matrix of concepts for which the "auspicious jades" were primary symbols.

Jade Disks in Archaeology

Before the advent of scientific archaeology in this century, most ancient jades known to connoisseurs were categorized according to the canonical prescriptions of Zhou and Han ritual specialists. Very little was known of the actual dates or origin of such forms as the large perforated *bi* disks and the hollow squared tubes called *cong*.

11. Ritual Disk, jade
H: 11.75 in. (30 cm.); D: 9.5 in. (24.2 cm.)
Eastern Han (2nd c.)
Tomb 43
Beilingtou Village, Dingzhou City, Hebei Province
Excavated 1969
Dingzhou City Museum

*Fig. 8 Bi disk from tomb of Prince Liu Sheng, Mancheng
County, Hebei Province.*

Since the development of Chinese
archaeology, however, our view of ancient
jades has changed considerably. We now
know that some of the most common shapes,
including *bi* disks, are among the most ancient
examples of the craft of working jade and
other hardstones. *Bi* have been found in
several prehistoric Neolithic cultures, especially the East Coast Liangzhu culture of the
areas around modern Shanghai, Nanjing and
Hangzhou.[23] Large numbers of *bi* disks and
cong tubes are found in graves dating from
the 4th and 3rd millenia B.C. The best-known
find, a grave near Changzhou in Jiangsu
Province, contained 57 of these "ritual jades,"
including 24 *bi* and 33 *cong*[24] Even though
we now know the actual origins of these
ancient forms, the meaning of their shapes
remains obscure. Indeed, these objects were
already archaic and mysterious in early imperial times.

Jade Disks in Han Burials

This *bi* disk was recovered from a large tomb
near modern Dingzhou City, Hebei Province,
an area that in Han times was the seat of the
Zhongshan kingdom.[25] The jade burial shroud
and palace furnishings from Mancheng, a site
further north in Hebei Province, also testify to
the wealth and extravagance of the imperial
princes of this region. Tomb 43 has been
tentatively attributed to one Liu Ch'ang who
reigned as Prince of Zhongshan from A.D. 141
to 174, at which time the fief was abolished.
Although the tomb was badly damaged by
the collapse of its vaulted roof, the contents
clearly were extraordinarily rich and included
a jade burial shroud similar to that of Princess
Dou Wan.

The disk may have been placed within
the shroud, as was the case with many *bi* at
the two Mancheng tombs. In addition to being
a symbol of Heaven, jade *bi* disks served in
early imperial times as an auspicious token to
be placed near the corpse within a tomb. The
jade shroud of Liu Sheng contained 14 disks,
while that of Dou Wan held 15 with another 12
affixed to her coffin. Lesser numbers of disks
as well as disks in other materials have been
found in many Han graves.

The most impressive of the late Zhou and
Han *bi* disks are those with rampant dragons
poised on the circumference. Dragons were
already an imperial symbol by this time and
were used on all kinds of objects manufactured
for imperial use in life or death. The Chinese
dragon, unlike its Western equivalent, is an
auspicious animal. It is a composite beast with
a snake's body and four animal legs, the feet
of a deer, the claws of a dog, and the scales

and whiskers of a fish.

The premier example of the dragon-disk is the uncanny *bi* disk now in the Nelson Gallery-Atkins Museum, Kansas City, said to have been unearthed at the Jincun site near Luoyang.[26] The Kansas City disk is characterized by a style of relief spirals on the body and the style of the dragons' jaws, eyes, curling crests, and tails common to jades said to come from Jincun. The maker of the Kansas City disk plays with the inherent sense of energy and imbalance that his rampant animals evoke through their poses. While one beast crouches, charged with potential energy, at the top of the disk, the other surges into motion, suggesting the possibility that the disk will actually begin to move in a lively counter-clockwise rotation. A third animal, its long body twisting within the confines of the two jade circles, also seems to be drawn up, poised like a serpent ready to strike.

The lineal descendant of the Kansas City *bi* disk is the disk from Tomb 1 at Mancheng *(Fig. 8)*.[27] Here two animals stand back to back, chests thrown out much like later chimeras and other stone guardian animals. Their lower bodies, however, join and ascend to create a pointed crest, curling bodies subordinated to an ornamental rhythm. The spiral pattern of the disk's body is now simplified and the central perforation is void.

Tomb 43 provides a third instance of this dragon-disk type, and evidence for the later history of the ornamental style exemplified by the Jincun and Mancheng jades.[28] On this disk two dragons confront each other clutching a ring in their jaws. The bodies are tightly composed, in contrast to the open work of the Jincun piece, and with the ring they form a compact, emblematic form. Two lesser animals climb the circumference at equally spaced points on a common level with the perforation. The pattern of relief spirals seen on the Kansas City and Mancheng disks has been still more simplified. The date of the Tomb 43 disk could be late Western Han and certainly is no later than Eastern Han.[29]

Such magnificent *bi* disks were created in Han times for solemn court ceremony or sacrifice, only to become the pride of a selection of jades interred in burials. More than the ubiquitous unadorned circular *bi* so common to grave archaeology, these specimens truly were symbols of Heaven.

1. A good exception to this rule is Howard J. Wechsler, *Offerings of Jade and Silk: Ritual and Symbol in the Legitimation of the T'ang Dynasty,* New Haven, 1985.

2. For an emperor's views on himself, see Jonathan D. Spence, *Emperor of China: Self-Portrait of K'ang-hsi,* New York, 1974.

3. See Robert L. Thorp, "Origins of Chinese Architectural Style: The Earliest Plans and Building Types," *Archives of Asian Art* 36(1983):22-39, and the same author's "The Architectural Heritage of the Bronze Age," in *Chinese Traditional Architecture,* ed. Nancy S. Steinhardt, New York, 1984, pp. 59-67.

4. Robert L. Thorp, "Architectural Principles in Early Imperial China: Structural Problems and Their Solution," *The Art Bulletin* 68.3(September 1986):360-378.

5. For a good pictorial introduction to this and other altar sites, see *Beijing gu jianzhu* [The Ancient Architecture of Beijing], Beijing, 1986.

6. "Excavation Report of the Tombs of Lord Meng of Huang and His Consort of the Early Spring and Autumn Period" (in Chinese), *Kaogu* [Archaeology], 1984.4:302-32.

7. *Zhongguo meishu quanji* [Encyclopedia of Chinese Arts], *Gongyi meishu bian* [Arts and Crafts], Vol. 5, *Qingtongqi* [Bronzes], Part II, ed. Li Xueqin, Beijing, 1986, Nos. 14-15.

8. On alloy recipes as they affect color, see W.T. Chase, "Bronze Casting in China: A Short Technical History," *The Great Bronze Age of China: A Symposium,* ed. G. Kuwayama, Los Angeles, 1983, pp. 100-123.

9. Li Xueqin, *Eastern Zhou and Qin Civilizations,* New Haven, 1985, pp. 85-86.

10. For example, early Spring and Autumn vessels from Luoshan (*Wenwu* [Cultural Relics] 1980.1:51-53), and Xinyang (*Wenwu* 1981.1:9-14), both in Henan Province.

11. "Spring and Autumn Period Chu Tombs at Xiasi, Xichuan County, Henan," (in Chinese) *Wenwu* 1980.10:13-19.

12. Zhao Shigang and Liu Xiaochun, "A Trial Interpretation of the Inscription on the Wang Zi Wu *Ding*" (in Chinese), *Wenwu* 1980.10:27-30.

13. *The Chinese Classics,* trans. James Legge, Vol. 5, *The Ch'un Ts'ew with the Tso Chuen,* reprinted Hong Kong, 1960, pp. 454-490.

14. Li Ling, "Who Was 'Chu Shu zhi Sun Peng'" (in Chinese), *Zhongyuan wenwu* [Cultural Relics from the Central Plains] 1981.4:36-37. See also Wen Bigui, "The Longcheng Site at Xiasi, Xichuan, Henan and the Chu Xi Settlement" (in Chinese), *Kaogu* 1983.6:542-544.

15. Wang Shimin, "Some Ideas about the Ritual System of the Upper Elite in the Western Zhou and Spring and Autumn Periods" (in Chinese), in *Wenwu yu kaogu lunji* [Essays on Cultural Relics and Archaeology], Beijing, 1986, pp. 158-66.

16. *Henan sheng bowuguan* [The Henan Provincial Museum], Zhongguo bowuguan [Chinese Museums], Beijing, 1982, Nos. 33-42; *Zhongguo meishu quanji, Gongyi meishu bian,* Vol. 5, *Qingtongqi,* Part II, Nos. 16-18.

17. See Robert L. Thorp, "The Sui Xian Tomb: Re-Thinking the Fifth Century," *Artibus Asiae* 43(1982-83):67-92.

18. *Shou Xian Cai Hou mu chutu yiwu* [Artifacts Unearthed from the Tomb of the Marquis of Cai at Shou Xian], Beijing, 1956, Pl. 4.

19. See *The Great Bronze Age of China,* ed. W. Fong, New York, 1980, No. 48, for an example from the Tianjin Museum. Another table is in the collection of the Metropolitan Museum of Art, New York.

20. Ren Changzhong and Wang Changqing, "The Casting and Restoration of the Bronze Altar Table with Cloud Patterns of the Spring and Autumn Period from Xiasi, Xichuan, Henan" (in Chinese), *Kaogu* 1987.5:474-478.

21. On the lost-wax method, see Hua Jueming, "The Origins and Development of the Lost Wax Method" (in Chinese), *Keji shi wenji* [Collected Papers in the History of Science and Technology] 13(1985):63-81.

22. "Brief Excavation Report of Tomb No. 2 at Leigudun, Suizhou, Hubei" (in Chinese), *Wenwu* 1985.1:16-36. See also *The Unearthed Cultural Relics from Leigudun, Suizhou, Hubei,* Hong Kong, 1984, Pl. 66.

23. Wang Zunguo, "Brief Account of the 'Jade Burials' of the Liangzhu Culture" (in Chinese), *Wenwu* 1984.2:23-35.

24. "Excavation of the Sidun Site at Wujin, Changzhou, Jiangsu in 1982" (in Chinese), *Kaogu* 1984.2:109-129.

25. "Excavation Report of Han Tomb No. 43 at Ding Xian, Hebei" (in Chinese), *Wenwu* 1973.11:8-20.

26. *Handbook of the Collections,* Kansas City, 1973, Vol. II, *Art of the Orient,* p. 23. On the Jincun tombs, see Li, *Eastern Zhou and Qin Civilizations,* pp. 29-32.

27. *Mancheng Han mu fajue baogao* [Excavation Report of the Han Tombs at Mancheng], Beijing, 1980, pp. 133-135.

28. *Hebei sheng chutu wenwu xuanji* [A Selection of Cultural Relics Unearthed in Hebei Province], Beijing, 1980, No. 267; *Zhongguo meishu quanji* [Encyclopedia of Chinese Arts], *Gongyi meishu bian* [Arts and Crafts], Vol. 9, *Yuqi* [Jades], ed. Yang Boda, Beijing, 1986, No. 193.

29. Yet another example of this type is known from a Han tomb at Ding Xian. See "Excavation Report of the Han Tomb at Beizhuang, Ding Xian, Hebei" (in Chinese), *Kaogu Xuebao* [The Journal of Archaeological Studies] 1964.2:127-159. Reproduced in *Zhongguo meishu quanji, Gongyi meishi bian* Vol. 9, *Yuqi,* No. 190.

2 THE OUTER COURT

The Last Dynasty

The Son of Heaven was also a head of state. He was a worldly ruler who shouldered many of the same responsibilities as those of monarchs in other cultures more familiar to Westerners, such as the kings of European history. The Son of Heaven presided daily at a court attended by the highest government officials. He celebrated major state occasions such as the New Year and oversaw such events as the dispatch of an army or the reception of a captured enemy leader. Like a European king, a Chinese emperor might receive foreign emissaries eager to establish cordial state-to-state relations. In all these activities, the unique Son of Heaven was a worldly ruler and, burdened with such duties, the theocrat acted as a senior bureaucrat.

In other ways, the Chinese sovereign differed from his European peers. A Son of Heaven would promulgate each year's new calendar, which was critical if the world and all its parts were to operate harmoniously. The emperor himself presided over the palace examination, which was the highest level of the civil service examination system. As an act of Confucian piety, a Son of Heaven might host a palace banquet to honor the most venerable men of his realm. These activities set a Chinese ruler apart from his Western equivalents.

Notes to Chapter 2 are on p. 94.

26. Dragon Throne and Cushion, gold lacquer on wood, silk
Throne, H: 65 in. (165 cm.); L: 46.75 in. (119 cm.);
W: 27 in. (69 cm.)
Cushion, L: 39 in. (99 cm.) W: 21.25 in. (54 cm.)
Qing (18th c.)
Shenyang, Liaoning Province
Shenyang Palace Museum

29. Dragon Screen, gold lacquer on wood
H: 7 ft. 3 in. (220 cm.); W: 6 ft. (185 cm.)
Qing (18th c.)
Shenyang, Liaoning Province
Shenyang Palace Museum

The Emperor at Court

Each imperial capital had its outer court where the Son of Heaven ruled. From the time of the First Emperor of Qin, high ministers assembled there to attend and advise the sovereign. The style of rule varied considerably over time and so the emperor's presence in the outer court changed accordingly.

The founder of the Western Han, Liu Bang (known as Han Gaozu, r. 206-195 B.C.), was a commoner by birth. When he assumed the throne, he became disgusted by the outrageous conduct of his cronies. Hacking at the columns of the palace hall with their swords and urinating in public was unseemly behavior for trusted companions turned high ministers of the new emperor. Among Liu Bang's most urgent tasks, therefore, was the creation of a court etiquette to insure a proper degree of dignity in the presence of the Son of Heaven. This etiquette regulated the actions of those who attended court and enhanced the authority and dignity of the emperor.

Through the post-Han period of division and into the Tang, Chinese rulers were generally first among social equals. High ministers at court came from the aristocratic families who regularly provided consorts to the throne. In such a society, the Son of Heaven had an advantage, but high ministers were still able to address him with directness. These centuries are notable for wise ministers whose sage counsel benefited the Son of Heaven and the state. Perhaps the most illustrious were the great Tang Taizong (r. 626-649) and his trusted but independent minister Wei Zheng.[1] Minister Wei could not always sway the strong-willed Taizong, but his ability to speak the truth and counterbalance the power of the emperor became a model for high officials in later periods. Taizong's reputation as an exemplary emperor rests as much on his ability to listen to Wei Zheng and other ministers as on his own accomplishments.

After the Tang, however, the equation changed fundamentally. The position of the Son of Heaven was so inflated and the status of the elite families sufficiently diminished that there developed an insurmountable barrier between the two. Few high ministers could resist the power of the throne. The Ming (15th-17th c.) rulers effectively instituted terror and cruelty in the ranks of officialdom. An official whipped and horribly mutilated to the verge of death was a persuasive demonstration of imperial despotism. An able Ming Son of Heaven was a supreme autocrat of a different order from his predecessors of the early imperial era.

Fig. 10 Hall of Supreme Harmony, Forbidden City, Beijing.

In the meantime, court etiquette and ceremony became more complex and stringent. What began in Western Han as a rowdy gathering of a commoner emperor and his cohorts ended as high theatre. Regulations dictated the different levels of court assemblies, the participants and their dress, deportment, and positions, the musical accompaniment, and the imperial regalia to be displayed. In spite of this suffocating etiquette, many Chinese emperors functioned as able administrators. They reviewed masses of documents, passed judgment on official appointments, retirements and punishments, and deliberated with their advisors on large-scale public works, military campaigns, and other matters of state. When a weak or underage sovereign sat on the throne and was manipulated by ministers, the empress dowager, or eunuchs, court gatherings could be a charade with only the appearance of normal rule.

The Three Great Halls of State

When the new Ming capital was constructed in Beijing in the first decades of the 15th century, the responsible officials recalled the achievements of previous dynasties for an architectural expression of the imperial institution. They devised a striking and timeless statement of grandeur and power and created a ritual stage for court theatre in which there was only one significant actor: the Son of Heaven. For 24 sovereigns of the Ming and Qing Dynasties, the Three Great Halls of State within the Forbidden City were that theatre.[2]

The entrance to the palace, the Noon Gate (Wu Men), is an imposing, even brutal, design *(Fig. 9)*. Twin arms extend from the gate at right angles to the wall and define a large courtyard in front of the palace. High above 40-foot (12 m.) walls rise five pavilions: four corner towers and a central gatehouse as large as a palace throne hall. Five portals penetrated this gate. The one at the center was reserved for the Son of Heaven, those on the left and right were used by imperial princes and high court officials; at the corners two more gates were for the normal traffic of the palace. The massive red-painted, crenellated walls were a formidable bulwark against attack. At the same time, they expressed the overwhelming power and physical force at the disposal of the emperor. Placed on the same central axis as the principal halls of the palace, the Noon Gate stood watch over the imperial and inner cities.

Fig. 9 Aerial view of Forbidden City, Beijing.

Fig. 11 *Throne in Hall of Supreme Harmony, Forbidden City, Beijing.*

The emperor could hold court here as well as inside the Forbidden City. In the courtyard below the Noon Gate prisoners of war would be presented to the throne. In Ming times, public lashings might take place here as a lesson to all. From his seat in the central gatehouse, the Son of Heaven could proclaim the new calendar or send out a military expedition. The sovereign was so remote from those assembled below that his words had to be echoed by those in immediate attendance. Their words in turn were repeated by others standing nearby until the command was relayed with enough volume by enough voices to be heard by the crowd below. When the imperial throne was in place atop the Noon Gate, the sovereign literally towered over his subjects. The gate itself became the throne of the Son of Heaven.

Within the Noon Gate lay a large courtyard of about seven acres, divided by the Golden River which was crossed by five marble bridges. Anyone attending court had by this point passed through a succession of gates aligned on the palace and city's north-south axis. The visitor moved through a sequence of carefully varied spaces, alternating broad yards and narrow avenues, his direction and field of vision controlled by the enclosing walls. Thus, the architecture prepared members of court for their entry into the grandest and most important space of all, the courtyard below the Hall of Supreme Harmony *(Fig. 10)*. As musicians played in the gatehouse, the officials crossed the bridges over the Golden River, passed through the gatehouse, and filed into the next courtyard.

Atop three marble-clad terraces, the Hall of Supreme Harmony loomed over the ten acres of courtyard below. Court was normally held at dawn and its business was to be concluded before the sun had fully risen. To those attending court, the hall would be darkly silhouetted against a lightening sky. Incense spewed from burners arrayed on the terraces below. Another orchestra with singers under the eaves of the hall performed as the officials took up their positions. Wearing court robes emblazoned with insignia of rank (Nos. **23-24**), they marched at a dignified pace, carefully scrutinized for any unseemly conduct or infraction of the dress code.

The Son of Heaven, borne on a sedan chair from the rear of the palace, mounted the terraces before the hall and, attired in appropriate court costume (Nos. **12-14**), ascended the throne. The emperor's seat on a high platform deep within the hall *(Fig. 11)* was well beyond the sight of anyone below the top terrace. The Son of Heaven's presence was proclaimed by his attendants carrying regalia in the courtyard (illustrated in No. **25**). Court began with the cracking of long whips. All present kowtowed repeatedly to the throne, kneeling and banging their foreheads on the pavement stones. High ministers allowed to approach the throne from the terrace outside the hall prostrated themselves repeatedly before conducting any business. With nobles and representatives from the ministries assembled before him, the Son of Heaven would conduct the myriad affairs of state.

The Outer Court

The Son of Heaven required a grand setting in which to perform the role of worldly ruler. In such a highly stratified society, every material expression of the imperial personage had to be the largest and best. Wherever he was, the emperor needed a throne and it required accessories befitting its occupant (Nos. **26-41**). Architecture and furnishings were produced to prescribed dimensions, materials, and decorative symbolic images. Similarly, a court assembly required particular costumes for all involved, not least the Son of Heaven (Nos. **12-24**) who donned different garments according to his activities. All court attire was produced according to the social rank and official status of the wearer. Every aspect of a dawn court announced the roles and relationships of the participants, from the lowliest pennant-carrying guardsman to the Son of Heaven seated on his throne.

Such architecture, furnishings, and costumes are extant only from the Ming and Qing periods (15th-20th c.). No imperial court architecture and few furnishings or costumes survive from the pre-Ming periods, but it may be presumed that the forms we know were heavily influenced by earlier dynasties. The objects in this unit therefore depict the court furnishings and costumes from the last dynasty, the Qing (1644-1911). This is the only portion of the exhibit that focuses on a single period while examining one theme. Most of the objects date from the reign of the Qianlong Emperor (r. 1735-1796). Much of the look of late imperial China is the result of Qianlong's efforts to refurbish the palace and other imperial establishments. Eighteenth-century court taste, a blend of native Chinese and Manchu habits and preferences, here represents late imperial China.

Although some related material exists in collections outside China, there are essentially only two sources for such exhibits: the Palace Museum in Beijing, and the Palace Museum in Shenyang (Liaoning Province) where most of our objects come from. Shenyang was the original seat of the Manchus and their capital before the conquest of China in 1644. Throughout the Qing, the Manchu emperors continued to occupy the palaces at Shenyang *(Fig. 15)*. As a result, those halls were furnished and equipped with the same categories of objects that were used in the Forbidden City and the other Qing palaces. Thus, the throne from Shenyang and its complement of accessories were produced by the same artisans who created the thrones of the Beijing palace. Indeed, some palace furnishings, including this throne, have moved back and forth between the two palaces. The Shenyang exhibits represent the mainstream of Qing court taste as well as objects in the Beijing palace collections.

14. Emperor's "Dragon Robe," silk
H: 54.75 in. (139 cm.); W (hem): 42 in. (107 cm.)
Qing (18th c.)
Shenyang, Liaoning Province
Shenyang Palace Museum

Nos. 12-24 Imperial Costume and Rank Insignia
Qing (18th c.)
Shenyang, Liaoning Province
Shenyang Palace Museum

Shou symbol

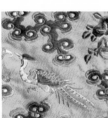

Pheasant

Paired dragons

Axe

Details from "Dragon Robe"

The costume of the Son of Heaven distinguished him from all others. Made from the finest woven and embroidered silk textiles embellished by gold thread, peacock feathers, and pearls, the emperor's robes incorporated special symbols of his unique status. Under the Qing, there were regulations and practices that combined native Chinese and Manchu traditions in garment construction and usage.[3] The Manchus adopted much from the Ming system of court dress including the dragon motif and the 12 symbols of authority. However, the Qing emperors knew that earlier non-Chinese regimes (the Liao, Jin, and Yuan) that had totally adopted Chinese dress and habits had not survived long, and they were determined not to repeat the same mistake. As a result, new styles of decoration and the selection of robes, hats, boots, and accessories of proper court attire were introduced.

During the Qing, cloth for the imperial robes was mainly made in Weaving Offices (Zhizao Ju) supervised by the Beijing palace but located in the silk industry cities of Jiangning, Suzhou, and Hangzhou. Designs for the robes were first created by artisans of the Imperial Household Department, approved by the Board of Rites and the emperor, and then sent to the weavers. Creating a single robe might have required almost thirty months. Both the gold work and the silk embroidery are estimated to have required more than a year each.[4] Within the palace were storehouses for the textiles as well as tailors. One scholar reports that as many as 10,000 robes of all kinds are still held in the palace collections.

The Emperor's Clothes
The most ornate court costume was ritual attire worn by the Son of Heaven as the unique, irreplaceable link between an all-powerful Heaven and the world. This included court attire *(chao fu)* and the imperial surcoat *(gun fu)*. The emperor's summer court attire (No. **12**) is a robe of light-weight yellow silk consisting of an apron-like skirt and a close-fitting jacket. Yellow was the usual imperial color, but other colors were used for special occasions such as sacrifices at the Temple of Heaven (blue), the Altar of the Sun (red), or the Altar of the Moon (white). The cut of the jacket may reflect the traditional wardrobe of the horse-riding Manchus who needed close-fitting clothing for warmth and freedom of movement. The right-over-left front closure of the jacket is probably a Chinese custom, but the long sleeves with flaring horsehoof cuffs may have been adapted from Manchu hunting dress. The black borders, cuffs, and collar were replaced by fur for the winter *(Fig. 12)*.

The repertoire of symbols on these robes establishes the virtues and cosmic role of a Son of Heaven. Here the Manchus followed well-established Chinese precedents. Foremost is a host of five-clawed dragons *(long)*, the species reserved for the imperial person. Court attire features dragons everywhere, large and small, frontal and rampant: on both the front and back of the jacket, on each shoulder, at the bottom jacket border, on the upper and lower areas of the skirt, and on the cuffs and collar. An additional 12 ancient symbols of authority established the Son of Heaven's role in the universe. John Vollmer writes:

Symbols for the sun and moon at the shoulder and for the constellation and mountain at the chest and back denote the four principal annual sacrifices made by the emperor. The fu *symbol and axe denote temporal power; the paired dragons and pheasant, dominion over the natural world. The water weed, libation cups, flame, plate of millet, and the mountain at the back symbolize the five elements of nature: water, metal, fire, plant life (by extension, wood), and earth.*[5]

These symbols originated in the early imperial era and were revived by succeeding dynasties for exclusive use on the emperor's robes. Adopting these emblems certified Manchu legitimacy within the framework of Chinese ideology.

Fig. 12 Portrait of Qianlong Emperor.

Detail of Emperor's Outer Robe, No. **13** (see p. 76)

*Fig. 13 Qing rank insignia as worn (see Nos. **23-24**).*

The emperor's outer robe (No. **13**) was worn over court attire for the most august state occasions. Cut shorter than the summer court robe and without an overlapping closure at the front, this traditional Chinese garment has straight cuffs. Four golden dragons within medallions are set off against the dark satin, with symbols of the sun and moon on the shoulders and stylized Chinese characters for "longevity" on the chest and back. Similar surcoats became required for all court members after reforms in the dress code during the reign of the Qianlong Emperor, about 1759. Rectangular rank insignia (Nos. **23-24**) were worn on surcoats by all officials *(Fig. 13)* after this time.

"Dragon robes" (Nos. **14** and **17**) were the most common palace dress and in the Qing system could be worn by both the emperor and empress. Unlike formal court robes, they are cut as long one-piece tunics using four panels of cloth. Dragon robes *(long pao)* preserve the overlapping closure and horse-hoof sleeves of court attire, however. Court regulations describe them as having nine dragons but only eight are visible. Some writers have hypothesized that the emperor's own body constituted the ninth, but in reality one dragon was embroidered on the inside of the robe.[6] Nine was a perfect and auspicious number associated with the emperor. Both dragons and the 12 symbols of authority float amid stylized, five-color clouds above an agitated sea with four rocky mountains of precious stone. These motifs themselves may have had cosmic significance as representations of the world-ocean and earth-mountain.

Court regulations prescribed that the emperor, empress, high officials, nobles, and civil and military officials of the upper ranks wear necklaces of 108 beads (No. **21**). Women of rank five and above were also required to add such jewelry to their court robes. Many semi-precious stones including agate, pearls, and coral were used for these necklaces, but this example is entirely jadeite. Like the pectorals of ancient times (Nos. **58-60**), court necklaces complemented formal attire and required a seemly deportment. Dress was completed by appropriate hats and footwear. Summer hats (No. **16**) were donned in the third lunar month and exhanged for winter head-gear in the eighth month.

The Qianlong Emperor's reign (1735-1796) was the great age of Manchu power, a time when the borders of China expanded to their maximum pre-modern dimensions. The emperor's armor (No. **18-19**) consists of iron plates riveted together and covered by dark silk. The helmet is surmounted by a special variety of pearl from the Songhua River of Heilongjiang Province that was reserved exclusively for the emperor and empress. The sword (No. **20**) was carried by the Qianlong Emperor during military reviews, hunts, inspection tours, and at the start of campaigns. Its handle is jade, while the scabbard was made from a tree bark with the appearance of golden lacquer.

The Imperial Seal

According to legend, Empress Wu of the Tang Dynasty changed the name of imperial seals to *"bao"* (treasure) because the former name sounded too much like the word for "death." No imperial document was complete or fully sanctioned without the imprint of the imperial seal, the final and literal stamp of authority. Seals were jealously guarded but few pre-Qing imperial seals are known. A Western Han seal discovered near Xi'an is perhaps the only surviving example from the early imperial era.[7] Already at that time, however, the basic form of imperial seals had been established. Jade was the favored stone, and they were generally square with a dragon-shaped grip on the top. The size of the Qing seals far exceeded that of earlier periods. In addition, Qing seals often carry legends in Manchu script as well as Chinese characters *(Fig. 14)*. During the Qing, the Hall of Union (the middle of the three rear palaces) was the repository for the emperor's 25 seals.

22. Qianlong Emperor's Seal, jade
H: 3.75 in. (9.5 cm.);
W (base): 5 in. (12.6 cm.); Wt: 6.8 lbs. (3.1 kgs.)
Qing (18th c.)
Shenyang, Liaoning Province
Shenyang Palace Museum

13. Emperor's Outer Robe, silk
H: 44.5 in. (113 cm.); W (hem): 41 in. (104.5 cm.)
Qing (18th c.)
Shenyang, Liaoning Province
Shenyang Palace Museum

16. Emperor's Hat
H: 8 in. (20.5 cm.); D: 11.75 in. (30 cm.)
Qing (18th c.)
Shenyang, Liaoning Province
Shenyang Palace Museum

15. Emperor's Boots
H: 18.25 in. (46.5 cm.)
Qing (18th c.)
Shenyang, Liaoning Province
Shenyang Palace Museum

17. Empress' "Dragon Robe," silk
H: 50.75 in. (129 cm.); W (hem): 44.75 in. (114 cm.)
Qing (18th c.)
Shenyang, Liaoning Province
Shenyang Palace Museum

19. Qianlong Emperor's Helmet
H: 13.75 in. (34 cm.)
Qing (18th c.)
Shenyang, Liaoning Province
Shenyang Palace Museum

20. Qianlong Emperor's Sword
L: 37.5 in. (95 cm.)
Scabbard, L: 35 in. (89 cm.)
Qing (18th c.)
Shenyang, Liaoning Province
Shenyang Palace Museum

23. Nine Rank Insignia for Civil Officials, silk
Sizes range from 9.25 x 10.25 in. to 13.25 x 13.5 in.
(23.5 x 26 cm. to 33.5 x 34 cm.)
Qing (18th c.)
Shenyang, Liaoning Province
Shenyang Palace Museum

Rank Insignia

The Ming Dynasty instituted a system of rank insignia for court officials using birds and animals to represent each level within the court bureaucracy.[8] Shortly after their conquest, the Qing emperors perpetuated the system, but because the Qing surcoat was cut down the middle *(Fig. 13),* insignia worn in front were made as two pieces, and only squares on the back were single pieces. These sets of civil and military insignia (Nos. **23-24**) were all sewn to the back of the surcoat. The civil ranks are represented by various birds and the military ranks are symbolized by animals. In the latter pecking order, both ranks seven and eight are represented by a rhinoceros. Unlike the Ming, the Qing insignia are brilliantly colored and feature a busy background as seen in the dragon robes.

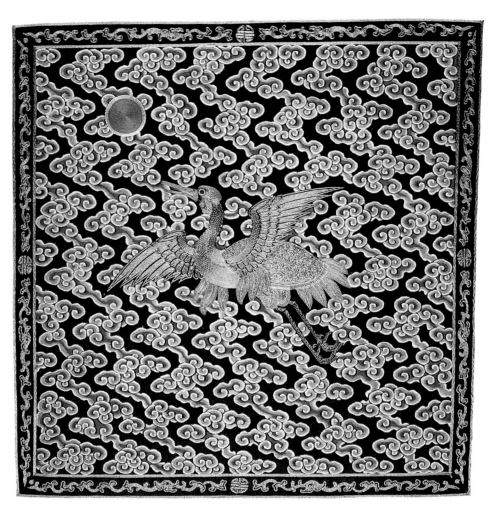

Rank insignia as worn

1. Crane
   xianhe

2. Golden pheasant
jin ji

6. Egret
lusi

3. Peacock
kongque

7. Mandarin duck
xichi

4. Wild goose
yunyan

8. Quail
anchun

5. Silver pheasant
baixian

9. Paradise flycatcher
lianque

24. Eight Rank Insignia for Military Officials,
silk
Sizes range from 9 x 10 in. to 16 x 16.75 in.
(23.2 x 25.2 cm. to 40.5 x 42.5 cm.)
Qing (18th c.)
Shenyang, Liaoning Province
Shenyang Palace Museum

1. "Unicorn"
   qilin

Rank insignia as worn

2. Lion
shizi

6. Tiger cat
biao

3. Leopard
bao

7, 8. "Rhinoceros"
xiniu

4. Tiger
hu

9. "Sea horse"
haima

5. Bear
xiongba

Accession Portrait of the Qianlong Emperor
(r. 1736-1795), ink and color on silk, hanging scroll
Palace Museum, Beijing

The fourth son of the Kangxi emperor, Qianlong (1711-1799) took the Manchu throne at age 25 and ruled for sixty years. This portrait is a collaborative work from several hands, including the Italian artist Giuseppe Castiglione (1688-1766), and ought to be compared with the aged Qianlong shown in figure 12.

Portrait of the Empress Xiaoxianchun, ink and color on silk, hanging scroll
Palace Museum, Beijing

One of 29 consorts and palace ladies of Qianlong, the Lady Fucha (1712-1748) was the Emperor's first Empress and was much beloved by him. She died at age 36 while returning with the Emperor from an imperial inspection tour of Shandong.

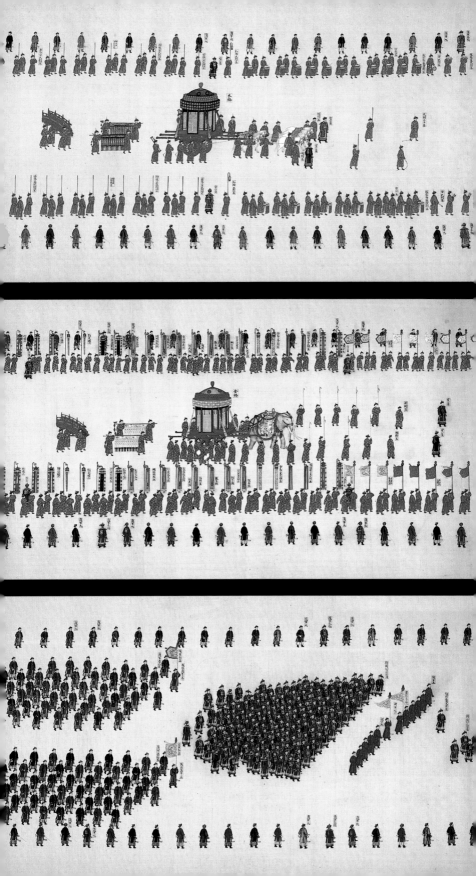

No. 25 "The Emperor's Honor Guard in Procession"
Qing (18th c.)
Shenyang, Liaoning Province
Shenyang Palace Museum

When the Son of Heaven moved from the inner palace, he was accompanied by an armed honor guard. In early imperial times, this guard included warriors bearing large shields (known as *lu*). As these entourages became more complex, a record (known as a *lu bu*) of the position of each member of the honor guard was needed. The latter phrase became the general term for an imperial honor guard. By the Tang and Song periods, the Son of Heaven's honor guard might entail thousands of attendants. The Song emperor Shenzong (r. 1067-1085) reportedly had an entourage of 22,000 on formal state occasions. Although the composition of the honor guard changed from dynasty to dynasty, the concept and nomenclature survived. In the early Qing Dynasty, however, the emperor's entourage was quite small: six attendants carrying banners, two with parasols, and six armed guards.

In 1748, the Qianlong Emperor promulgated new regulations for the mature Qing protocol governing the imperial honor guard. Under these regulations, there were four versions of the honor guard. The emperor was to be accompanied by 104 attendants and guardsmen when he moved out of the Forbidden City into the confines of the Imperial City. For movements outside the Imperial City, the entourage grew to 152 attendants. Formal court assemblies, however, demanded more extensive demonstrations of imperial grandeur. For a full-scale court, the honor guard was increased to more than 560 attendants who would take their places along the central axis between the south palace gate and the Hall of Supreme Harmony during the morning audience. Still more solemn occasions such as the annual sacrifices at the Circular Mound of the Temple of Heaven, by this same logic, required an even more lavish display of imperial authority. For such events, the honor guard was augmented to a total of 660 attendants and guardsmen. Known as the Da Jia Lu Bu, this most complete imperial honor guard is the subject of the hand scroll in this exhibit (No. **25**).

The scroll was painted by a committee of court artists under the general direction of one Wu Gui. It commemorates the winter solstice visit of the Qianlong Emperor to the Temple of Heaven in 1748 for the annual sacrifice to Heaven. The artists set themselves a challenging task. Rather than simply recording the regalia and chariots of the emperor, they created a total description in pictures and text of the 3,766 participants in this grandest of imperial honor guards.

Their artistic vision became 56 feet (17 m.) of documentary painting of the highest caliber. As a "newsreel" of the event, this is as complete and accurate a picture of an 18th-century emperor's honor guard as one could wish for. As the viewer follows the procession from right to left, he encounters each member of the honor guard. All are depicted in proper dress and carry their assigned imperial regalia: more than 140 pennants, dozens of canopies, over 50 banners, plus weapons, fans, musical instruments, and the other paraphernalia that accompanied the Son of Heaven when he left the palace. The entire procession marched in clusters around elephant-drawn chariots. When the Son of Heaven finally makes his appearance toward the end of this scroll, he has been preceded by hundreds of attendants, guardsmen, and several chariots. Even then, the emperor is hidden behind the curtains of his palanquin. Cartouches throughout the scroll name the official rank of each member of the honor guard.

On the following page, "Emperor's Palanquin" (section from No. **25**)

25. "The Emperor's Honor Guard in Procession" (Da Jia Lu Bu), by Wu Gui et al., hand scroll (three sections)
L: 56 ft. (1,745 cm.); H: 19.25 in. (48.9 cm.)
Qing (18th c.)
Shenyang, Liaoning Province
Shenyang Palace Museum

Nos. 26-41 Imperial Palace Furnishings
Qing (18th c.)
Shenyang, Liaoning Province
Shenyang Palace Museum

Throughout the Qing Dynasty, the Manchu emperors continued to use the palaces at Shenyang, the modern capital of Liaoning Province. The palace halls were remodeled and refurbished several times to bring their furnishings up to the same standard that the court enjoyed in Beijing. Nonetheless, these halls stand apart from the more familiar architecture of the Forbidden City. The most distinctive feature of the Shenyang Palace is the eastern precinct with its polygonal throne hall at the north and smaller halls for each of the eight Manchu banners arrayed before it *(Fig. 15)*. Although the Shenyang palace was first designed in emulation of Ming architecture, the Manchu builders modified the Chinese style in several characteristic ways. None of the halls of state was elevated on a three-tiered terrace as seen in the Forbidden City, but residential halls were built with multiple stories, a practice almost unknown in Beijing. Roofs in the Shenyang palace are multi-colored rather than the uniform yellow of the Beijing palace. Grotesque monster masks punctuate the brackets under the eaves of the Shenyang halls.

The Shenyang palaces were architecturally distinctive, but their furnishings were consistent with the styles of the capital. Indeed, the palace furnishings were made in the same workshops in the southeast that supplied the Forbidden City. Among the most critical of palace furnishings were the thrones, the literal seats of power where the Son of Heaven engaged in the business of rulership. The throne ensemble displayed here is typical of that used by the Qing Son of Heaven for court business.

Like palace architecture, thrones were constructed according to strict regulations within a total system in which all palace halls were ranked. The highest ranking hall, the Hall of Supreme Harmony in Beijing *(Fig. 10)*, exceeded all others in scale, dimensions of timbers, decoration of its tile roof, and in its throne ensemble. Raised on a platform almost seven feet (2 m.) off the floor, this throne *(Fig. 11)* was backed by a seven-panel screen. Both screen and throne were covered with carved dragons in gold lacquer. A similar throne sits in the Palace of Heavenly Purity (Qianqing Gong), the first of the three rear palaces and the emperor's normal residence during the Ming and early Qing. Here a five-panel screen stands behind the seat.

Our throne shares the same style of carved dragons covered in gold lacquer but is intended for a smaller throne hall. The accompanying screen is designed as three panels, a step down from the five-panel type used in a more formal hall. In Shenyang, this throne could have been installed in either the Dazheng Hall or the Chongzheng Hall. In the Beijing Forbidden City, this throne would have

been appropriate to audiences in the Gate of Heavenly Purity or the Hall of Mental Cultivation when the emperor busied himself with paperwork and deliberations with his high ministers. Both the throne and screen are made in parts so they could be disassembled for moving. The desk and its writing equipment (No. 30) were used by the emperor in his role of supreme bureaucrat, shuffling the memorials and palace documents that passed before him every day.

A throne ensemble demanded a repertoire of accessories. Some were practical and others were symbolic of the roles and virtues of the ruler. Thrones were equipped with padded cushions and two accessories: a jade scepter known as a *ru yi* (No. **27**) and a carved red-lacquer spittoon in the shape of a persimmon (No. **28**) (for a more prosaic but necessary function in Beijing's parched environment). The names of these two objects were the basis for a pun. The words for "persimmon-shape" sound like that for "affairs of state"; the name *ru yi* literally means "as you will" or "according to your wish." Thus, together the two objects embody the wish that the emperor might manage all affairs according to his will.

Fig. 15 Shenyang Palace, Liaoning Province.

26. Dragon Throne and Cushion, gold lacquer on wood, silk
Throne, H: 65 in. (165 cm.); L: 46.75 in. (119 cm.); W: 27 in. (69 cm.)
Cushion, L: 39 in. (99 cm.) W: 21.25 in. (54 cm.)
Qing (18th c.)
Shenyang, Liaoning Province
Shenyang Palace Museum

29. Dragon Screen, gold lacquer on wood
H: 7 ft. 3 in. (220 cm.); W: 6 ft. (185 cm.)
Qing (18th c.)
Shenyang, Liaoning Province
Shenyang Palace Museum

Detail of arm from "Dragon Throne," No. **26** (see p. 92)

Every throne required a proper rug such as the magnificent carpet from Xinjiang Autonomous Region (No. **41**) dominated by silk threads of red, orange, and yellow interwoven with strands of gold and silver. This particular carpet was presented to the palace in the Qianlong reign. Placed on a low platform, the rug defined the emperor's own space and also offered warmth and comfort.

Auspicious animals flank the throne itself. Closest are two *cloisonne* elephants symbolic of universal peace (Nos. **31-32**), which seems to have been standard with imperial thrones during the Qing. At either side are gilt bronze single-horned scaled creatures called *lu duan* (Nos. **33-34**). Such beasts appear when a virtuous and sage ruler is on the throne and the ranks of officialdom emulate the ruler's high standard of conduct. These beasts are also common to most throne hall ensembles. The crane candle holders (Nos. **35-36**), also *cloisonne,* are symbolic of long life but also supply needed light. Completing the ensemble are two pairs of incense burners. One pair of cylindrical burners has a pavilion roof and coiled dragons (Nos. **37-38**); the others are *cloisonne* tripods (Nos. **39-40**). The highly perfumed atmosphere of the court further augmented the presence of the emperor. These accessories were used for most thrones, but unlike the seats and screens they do not vary appreciably in scale or workmanship from one setting to another.

1. See Howard J. Wechsler, *Mirror to the Son of Heaven: Wei Cheng at the Court of T'ang T'ai-tsung,* New Haven, 1974.

2. On the Forbidden City, see Wan-go Weng and Yang Boda, *The Palace Museum Peking: Treasures of the Forbidden City,* New York, 1982, Ch. 1, and Yu Zhuoyun, ed., *Palaces of the Forbidden City,* New York, 1984, pp. 48-71.

3. John E. Vollmer (*In the Presence of the Dragon Throne: Ch'ing Dynasty Costume in the Royal Ontario Museum,* Toronto, 1977, pp. 15-28) makes a case for the Manchu contribution to court attire. Verity Wilson (*Chinese Dress,* London, 1986) disputes some of Vollmer's assertions.

4. Wilson, *Chinese Dress,* p. 98.

5. Vollmer, *In the Presence of the Dragon Throne,* p. 58.

6. *Zhongguo fushi wuqian nian* [Five Thousand Years of Chinese Costume], Hong Kong, 1984, p. 174.

7. Qin Po, "Discovery of a Jade Seal of a Western Han Empress and a Bronze Brazier Dated Ganlu 2" (in Chinese), *Wenwu* 1973. 5:26-29.

8. Schuyler Cammann, "The Development of the Mandarin Square," *Harvard Journal of Asiatic Studies* 8 (1944) : 71-130.

41. Carpet, silk
12.2 x 12.2 ft. (372 x 372 cm.), with 5.5 in. (14 cm.) fringe
Qing (18th c.)
Xinjiang
Palace Museum, Beijing

a.

30. Writing Set
a. Water basin and dipper, D: 3.5 in. (9.3 cm.)
b. Ink stone, L: 12.5 x 9.5 in. (32 x 24 cm.)
c. Brush tube, 6 x 3.5 in. (15.2 x 9.3 cm.)
d. Jade ink stand, H: 1.25 in. (3.3 cm.)
   Ink stick, D: 4.75 in. (12.2 cm.)
e. Two ivory brushes, L: 9.25 in. (23.5 cm.)
   Jade brush stand, H: 3.25 in. (8.3 cm.);
   L: 7.75 in. (19.7 cm.)
Qing (18th c.)
Shenyang, Liaoning Province
Shenyang Palace Museum

b.

c.

d.

e.

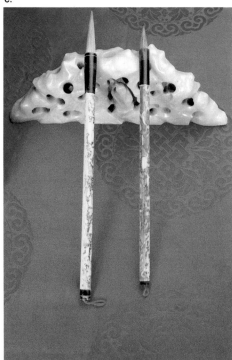

27. Scepter, jade
L: 17 in. (43.5 cm.)
Qing (18th c.)
Shenyang, Liaoning Province
Shenyang Palace Museum

28. Spittoon, carved red lacquer
H: 3 in. (7.5 cm.); D: 6 in. (15 cm.)
Qing (18th c.)
Shenyang, Liaoning Province
Shenyang Palace Museum

31, 32. One of a Pair of Elephants, *cloisonne*
(32 not shown)
H: 15.75 in. (40.3 cm.); L: 11.25 in. (28.5 cm.)
Qing (18th c.)
Shenyang, Liaoning Province
Shenyang Palace Museum

35, 36. One of a Pair of Crane Candlesticks,
cloisonne (36 not shown)
H: 4 ft. 4 in. (133 cm.); D: 8.25 in. (21 cm.)
Qing (18th c.)
Shenyang, Liaoning Province
Shenyang Palace Museum

37, 38. One of a Pair of Incense Burners,
gilt and inlaid bronze (38 not shown)
H: 41 in. (104 cm.); D: 10.25 in. (26 cm.)
Qing (18th c.)
Shenyang, Liaoning Province
Shenyang Palace Museum

39, 40. One of a Pair of Censers, *cloisonne*
(40 not shown)
H: 41 in. (104 cm.); D: 31.75 in. (81 cm.)
Qing (18th c.)
Shenyang, Liaoning Province
Shenyang Palace Museum

3 THE TEMPLE

The Emperor and the Three Teachings

Notes to Chapter 3 are on p. 120.

As "Son of Heaven," the emperor was both secular ruler and theocrat. His ritual roles (summarized in Ch. 1) did not fulfill all his religious obligations, either as an embodiment of the state or as an individual. In carrying out his duties as supreme ruler, the emperor also had to serve as a moral teacher and patron of learning. Through his personal attention to the writings of the sages, the Son of Heaven promoted upright conduct among those who served him and the state. By patronizing the two major religious traditions, Buddhism and Taoism, the emperor gained merit above and beyond the call of his ideological duty. Not all emperors patronized these faiths, but private devotions were often a part of life in the Inner Court.

The term "Three Teachings" refers to three great philosophical and religious traditions: Confucianism, Buddhism, and Taoism (see pp. 25-29 for summary of the Three Teachings). In the early periods, Buddhism was a catalyst to the development of religious Taoism and state-sponsored rites that elevated Confucius to the status of sage. In the later dynastic periods, the outward expressions of worship and imperial donations and patronage were similar for each of these traditions. Building or refurbishing a temple hall, commissioning images or murals, sponsoring publications, and underwriting religious observances for each of the Three Teachings became the objects of imperial support in many periods.

Confucianism

The oldest of the Three Teachings in China was Confucianism. Confucius was the sage known as Master Kong (Kong Fuzi, 551-479 B.C.) who lived in the ancient state of Lu (modern Shandong Province). Confucius held office for only a short time, but gained his lasting fame for the philosphical and political teachings which his disciples, who numbered as many as 3,000, transmitted to later ages.[1] *The Analects* are a compilation of sayings and exchanges between Confucius and his disciples compiled at some point after the death of the Master.[2] It was not until the Han (2nd-1st c. B.C.) that Confucian teachings became a state orthodoxy through imperial sanction. Many scholars from Shandong Province were given positions at court to teach the proper interpretation of the Classics (such as the *Book of Poetry* or *Book of Documents*), some of which were thought to have been edited by the Master. By promulgating authorized versions of those writings (later cut in stone at the Eastern Han capital), the court elevated the status of Confucius. Gradually rites were conducted both at court and at Confucius' native place, modern Qufu in Shandong Province. Temples were erected for such ceremonies, and most major cities in China today still have their Confuciuan temple (Wen Miao), which often now serves as the local museum.

The Classics and the writings of Confucius and his major followers became an integral and essential part of the curriculum of all educated men, and the ideas of the Master penetrated all aspects of Chinese elite society and thought. There were alternative interpretations and applications of these canonical works in different periods, but as a body of thought Confucianism is remarkably unitary. Foremost among the values the Master promoted was humanity or benevolence *(ren)*:

Fan Chi asked about humanity.
Confucius said: "Love men."   Analects *XII.22*

Zi Gong asked: "Is there any one word that can serve as a principle for the conduct of life?"
Confucius said: "Perhaps the word 'reciprocity': Do not do to others what you would not want others to do to you."   Analects *XV.23*

At the core of Confucian teachings were human relationships. Throughout his sayings there is a strong belief in a natural moral order, a conviction that man can learn righteous conduct and that the past can serve as a model for human action.

44. Pentad Niche, painted stone
H: 40 in. (102 cm.); W: 22 in. (56 cm.)
Tang (7th c.)
Changzhi County, Shanxi Province
Shanxi Provincial Museum

Confucianism later developed along several courses. As a rich philosophical system, it gave rise in the Tang and Song dynasties (7th-13th c.) to a school of philosophical investigations now called Neo-Confucianism. Because he had become the patron saint of learning and teachers, many projects to publish and disseminate the Classics were carried out in the name of the Master. To emphasize the relevance of the past, rites to honor the sage became a part of the annual calendar. The great Confucian Temple at Qufu was built, rebuilt and refurbished perpetually by successive dynasties with similar provincial and local patronage. Yet the Confucian tradition did not develop a great need for devotional images, nor did it generally require large quantities of figural art of any kind. In addition to the Confucian temples and their ritual equipment, the major artistic expressions of Confucianism were steles (stone monuments) and publications.

Fig. 17 Altar of East Main Hall of Foguang Temple, Mount Wutai, Shanxi Province.

Fig. 16 Buddha Vairocana, Longmen, Luoyang, Henan Province.

Buddhism

Buddhism arrived in China over a period of several centuries from the Han onward. An ancient and highly evolved religious and philosophical system, it offered many attractions to the Chinese population at every social level. Although early Buddhism in South China gained the support of the gentry and stayed aloof from the state, in North China Buddhist clerics became a part of the state bureaucracy, and Buddhism was used by non-Chinese dynasties to maintain social and political control. In the great age of Buddhism in China, the Tang (7th-9th c.), there were new levels of court involvement.[3] Some emperors were raised as devout Buddhists and became generous patrons when they ascended the throne. The cosmopolitan age of Tang China was open to renewed contacts with the ancient centers of Buddhism in India, and new sects took root and flourished alongside older devotional creeds. Although sectarian competition certainly existed in Tang China, Chinese believers were generally open-minded toward the different strains of Buddhist thought and practice.

Imperial patronage ranged from establishing major temples and dedicating important pagodas and images to translation projects and other learned activities. Under the Empress Wu (ca. 684-705), Buddhist prelates promoted the idea that the earthly ruler was to be identified with the Buddha, and sutras (sacred writings) to support this idea were circulated. The height of imperial patronage at the Longmen cave chapels *(Fig. 16)* coincides with this phase of court preoccupation with Buddhism.

Buddhism was not unopposed in the Tang. Taoist leaders gained an equal footing before the court, and critics of the wealth, power, and alien character of Buddhism prevailed in 845 when a thorough persecution of the faith was ordered. Most temples and their contents were destroyed, monks and nuns were returned to lay life, and the land and wealth of the "church" was confiscated by the state. The Main Hall at Foguang Temple *(Fig. 17)* is one of the few temple buildings to survive this historic low point of the Buddhist Law within China.

Taoism

The third Teaching, Taoism (or Daoism), is a more complicated phenomenon to analyze, especially when considered over the span of imperial times. Before unification, the teachings associated with Lao Zi (Lao Tzu) and Zhuang Zi (Chuang Tzu, 369-286 B.C.) were among the many competing schools of political, social, and philosophical thinking that characterized the late Bronze Age.[4] Other schools shared many of their ideas, but in general Taoist thinkers provided a healthy antidote to the sober pronouncements of the Confucians. *Lao Zi* is the most enigmatic and most inspired of all early Chinese philosophical writings and has the distinction of having been translated into Western languages several dozen times. Where the *Lao Zi* is cryptic and illusive, the text named after Zhuang Zi is full of wit, paradox, and fable, expressing a healthy contempt for the proprieties of society.

In the early imperial era, disciples of the two Masters were joined by a diverse company of adepts and teachers of such arts as breath control, calisthenic regimens, alchemy, and other esoteric knowledge that promised the initiate longer life or even immortality. At the same time, Taoist thought was bound up with the political and philosophical programs of the so-called Legalists and, in addition, began to assume a role as a popular, sometimes millenarian, religion. We should differentiate between "philosophical" and "religious" Taoism, but even more categories are needed.[5] The 2nd-century B.C. tomb at Mawangdui contained a small library of silk books including an early version of the Lao Zi and texts associated with other strains of Taoism. There was also a manual of breathing exercises to increase longevity and other tracts typical of the great intellectual diversity of the age.

Imperial patronage of Taoism followed paths similar to those already described for Buddhism, and in some eras Taoist images and shrines were constructed on a par with Buddhist temples. Lao Zi, however, never attained the official status accorded to Confucius, nor was image-making so common in this tradition as in Buddhism. Still, major Taoist temples became the site of large mural decoration, and the Taoist Canon was finally published under imperial sponsorship. The Taoist pantheon was populated with a wide assortment of deities, from the supreme Jade Emperor to the lowest clerks and lackeys of the subterranean bureaucracy. These personages were also accommodated into Buddhist art and belief (see Nos. 53-57). In the late imperial period, the Taoist establishment had assumed many of the attributes of the rival Buddhist "church."

Although all three Teachings may be both religious and philosophical, they are not mutually contradictory and do not necessarily overlap. In many ways the range of topics and concerns that are "Confucian" and "Taoist" are complementary, and Buddhism offers still other compensations. The degree of their interaction is only now becoming evident, but Buddhism, basically a foreign religion, adapted as much to Chinese thought and traditions as the two native Chinese teachings accommodated themselves to Buddhism.

The Temple

The works selected for this portion of the exhibition are representative of imperial relationships to the Three Teachings. The Buddhist pagoda tiles and suites of stone images and paintings are typical of the artistic impact of court patronage. But there were imperially sponsored stone steles (Nos. 47-50) for all three traditions and here they must represent, however minimally, the imperial patronage of non-Buddhist establishments. Our selection of exhibits argues, implicitly, that more of aesthetic worth survives from the Buddhist tradition in such arts as sculpture and painting. However, more exposure to artistic enterprises linked to state Confucianism and Taoism is needed before this judgment can be considered conclusive.

Because architecture is not easily transported, the exhibits can only hint at the richness of a temple environment. The layout of the gallery copies the general plan of a Buddhist temple precinct. The pagoda with its reliquary (Nos. 51-52) was essential in any large temple, while the yards on both sides of the main axis were often given over to rows of steles. A major hall usually had mural decoration and could display ensembles of portable scroll paintings (Nos. 53-57). Within the temple's main devotional hall, an altar platform filled with sculpted images (Nos. 42-46) dominated the interior and provided the focus for worship. Confucian and Taoist temples share at least the general plan of a Buddhist temple, but without the pagoda.

42. Standing Bodhisattva, stone
H: 22.5 in. (57 cm.)
Tang (late 7th-early 8th c.)
Huata Village, Taiyuan, Shanxi Province
Excavated 1954
Shanxi Provincial Museum

Nos. 42-46 Buddhist Sculpture
Tang (7th-8th c.)
Taiyuan City, Taigu County, Changhzi County,
Ruicheng County, Shanxi Province
Shanxi Provincial Museum and Ruicheng
County Museum

The impact of Buddhism on the arts was so profound that the course of stylistic developments was irrevocably altered. It is impossible to conceive of the history of Chinese painting, sculpture, and architecture without reference to the Buddhist monuments that highlight the centuries after the fall of the Han (3rd c.). Although notable secular works in all three arts survive, it is Buddhist sites and monuments that preserve the greatest works of Chinese art from these centuries. The quality and quantity of what survives, however, is but a dim reflection of the original whole. Natural calamities and religious persecutions destroyed vast quantities of images, paintings, and temples, especially in the mid-9th century.

All three of the fine arts—painting, sculpture, and architecture—reached a mature stage in Buddhist works of the Tang period. Innovations in figural painting during the 5th and 6th centuries (see the copy of the wall painting from the tomb of Lou Rui, Nos. **117-125**) resulted in a fresh stage of advanced naturalism. Many of the greatest painters of the period were best known for their contributions to the walls of Buddhist temples, and contemporary critics were astounded by the technical skill and artistic vision of these masters of the brush. The greatest of Tang figure painters, Wu Daozi (active about 710-760), was supreme both for his extraordinary technical finesse and for his creativity as a painter of Buddhist deities, guardians, and hells.

Architecture flourished no less. Although no major temple survives from the early Tang, the two oldest surviving timber halls are confident, vigorous expressions of a sophisticated architectural system. The larger of these two, the East Hall at Foguang Temple on Mount Wutai dated before 857, gives a good impression of a major Tang monastery *(Fig. 17)*. Complementing these survivors in timber are a large number of masonry pagodas of every size and design, from the Great Goose of Xi'an (Shaanxi Province) to the "Forest of Tomb Pagodas" at Shaolin Temple (Henan Province).[6]

Tang sculpture represents the classic age of this art form in China. It has been remarked that a Tang sculptor could create the effects of any material, from soft human flesh to transparent gauze, in any media, whether wood, dry lacquer, metal, or stone. Complete technical mastery was matched by utter confidence, convincing naturalism, a high sense of drama, and exquisite taste. Tang sculpture sets the standard against which all earlier and later achievements are measured. Although many of the greatest works in wood, dry lacquer, and clay have probably perished, major statements still survive in metal and stone. Tang cave chapels, such as the Longmen *(Fig. 16)* and Tianlong Shan sites, are encyclopedias of Buddhist sculpture of the period, even more valuable because of the imperial patronage that created them.[7]

Any sizeable Buddhist temple constructed during the Tang had a complement of images installed on its altars. Often, however, it is only those images of durable materials that have survived. Many stone images were looted from cave chapels in the decades prior to World War II and tend to dominate Western collections, but there are equally as many stones from abandoned temple sites. Archaeologists and peasants have been unearthing large numbers of Buddhist images of stone and metal since 1949. Many fell victim to iconoclasm and were decapitated or disfigured before they were buried. Yet many others have emerged from their centuries of sleep underground in immaculate condition. Among all the provinces of China, Shanxi has yielded some of the most important recent finds, especially of the Tang.

The two stone images of seated Buddhas (Nos. **45-46**) have a common but uncertain origin. Both were given to the local authorities by a peasant who had been their keeper for 30 years.[8] These two Buddhas are seated on well-carved pedestals that rise from octagonal plinths with lotus-petal decoration. In each case, the sculptors have taken great pains to carve the falling drapery over the platform so that upright lotus petals underneath the cloth are clearly indicated. The Buddhas themselves are clad in monk's dress covering both shoulders. The proper right hands (now broken) probably were lifted in a gesture of charity; the left hands rest at the knee. A snail-curl hair style unifies the images, and both once had haloes behind their heads. Both images are dated by inscriptions to the first decade of the 8th century *(Fig. 18)*, and their style is consistent with other monuments of the period. In spite of their likely origin in southern Shanxi Province, there is nothing provincial about their style or workmanship. The plumpness of the facial features and suavity of the drapery as it interacts with the underlying forms of the body link these images to the finest products of imperial patronage, such as the reliefs from the Terrace of Seven Jewels (Qibao Tai) dedicated in the late 7th century by Empress Wu.

The standing bodhisattvas (Nos. **42-43**) that attend the Buddhas are a study in contrasts.[9] Each bodhisattva, a being on the brink of enlightenment, is dressed in the manner of an Indian prince, with bare chest and long skirt. They assume "hipshot" poses in which the weight of the body is shifted onto one stiff leg. The smaller bodhisattva from a former temple site at Hauta Village near Taiyuan (No. **42**) was unearthed in 1954 with a large number of stones.[10] Complete except for its hands, it is as suave a combination of naturalism and ideal proportions as the seated Buddhas. Patches of applied gilt still survive on the skirt. The larger, headless torso (No. **43**) was unearthed at another abandoned temple site in Taigu County. Heavy-set and voluptuous, this figure seems to be later in date than the two Buddhas and small bodhisattva. The sculptor was as concerned with the generous volumes of the figure as with the intricacies of the fall of its skirt. This figure anticipates a later Tang taste for ponderous, fleshy images.

The polychrome pentad niche (No. **44**) from Changzhi County is one of the best preserved examples of this sculptural form. The niche is shaped like a boat with the Buddha seated in the middle flanked by two standing bodhisattvas and two monk disciples. The Buddha assumes the so-called European pose with both legs hanging (rather than a cross-legged, lotus position) and makes the gesture of reassurance ("Have no fear") with his left hand. The two bodhisattvas stand relaxed in gentle S-curve postures; like the Buddha, they have round haloes behind their heads. All the images retain traces of color, but it is uncertain how much of that pigment is original. On the lower exterior face of the niche are earth spirits and a pair of lions, emblematic of the Buddha's royal status, with a flaming jewel between them. The facial expressions of each image are varied: the Buddha solemn, the bodhisattvas compassionate, the disciples adoring.

*Fig. 18 Rubbing of inscriptions on stone Buddhas (Nos. **45** and **46**).*

43. Standing Bodhisattva Torso, stone
H: 44 in. (112 cm.)
Tang (8th c.)
Taigu County, Shanxi Province
Shanxi Provincial Museum

45. Seated Buddha, stone
H: 31 in. (79 cm.)
Tang (dated to Chang'an reign, 701-704)
Ruicheng County, Shanxi Province
Ruicheng County Museum

46. Seated Buddha, stone
H: 35.75 in. (91 cm.)
Tang (dated to Jinglung reign, 707-709)
Ruicheng County, Shanxi Province
Ruicheng County Museum

聖人知孝之可以教人也故因嚴

之本歟經曰昔者明王之以孝理

于四海歟嗟乎夫子沒而微言絕

雅頌分為四詩丟聖逾遠源流益

必騁殊軌轍是以道隱小成言隱

之領袖夐龤劉邵抑又次焉劉炫

然分註錯經理亦條貴寫之琬琰

意有蒸明具載財文繁略之又義

Nos. 47-50 Calligraphy Rubbings
Tang (7th-8th c.)
Steles from Xi'an, Shaanxi Province; Taiyuan, Shanxi Province
Overseas Archaeological Exhibition Corporation

Few cultures have accorded the written word as much attention as China. Throughout its exceptionally long history, the Chinese writing system has been a powerful force for cultural identity and unity. The continuity of the system, in spite of several thousand years of linguistic change in the spoken languages, has been a crucial element in the strong consciousness of the past and its relevance that has permeated Chinese society to this day. A modern English speaker may trip over Shakespeare, labor at Chaucer, and find himself completely mystified by *Beowulf,* but a person literate in modern Chinese can read texts written as long ago as the time of Confucius (551-479 B.C.) and will recognize at least some characters of early Bronze Age inscriptions.

49. "The Stone Terrace Classic of Filial Piety," by Tang Xuanzong (r. 712-756),
rubbing (detail)
H: 11 ft. (338 cm.); W: 4 ft. 6 in. (137 cm.)
Tang (dated 745)
Overseas Archaeological Exhibition Corporation, Beijing

Chinese Language and Writing
The writing system became a potent tool for those in authority, probably as early as the late Shang period when the oldest preserved inscriptions were made. Even at this early date, the writing was sophisticated beyond any simple "pictographic" system. Chinese characters, then as now, are visual representations of words, units of meaning rather than carriers of sound. It is precisely for this reason that speakers of different Chinese languages (by custom called dialects) can communicate in writing even though each language assigns different phonetic values to the characters. The sophisticated writing system and its role in politics and religion served to define a specifically "Chinese" world in distinction to the many peoples in and around China who did not share the language or its writing. The exportation of Chinese characters to other East Asian peoples in turn was a conduit for the transfer of large portions of Chinese culture, still much in evidence in modern Southeast Asia, Korea, and Japan.

The normal tool for writing was always a hair brush with fluid ink. The Chinese brush was perfected in the Bronze Age and has not changed appreciably since.[11] Bamboo slips and silk rolls were the writing materials during ancient times until scribes turned to a revolutionary invention: paper. By the early imperial era, the first centuries A.D., paper was fast becoming the standard medium for all writing. The graphic writing system divided into three script types during the early imperial era: Regular, or Standard Script; Semi-cursive, or Running Script; and Cursive, or Draft Script. The appreciation of fine writing, of calligraphy as an art that mirrors the personality of its creator, can also be traced to this era. Well-known calligraphers became increasingly influential in the post-Han centuries, and their stylistic tastes and habits seriously affected the writing system. Although no new script types developed, many stylistic traditions thus emerged within each script type.

Calligraphy of the Two Wangs
Few subjects have engaged Chinese scholars as long or as intensely as the calligraphy of Wang Xizhi (307-365) and his son, Wang Xianzhi (344-388). Called the "Sage of Calligraphy," Wang Xizhi became the prototype of the Chinese cultured gentleman skilled at the arts, able to transform a received tradition and create a style of his own. Wang's handwriting was highly praised by early critics and became the most important model for fine calligraphy during the Sui and Tang dynasties. The Tang emperor Taizong (r. 626-649) did

more than anyone before or after to establish Wang's writing as the ultimate standard for all time. The emperor took Wang's style, especially in Regular and Semi-cursive Scripts, as a personal model, and himself became an accomplished calligrapher within the tradition. Taizong's knowledge of Wang's writings derived from an ambitious program of collecting and copying original specimens and early copies, and his mentor in calligraphy, Yu Shinan (558-638), was a leading proponent of Wang's Regular Script.[12]

Two works by Taizong are generally regarded as reliable examples from the emperor's hand: the "Inscription for the Hot Spring" and the "Inscription for the Jin Shrine" (No. **48**).[13] The latter was written by the emperor in 646 and then cut and erected at the shrine, which is located in the western suburbs of Taiyuan (Shanxi Province). Although the text is written in Semi-cursive Script in which strokes are connected, some influence from Regular Script can be seen in the independence of each character. There is a softness and buoyancy to the writing that contrasts with the austere Regular Script of Yan Zhenqing (No. **50**). The content of the inscription extols the political virtues of the ancient Zhou house and the civil and military strengths of the contemporary Tang regime.

The fascination with Wang's writings led to an ambitious project under the third Tang emperor, Gaozong (r. 649-683). Wang's writings had been collected in great number by Taizong, and many hand copies were produced by a fastidious tracing technique. In order to circulate and promote Wang's writings, it was decided to extract characters from Wang's calligraphy and use them to write the "Preface to the Holy Teachings" (No. **47**), a text composed by Taizong to eulogize the great traveler-monk Xuanzang (ca. 596-664) who had journeyed to India, the fountainhead of Buddhism. This text was 1,900 characters long, so that the entire compilation was a kind of calligraphic encyclopedia of Wang's style. The new version thus became known as the "Preface to the Holy Teachings Compiled from Characters Written by Wang Xizhi." The stone survives today in the Forest of Steles in the Provincial Museum at Xi'an.[14]

Like the "Jin Shrine" text, the "Preface to the Holy Teachings" was written in Semi-cursive Script, which elevated the status and utility of this type to a par with the more formal Regular Script. Semi-cursive Script simplifies individual strokes and even whole characters by connecting lines and dots and by abbreviating forms. Ligatures, the filaments of ink that appear between strokes and dots, are produced when the tip of the brush continues to move lightly over the paper surface in a connecting movement. In actual brush writing, adjacent characters are also joined by ligatures. The cutting of the stone is so expert that even these nuances are faithfully reproduced. Even more than in the formal script types, the reader of a specimen of Semi-cursive script can re-experience the act of creation, as the eyes follow the traces of the brush and the implied subtle movements of the writer's hand.

Stone Monuments and Rubbings

The inception of inscriptions cut into stone seems to correlate with the widespread use of iron tools in the later Bronze Age, particularly in the state of Qin which was to unify China in 221 B.C. The earliest stone inscriptions are associated with Qin, as seen on the "Stone Drums" now in the Palace Museum, Beijing, and stones bearing texts written for the First Emperor now known mainly from rubbings. By their very nature, stone-cut inscriptions are a public statement of monumental scale. The writing first used was the then-standard Seal Script, but Regular Script later became the usual choice. Clerical Script, a precursor to Regular Script, was widely used on stone monuments in the Han period, and both it and Seal Script continued in conjunction with Regular Script in later periods. It was only much later, during the Tang period (7th-9th c.), that Semi-cursive and Cursive Scripts were employed on large-scale public monuments.

Stone monuments (or steles) were erected for a variety of purposes, generally to commemorate an event or person. Stones produced for the First Emperor record his visits to different parts of the newly unified realm. In Han times, steles were used both for authorized versions of the Confucian Classics and for mortuary inscriptions. During the post-Han centuries, stones became a part of Buddhist and Taoist temples and cave chapels, as pious acts were recorded for posterity. By the Tang, stone inscriptions had become another of the Son of Heaven's political and moral tools. Major inscriptions for large and impressive steles were commissioned during the early Tang reigns by each emperor (Nos. **47-49**).

A logical consequence of the tools and techniques of writing available in early imperial times was the invention of rubbings or ink squeezes. All the necessary elements were at hand: incised inscriptions, paper, and ink. The virtue of a rubbing is that it is an exact, mechanical copy of the carved inscription, an impression much like a print taken from a woodblock. Thin paper is pushed into the intaglio recesses on the stone surface. A pad with ink is then pounced across the paper, leaving dark ink on all the raised and level uncut areas. When the paper is peeled away, recessed areas appear white against the solid ink ground. The rubbing will pick up the original cutting of the stone, and any damage on the surface as well. Rubbings began to be used to "publish" examples of fine calligraphy by at least the Tang period and were promoted even more under the Song and later dynasties.

The "Classic of Filial Piety" Rubbing. The Son of Heaven was a moral teacher who was charged to promote orthodox learning and the Classics of the Confucian tradition. As early as the Han and Wei dynasties, authorized versions of the Classics were cut into stone on imperial order, and some fragments of the "Stone Classics" from those eras still survive. The more ambitious Tang effort resulted in the "Kaicheng Era Stone Classics," a collection of 114 stones which took seven years to produce. Individual classics were also studied by the imperial person, and at imperial command debates at court were convened on matters of philosophy and ritual in which these writings were the final authorities.

A unique example of imperial involvement with a Confucian classic is the "Stone Terrace Classic of Filial Piety" (No. **49**) produced by and for the Tang emperor Xuanzong (r. 712-756) in 745.[15] This stele takes its name from its unusual square shape and position on an elaborate stone plinth. Four large blocks of stone, nearly 20 feet (6 m.) tall, were carved to form a great stone pillar, covered by an impressive cloud-bedecked cap. The stones were first set up at the Tang Academy but were moved twice in the 10th and 11th centuries, coming to rest in 1090 at their present location. This stele thus became the first "exhibit" of the Forest of Steles, China's first museum.[16]

The emperor wrote out both the text of the "Classic of Filial Piety" and a commentary of his own creation. The emperor's preface and the proper text were brushed in Clerical Script, a type that bridged the period from the archaic Seal Script of the Bronze Age to the Regular, Semi-cursive and Cursive Scripts that came

into wide use during the early imperial era. This script type is notable for plump characters with flaring horizontal and diagonal strokes. Many horizontal strokes flex upward, which lends a feeling of buoyancy to the vertical columns. This was the first script type that actually demonstrated the potentials of a pliant brush, and its choice here was an attempt to find writing appropriate to an ancient text. The commentary is written in smaller characters in double columns placed at intervals throughout the main text.

The "Stele for the Guo Family Temple" Rubbing. The Tang was an age of great calligraphers. Among the later figures, the writings of Yan Zhenqing (709-785) became a paragon of Regular Script (No. **50**). Yan's writing was characterized by its tartness and severity, and represents an early challenge to the orthodox tradition of the two Wangs. Yan's style avoids the suavity of the Wangs' writings and instead is modeled on epigraphic stone inscriptions from the period of the Northern Dynasties. In this case, a brush style was derived from writing developed in cutting stone inscriptions and then, by a turnabout common in art, was applied to stone inscriptions as an alternative to the conventional brush-writing of the day.

The "Stele for the Guo Family Temple" (No. **50**) was inscribed in 764 on behalf of the great general Guo Ziyi (697-781) to memorialize his father. The text records the family genealogy and official positions. General Guo had served with great distinction under four Tang emperors. Yan's participation in the creation of a family temple is another example of imperial patronage directed outside the palace. The heroic and bold script was created by Yan and perpetuated by his followers to differentiate their "Northern" tradition from the softer, more refined "Southern" tradition of the two Wangs. The individual strokes form a brushed equivalent of a chisel's path, yielding a crisp and firm definition to each stroke.

47. "Preface to the Holy Teachings Compiled from Characters Written by Wang Xizhi,"
rubbing (detail)
H: 8 ft. 7 in. (262 cm.); W: 45.5 in. (116 cm.)
Tang (dated 672)
Overseas Archaeological Exhibition Corporation, Beijing

48. "Inscription for the Jin Shrine," by Tang Taizong (r. 626-649), rubbing (detail)
H: 7 ft. 1 in. (217 cm.); W: 4 ft. 3 in. (133 cm.)
Tang (dated 646)
Overseas Archaeological Exhibition Corporation, Beijing

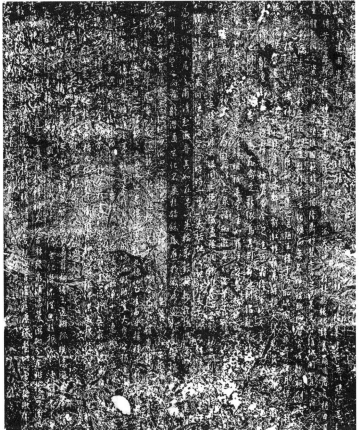

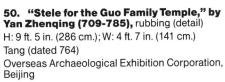

50. "Stele for the Guo Family Temple," by Yan Zhenqing (709-785), rubbing (detail)
H: 9 ft. 5 in. (286 cm.); W: 4 ft. 7 in. (141 cm.)
Tang (dated 764)
Overseas Archaeological Exhibition Corporation, Beijing

51. Arched Door Frame from Bao'en Temple Pagoda, glazed tiles

Top, Feiyang, H: 20 in. (51 cm.)
Middle, Lion, H: 17.25 in. (44 cm.)
Bottom, Elephant, H: 19.5 in. (50 cm.)
All 19 in. (48 cm.) wide, 15.7 in. (40 cm.) thick
Ming (ca. 1412–1428)
Liuli Kiln Site, Jubao Shan, Nanjing, Jiangsu Province
Excavated 1959
Nanjing Museum and Nanjing City Museum

Line drawing of Arched Door Frame, showing location of tiles

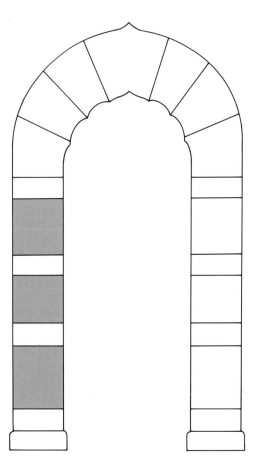

No. 51 Arched Door Frame from Bao'en Temple Pagoda
Ming (ca. 1412-1428)
Liuli Kiln Site
Jubao Shan, Nanjing, Jiangsu Province
Excavated 1959
Nanjing Museum and Nanjing City Museum

Perhaps the greatest monument of early Ming Buddhism was the pagoda constructed at Bao'en Temple just south of the capital at Nanjing. Regarded as one of the "Seven Wonders of the World" by foreign visitors of the 19th century, this edifice was an imperial commission built "to the standards of the Inner Palace" (in the words of a stone monument).[17] It was first proposed during the reign of the founding Ming emperor (Hongwu, r. 1368-1398), but work did not begin in earnest until 1412, the tenth year of the reign of his grandson, the Yongle emperor. It is recorded that at least 2.5 million ounces of silver flowed from the imperial purse to underwrite this project. Eunuchs and palace officials were charged with supervision of this ambitious project, and at times as many as 100,000 workers may have been employed.

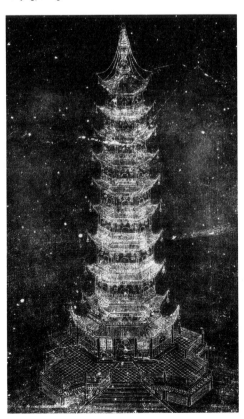

Fig. 19 Rubbing of rendering of the Bao'en Temple Pagoda, Nanjing, Jiangsu Province.

The temple and its pagoda were dedicated 16 years later in the third year of the fourth emperor, Xuande (1428). Although the temple's wooden-frame compounds and halls burned in 1566, the brick pagoda survived until 1856, when it was destroyed during the Taiping Rebellion. Today, all that remains of this monument are bricks and tiles (No. **51**).

The pagoda was an octagonal structure built nine stories high *(Fig. 19).* The exterior walls were white glazed bricks decorated with five-colored glazed tile ornaments for red balconies, green bracketing and doorways, and yellow eaves. All bricks and tiles were produced by the imperial kilns nearby in triplicate so that adequate replacements would always be available; one set was used in construction, the other two buried for later use. A peculiarity of the design was that the number of bricks required for each story was identical; as the tapering pagoda rose, the bricks employed were proportionately smaller.

Construction was also unusual. After the first level was complete, earth was mounded up around it to create a working stage for the masons. Once the second level was finished, the process was repeated so that both lower levels were encased in earth. By the time the topmost, ninth level was reached, the construction workers were standing on a pile of earth eight stories tall. After the entire structure was finished, this earth was then dug away, revealing a full nine-story pagoda. Nineteenth-century Western visitors estimated the height of the pagoda to be 260 feet (nearly 80 m.). The pagoda was outfitted inside and out with 146 niches for oil lamps that were lit at night and created a glow that could be seen for miles away. The oil for these lamps came from the imperial palace, another sign of the Son of Heaven's virtue as a patron of the Buddhist Law. The gilt finial that was mounted atop the pagoda included a cast-iron basin 12 feet (3.5 m.) in diameter, while 152 bells were at the eaves to ring in the wind. These exterior decorations and the interior furnishings do not survive, but they suggest something of the splendor of the establishment in its prime. A placard under the eave of the pagoda proclaimed it the "First Pagoda" (Di yi ta), which is surely no exaggeration.

The tiles (No. **51**) are portions of an arched door frame. Each story of the pagoda had four doorways, one aligned with each cardinal direction, as well as windows, bracketing, and eaves of glazed tile. All these features simulated wooden structural elements. Although the Bao'en Temple pagoda is lost, one can see much the same effect in the "Flying Rainbow" pagoda of the Guangsheng

Temple in Hongtong County (Shanxi Province).[18] This structure was erected about 1515-1527, a century later than the Nanjing pagoda, but it is another masterpiece of Ming glazed-tile decoration, a tradition especially strong in Shanxi Province. Its height, however, is approximately 100 feet less than the lost Nanjing pagoda. The decorative program for the Bao'en Temple pagoda was influenced by recent innovations in Buddhist art, especially the Lamaist styles of Tibet and Mongolia.[19]

In 1958 and 1959, the Nanjing City Museum and Nanjing Museum explored a site on Jubao Shan south of Nanjing City.[20] Their investigations revealed 60 kilns established under the early Ming to manufacture roof tiles and other pottery required for the Ming palace and the tomb of the founding emperor. Construction commenced in about 1366, before the formal establishment of the new dynasty, so the kilns probably were in use for several decades before the imperial order to begin work on the Bao'en Temple.

The kilns were a part of the Ministry of Works and one of five factories engaged in specialized production of architectural materiel. The glazed-tile factory had several yards in operation at any one time with about 1,700 skilled artisans assigned to it. In principle, these artisans were expected to work for about three months at a time once every three years. In practice, for large construction projects the artisans worked for much longer periods without respite. Inscriptions on the Bao'en Temple pagoda tiles name various low-level managers at the kiln yards and include registration numbers that indicate where the tiles were to be used in the pagoda. The clay used for these tiles was of a superior-quality white earth from Taiping County, over 40 miles (70 km.) away. According to official regulations published in 1393, each kiln was to be large enough to fire 280 "second-grade" roof tiles at one time with seven workers in attendance. Keeping the kilns at Jubao Shan in production would have required at least 400 or 500 workers. The pottery shops employed the remaining 1,200 artisans, working with molds and dipping the tiles into the glaze. Each tile required two firings: a first bisque firing and a second firing after glaze had been applied. Only a few of the tiles found at the Jubao Shan site were glazed, suggesting that there was little waste in the last stage of production.

Recent investigations in the vicinity of the lost pagoda have uncovered clues as to the two buried sets of tiles, and it has been proposed to reconstruct the lost monument using these tiles.

No. 52 Reliquary from Hongjue Temple
Ming (ca. 1436-1450)
Hongjue Temple
Niushou Shan, Nanjing, Jiangsu Province
Excavated 1956
Nanjing Museum

Niushou Shan (Ox Head Mountain) is a well-known scenic spot south of Nanjing. In addition to several ancient Buddhist temples, the mountain boasts two imperial tombs of the Southern Tang Dynasty (10th c.).[21] Hongjue Temple was built on the mountain about 1436-1450, and one of its pagodas, now lost, was outfitted with a reliquary (No. **52**) during that time by one Li Fushan, a eunuch official of the capital. Workers probing at the site of the destroyed pagoda in the summer of 1956 uncovered the stone chamber within the foundations where the reliquary had been deposited.[22]

This find is another testament to the impact of Lamaist or Tibetan Buddhist decorative motifs on early Ming Buddhist art. The reliquary is a gilt bronze miniature *dagoba,* the Himalayan form of the Indian *stupa* and a development parallel to the Chinese multi-storied pagoda. Four vase-shaped doors allow access to the interior, which contains Buddha images; the *dagoba* is surmounted by a bell-shaped dome with multiple layers of canopies below the finial. Such adornments were certainly a part of the lost Bao'en Temple brick pagoda as well. Surrounding the *dagoba* are four blue-and-white porcelain urns used to store fragrant herbs. The entire ensemble sits on a square stone base carved with stylized mountains and guardian spirits. The front face is adorned by two strong men, the right side a pair of lions, the left side two horned deer, and the rear dragons amid clouds. A reclining Buddha representing the Mahaparinirvana (the Great Decease or Death of the Buddha), also of gilt bronze, has been accommodated in a niche below the *dagoba*. The inscription records the donation by the eunuch Li Fushan as an act of "perpetual offering" *(Fig. 20).*

Detail of Reliquary, No. **52**

52.   Reliquary from Hongjue Temple, gilt bronze on stone base
H: 20 in. (51 cm.); W: 15 in. (38 cm.) square; Wt: 136.7 lbs. (62 kgs.)
a. Four blue-and-white jars, H: 3.75 in. (9.5 cm.)
b. Gilt image of Buddha
c. Gilt bronze miniature inner coffin
d. Bronze miniature outer coffin
Ming (ca. 1436-1450)
Hongjue Temple, Niushou Shan, Nanjing, Jiangsu Province
Excavated 1956
Nanjing Museum

Fig. 20   Rubbing of inscription by Li Fushan on reliquary of Hongjue Temple, Nanjing, Jiangsu Province.

一切太子王子等衆
府第四十七雒管帝主

53. "Former Emperors, Heirs and Princes,"
silk hanging scroll
H: 46.5 in. (118 cm.); W: 24 in. (61.2 cm.)
Ming (ca. 1460)
Baoning Temple, Youyu County, Shanxi Province
Shanxi Provincial Museum

Nos. 53-57 Buddhist Paintings
Ming (ca. 1460)
Baoning Temple
Youyu County, Shanxi Province
Shanxi Provincial Museum

Baoning Temple is situated in the seat of Youyu County in northern Shanxi Province, some 74 miles (120 km.) west of Datong. This region was important for border defense throughout the later dynasties. In 1449, the Ming emperor Yingzong made the foolish decision to lead his army into battle against the Oirat Mongols, a strategem which led to his capture at a place called Tumu.[23] This shocking development sent tremors throughout the court. Officials at the capital had to regroup and select a new emperor, subsequently known as Jingdi, who reigned until 1457 when Yingzong was returned to the throne. This incident may explain why the Ming court took a special interest in this part of China. In 1460, Baoning Temple was founded, and an imperially commissioned suite of paintings was given to the temple. Chinese scholars speculate, with reason, that the temple and the paintings were designed to "show the flag" in this region after the disaster of 1449.[24]

The "Water and Land Assembly"

The set now consists of 139 hanging scrolls. Cartouches at the top corner of each scroll name deities and spirits associated with a religious ceremony known as the "Water and Land Assembly," a major rite on behalf of the souls of the dead. Later inscriptions on the mounting silk reveal that the paintings were by imperial commission, and their quality endorses that view. This suite of paintings remained at the temple until World War II, when they were taken away for safekeeping. In 1955 they came into the care of the Shanxi Cultural Relics Administration and now are held by the Provincial Museum in Taiyuan.

The origins of the ceremony of the Water and Land Assembly are said to extend to India at the time of the Buddha's beloved disciple Ananda. Ananda once had a dream in which a "hungry ghost" appeared before him begging for food. He thereupon awoke and laid out offerings on both water and land for itinerant hungry ghosts. The ceremony became an elaborate rite in China and frequently was sponsored by the Son of Heaven to win the release from purgatory of a loved one, or to assuage the souls of victims of a natural disaster or wartime calamity. Notable assemblies were convened at the capitals under the Tang, Song, and Yuan. The largest event recorded may be the assembly patronized by the Ming emperor in 1581 at which 1,000 Buddhist monks officiated to release the souls of the dead from purgatory. All these assemblies required an encyclopedic representation of the Buddhist pantheon, either as painted or sculpted images. The iconography of these images was described in texts and then codified by the court and temple artisans charged with their production. It is likely that the 1460 ensemble commissioned for the Baoning Temple embodies the content and compositions of earlier paintings made for imperial patrons and, as such, they are important reference works for Buddhist painting subject matter.

The scrolls of the Baoning Temple ensemble can be analyzed as several iconographical units. Central to the set and the assembly are the images of nine Buddhas and ten Great Bodhisattvas. Arrayed at left and right are ten Bright Kings (Vidyaraja), wrathful deities in excited, energetic poses, brandishing weapons and emanating fiery body auras. They in turn are flanked by the 16 Great Arhats, most disciples of the Buddha, rendered in pairs, two per scroll. The major portion of the suite, however, is devoted to a true pantheon from the Buddhist universe as it was perceived in late imperial China. Deities of the heavens, the stars and planets, the earth and its great waters, various protectors and divine guardians, and bureaucrats are all represented, usually in small groups on each scroll. Indian and Central Asian deities, such as Indra and the Guardian Kings of the Four Directions, are pictured among the scrolls in this part of the suite, but all are rendered as Chinese rulers, court ladies, generals, or the like. The deities of the major constellations and the spirits of the days of the week and hours of the day are all assembled as if they were court officials in high mufti at a morning convocation.

As a total representation of the forces of the Buddhist universe, the suite also incorporates representatives of lesser realms within the hierarchy of existence. Here we find groups of worldly rulers and their consorts (Nos. **53-54**), sages of Confucianism and Taoism (Nos. **55-56**), and such unlikely personages as entertainers (No. **57**). This segment of the ensemble also includes narrative paintings illustrating the torments of hell and the myriad misfortunes of the human world.

The depiction of the "Former Emperors, Heirs, and Princes" (No. **53**) includes six emperors carrying jade tallies in the lower portion of the scroll, an heir dressed in white at the left, and four princes attired in red at the top. In spite of their repetitive, static poses, these rulers are clearly distinct personalities. Eight women are portrayed within the ensemble of "Former Consorts and Palace Ladies" (No. **54**), each clothed in different costume and jewelry. The large figure at the lower left is an empress with her fan-bearing attendant behind her. Another favored lady is shown at the center of the remaining figures, while the others are probably women attendants of the palace. A company of seven practitioners of the alchemical arts that produced elixirs of long life occupy the lower portion of the third scroll (No. **55**). Their robes and regalia are as elaborate as any worn at the imperial court, for they have ascended to an other-worldly sphere. The smaller figures at top, on the other hand, appear to be recluses cultivating their virtue amid rustic surroundings suggested by their fishing creels and flutes. The next scroll (No. **56**) is similarly divided into upper and lower registers. Below, seven literary scholars ranging from young to old exemplify the accomplishments of a Chinese gentleman, from music to martial arts. Other occupations are represented by the five remaining figures dressed in yellow and blue at top, including a painter holding what may be a portrait of the artist of these scrolls. The final scroll (No. **57**) depicts masters of various trades at the top level: a fortune teller at left, an eye doctor beside him, a public scribe, and several tradesmen. Below are the members of an acting troupe that could perform both drama and variety acts.

Wall Paintings. By reference to another Ming temple, it can be established that the 139 hanging scrolls of the Baoning Temple reproduce the iconography of proper mural decoration. The Pilu Temple located north of Shijiazhuang (Hebei Province) contains a rear hall with its walls covered by a full-scale depiction of the Water and Land Assembly.[25] The paintings in the rear hall probably date from around 1495. The walls, covered with almost 1,400 square feet (130 sq. m.) of paintings, are almost 10 feet (3 m.) tall and are filled with about 500 images of the deities and spirits required for the Water and Land Assembly. The two sides of the south wall flanking the central doorway are given over to the human realm. There are depictions of former emperors and the like as found in the Baoning Temple set. The east and west walls each portray about 130 to 140 deities and protectors of the heavenly and terrestrial realms, while the north wall, also divided by a doorway, holds the renderings of the Bright Kings and other beings that flank the Buddhas and Great Bodhisattvas of the Baoning Temple suite. One can infer that the altar platform of the hall itself would have carried sculpted images as the focus of the assembly. In both cases, the basic imagery of the paintings was determined by manuals of practice. On a portable hanging scroll, the subject matter had to be subdivided, while on the expansive surfaces of large walls the deities could be assembled in grand convocations. In spite of their compositional differences, however, the two sets of paintings share much in details such as clothing and regalia. For a modern viewer, they each provide fascinating glimpses into the world of 15th-century Ming China.

1. On Confucius, see Frederick W. Mote, *Intellectual Foundations of China,* New York, 1971, Ch. 3, and H.G. Creel, *Confucius and the Chinese Way,* New York, 1960.

2. The standard English version is Arthur Waley, *The Analects of Confucius,* London, 1938.

3. For a history of Buddhism and the court, see Stanley Weinstein, *Buddhism under the T'ang,* New Haven, 1987.

4. Mote, *Intellectual Foundations,* Ch. 4.

5. Herrlee G. Creel, "What Is Taoism?" in *What Is Taoism and Other Studies in Chinese Cultural History,* Chicago, 1970, pp. 1-24.

6. For an introduction, see Liang Ssu-ch'eng, *A Pictorial History of Chinese Architecture,* Cambridge, Mass., 1984, pp. 124-165.

7. On Longmen, see *Longmen shiku* [The Grottoes at Longmen], Beijing, 1980. The Tianlong Shan site has not yet received recent publication.

8. Li Hurang and Xue Zhengmin, "Three Stone Buddha Images from Ruicheng, Shanxi" (in Chinese), *Wenwu* [Cultural Relics] 1983.7:88.

9. *Shanxi shidiao yishu* [Sculptural Art of Shanxi], Beijing, 1962, Nos. 42, 45.

10. Guo Yong, "Brief Excavation Report of Stone Images Discovered in the Western Suburbs of Taiyuan, Shanxi" (in Chinese), *Wenwu* 1955.3:79-30.

11. For the materials of writing, see T. H. Tsien, *Written on Bamboo and Silk: The Beginnings of Chinese Books and Inscriptions,* Chicago, 1962.

12. On the tradition of Wang Xizhi, see Lothar Ledderose, *Mi Fu and the Classical Tradition in Chinese Calligraphy,* Princeton, N.J., 1979, pp. 12-28.

13. *Shodo Zenshu* [Compendium of Calligraphy], Tokyo, 1966-1969, Vol. 7, Pls. 86-89.

14. *Shodo Zenshu,* Vol. 8, pp. 33-40 and Pls. 50-57. *Xi'an Beilin shufa yishu* [Calligraphic Art at the Forest of Steles, Xi'an], Xi'an, 1984, pp. 44-45.

15. *Shodo Zenshu,* Vol. 8, Pl. 91.

16. In 1973 workers at the Beilin restoring this stele discovered a small cache of objects within the stones. The cache included a 12th-century rubbing of the "Preface of the Holy Teachings Compiled from Characters Written by Wang Xizhi." See Liu Zuichang and Zhu Jieyuan, "Nuzhen Documents, a Southern Song Rubbing of the Complete Preface to the Holy Teachings Compiled from Characters Written by Wang Xizhi, and a Print Discovered in the Beilin at Xi'an" (in Chinese), *Wenwu* 1980.5:1-6.

17. Zhang Huiyi, *Jinling Da Bao'en Si Ta Zhi* [Records of the Pagoda at Bao'en Temple, Jinling], Shanghai, 1937. See also Wang Yongping, "The World-renowned Glazed Tile Pagoda of Bao'en Temple, Nanjing" (in Chinese), *Zhongguo gudu yanjiu* [Research on the Ancient Capitals of China], No. 2, Hangzhou, 1986, pp. 208-216.

18. Illustrated in Liang, *Pictorial History of Chinese Architecture,* Fig. 72. Also in Liu Dunzhen, ed., *Zhongguo gudai jianzhu shi* [A History of Ancient Chinese Architecture], Beijing, 1980, pp. 360-362, and *Ancient Chinese Architecture,* Beijing, 1982, Pls. 164-165.

19. Seen at the Cloud Terrace at Juyong Guan north of Bejing. See Liu, *Zhongguo gudai jianzhu shi,* pp. 273-274, and *Ancient Chinese Architecture,* Pl. 127.

20. "The Ming Period Glazed Tile Kilns at Jubao Shan, Nanjing" (in Chinese), *Wenwu* 1960.2:41-48. Published in *Jiangsu sheng chutu wenwu xuanji* [A Selection of Cultural Relics from Jiangsu], Beijing, 1963, No. 218 and *Nankyo hakubutsuin ten* [Exhibition of Treasures from the Nanjing Museum], Tokyo, 1981, No. 112.

21. Nanjing Museum, *Nan Tang er ling fajue baogao* [Excavation Report of the Two Imperial Tombs of the Southern Tang Dynasty], Beijing, 1957.

22. Cai Shujuan, "Cultural Relics Discovered in the Pagoda of Hongjue Temple, Niushou Shan, Nanjing" (in Chinese), *Wenwu* 1956.11:73.

23. Frederick W. Mote, "The T'u-mu Incident of 1449," in *Chinese Ways In Warfare,* ed. Frank J. Kierman, Jr., Cambridge, Mass., 1974, pp. 243-272.

24. Wu Liancheng, "Water and Land Assembly Paintings of the Baoning Temple in Youyu, Shanxi" (in Chinese), *Wenwu* 1962.4-5. *Baoningsi Mingdai shuilu hua* [The Ming Water and Land Assembly Paintings from Baoning Temple], Beijing, 1985.

25. *Pilu Si bihua* [Wall Paintings of the Pilu Temple], Shijiazhuang, 1984.

54. "Former Consorts and Palace Ladies,"
silk hanging scroll
H: 46.5 in. (118 cm.); W: 24 in. (61.5 cm.)
Ming (ca. 1460)
Baoning Temple, Youyu County, Shanxi Province
Shanxi Provincial Museum

56. "Former Confucian Worthies and Sages," silk hanging scroll
H: 46.5 in. (118 cm.); W: 24.5 in. (62 cm.)
Ming (ca. 1460)
Baoning Temple, Youyu County, Shanxi Province
Shanxi Provincial Museum

57. "Former Masters of Professions and Arts," silk hanging scroll
H: 46.75 in. (119 cm.); W: 24.5 in. (62.5 cm.)
Ming (ca. 1460)
Baoning Temple, Youyu County, Shanxi Province
Shanxi Provincial Museum

4 THE INNER COURT
Life in the Palace

The Inner Court, more than any other unit of this exhibition, involves all the arts of each period. This was for reasons both ideological and practical. In the orthodox view, "all under Heaven" belonged to the emperor: all land and property, all resources and talent, all exotica and rarities. Tribute from throughout the realm was forwarded to the palace on a regular basis, whether it was a new crop of fresh litchis from the south or the discovery of a rare animal or other wonder. Similarly, the finest craftsmen and their wares were assembled at court, and palace or state factories produced goods of the finest quality for the imperial wardrobe, table, and apartments. The Son of Heaven had unparalleled access to the most precious materials, the cleverest hands, and the most talented designers. Such was the natural order of things.

On a practical level, the palace was a small city with all of the needs of a city. It was inhabited not only by the emperor and his immediate family, but also by a large staff of eunuchs and palace ladies. It was an extended household of the largest scale, as each empress, consort, prince, or princess staffed and furnished his or her own mansion within the walls. Within this small city, the standard of living was as high as could be rationalized. Waste and extravagance were not necessarily the norm, but the gap between life in the palace and life outside its walls was always enormous. Nonetheless, the conspicuous consumption of the Son of Heaven and the residents of the palace was an economic boon to some producers of goods and services.

Notes to Chapter 4 are on p. 160-61.

89. Lady's Phoenix Crown, gilt silver
D (approx.): 7.75 in. (20 cm.)
Qing (17th c.)
Jurong County, Jiangsu Province
Excavated 1967
Zhenjiang City Museum

The Development of Palace Plans

The Son of Heaven's palace evolved rapidly during the early imperial era. While the Qin First Emperor moved among a network of several hundred dispersed palace halls spread over a broad area in the modern Xianyang-Xi'an region, the Han emperors consolidated their residences within a "palace city" they named Chang'an.[1] The site chosen had previously served as a Qin detached palace so court architects simply added other palaces nearby and enclosed them within walls. Separate palaces were inhabited by the reigning Son of Heaven, the retired empress, and the heir. Each was further subdivided into smaller compounds. The capital population was excluded from the palace city, except for the area reserved for the markets, so residential quarters grew up outside the walls.

Immediately after the Han, during the short-lived Wei regime (A.D. 220-265), an imperial capital was laid out for the first time in accordance both with custom and canonical prescriptions at Ye (north of modern Anyang, Henan Province).[2] In this design, the palace was at the center of the rear half of the rectangular city, flanked by a residential quarter for the elite and a large park. These three units on the north were divided from the southern half of the city by a main east-west thoroughfare. One set of walls contained the whole so that for the first time a full-scale imperial capital was created anew with all its parts unified. Court business took place in halls near the north-south axis, with residences behind and to the east. Imperial warehouses, stables, and other facilities were located in the park.

The greatest of the early imperial capitals, the Sui and Tang city of Chang'an (at modern Xi'an), was much indebted to the rationalized design of Ye and rigorously followed the idea of a rear central position for the palace.[3] At Sui and Tang Chang'an, the seat of authority was placed at the culmination of a long avenue on an axis extending about three miles (5 km.) from the central south gate of the outer wall. Across this axis stood the Imperial City (Huang cheng), a governmental center for the state ministries and altars. The Palace City (Gong cheng) behind it was divided into three areas: the Palace of the Supreme Ultimate where the Son of Heaven ruled and resided, the palace of the heir on the east, and secondary palaces on the west. A park adjoined the Palace City on the north. This centralized location was quickly found too confining, and early in the Tang a new site just outside the city wall on the northeast was chosen for the Son of Heaven's abode. The

new Great Bright Palace (Da Ming Gong) merged a formal outer court in front with a park-like setting for several dozen residential palaces at the rear.[4] Its elevated position allowed a view of the entire Tang capital stretching out to the south and west.

The Forbidden City

Under later dynasties, the design of imperial capitals underwent numerous refinements, and several competing traditions can be detected in their plans. The strictest application of canonical Chinese precepts ironically was achieved under the Mongols in a design that placed the imperial and palace cities at the front center in nested rectangles surrounded on three sides by the capital's wards for the resident population.[5] Palace halls were built on both sides of a large lake system, permitting the Mongol Khan-Son of Heaven to enjoy the pleasures of rulership without leaving his palace. After the Ming inherited the site and constructed a new capital on it, much the same location continued for the imperial palaces, but the outer city walls were shifted southward so that the palace was now somewhat more centrally located. The lakes developed by the Mongols survive today in the North, Middle and South "Seas" (Bei Hai, Zhong Hai, Nan Hai) of modern Beijing.

In the grand design of the Ming Forbidden City, the Three Rear Palaces were on axis behind the Three Great Halls of State.[6] These residential halls mimic the outer court in their general design of marble-tiered platforms and in the shapes of the halls and roofs. However, the scale has been reduced and the yards are more intimate, though still grand. In the front hall (the Palace of Heavenly Purity), the Ming emperors resided and transacted their daily business, and the empress lived in the rear Palace of Earthly Tranquility. The intermediate Hall of Union was the site of their nuptials. The galleries surrounding the yard of the Palace of Heavenly Purity housed the emperor's study and offices for court physician, chief eunuch and other necessary services.

The halls on the central axis were only part of the Inner Court. Secondary palace courtyards were built on both the east and west, gradually filling most of the rear area of the Forbidden City. After the long 60-year reign of the Qing Kangxi Emperor (1662-1722), his successor would not take up residence in the front of the Three Rear Palaces and instead remodeled a compound off the axis to the west, the Hall of Mental Cultivation *(Fig. 21).* As with the Tang, the seat of authority and most day-to-day activities revolving around the emperor then shifted away from the strict formality of the main axis.

However, much of the time the Qing emperors did not reside within the walls of the Forbidden City. There were the halls surrounding the string of lakes just west of the palace (see No. **96**), an extensive suburban palace complex called the Yuan Ming Yuan (of which the surviving Summer Palace is but a small part), and another palace city north of Beijing at Chengde which was a refuge from the stifling heat of the summer. In addition, there was the original Manchu capital at Shenyang (Liaoning Province). Thus, in making an annual cycle of progresses from one palace to another, the emperor rarely occupied the central axis of the Forbidden City.

The Inner Court

Like any household, the palace required the furnishings and necessities of daily life. Within the Household Office, various bureaus procured or produced everything from the furniture, rugs, lamps, spittoons, cushions, and bedding, to fresh food and wine, incense, coal, and toilet paper. Little of this survives, mainly because so much of it was consumed in its own day. The best evidence of these processes are artifacts used in the operation of the Qing household from the 17th through the early 20th centuries.[7] Generally, however, what we know of pre-Qing imperial household furnishings is limited to objects that were consigned to tombs. The *hu* vessel, phoenix lamp, and cups from the Mancheng tombs (Nos. **111-113**) were palace furnishings used at Han Chang'an and later transferred to the Prince and Princess of the Kingdom of Zhongshan.

So much material in this category exists from so many periods that the curatorial process is especially arbitrary for the Inner Court exhibits. The jade and hardstones (Nos. **58-62**) and small bronze sculptures (Nos. **63-65**) are merely a few examples of a remarkable volume of luxury goods available from the pre-imperial eras, while a few brilliant works of Han lacquer, Tang silver, or Song porcelain represent only the smallest tips of their respective icebergs. A dozen paintings do not a history of Chinese painting make, nor can a few examples of jewelry tell the complete story of court taste. In every case, a special exhibition could be mounted for each of these categories.

Gathering these objects together, however, helps us to recreate the colors, textures, and shapes of a lifestyle that is now lost. Without bringing the palaces to the exhibition visitor, we can suggest by specific examples what "imperial quality" meant and what life in the inner court was like. In this way, we can bring the modern Western visitor into the everyday world of the Son of Heaven.

Fig. 21 Gate to Hall of Mental Cultivation, Forbidden City, Beijing.

62. Necklace, rock crystal and agate
L (approx.): 15 in. (38 cm.)
Eastern Zhou (6th c. B.C.)
Tomb 1 at Langjiazhuang
Linzi City, Shandong Province
Excavated 1971
Shandong Provincial Museum

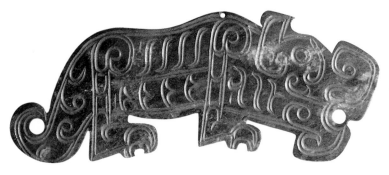
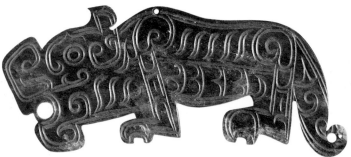

58. Pair of Tigers, jade
L: 5 in. (12.7 cm.); W: 2.5 in. (6.2 cm.)
Eastern Zhou (7th c. B.C., not later than 648 B.C.)
Tomb of Lady Meng Ji
Baoxiangsi, Guangshan County, Henan Province
Excavated 1983
Xinyang District Cultural Relics Administration

59. Pair of Human-headed Snakes, jade
D: 1.5 in. (3.8 cm.)
Eastern Zhou (7th c. B.C., not later than 648 B.C.)
Tomb of Lady Meng Ji
Baoxiangsi, Guangshan County, Henan Province
Excavated 1983
Xinyang District Cultural Relics Administration

60. Fish, jade
L: 2.25 in. (6 cm.); W: 0.75 in. (2 cm.)
Eastern Zhou (7th c. B.C., not later than 648 B.C.)
Tomb of Lady Meng Ji
Baoxiangsi, Guangshan County, Henan Province
Excavated 1983
Xinyang District Cultural Relics Administration

Nos. 58-61 Early Jade and Hardstone Carvings
Eastern Zhou (7th c. B.C., not later than 648 B.C.)
Tomb of Lady Meng Ji
Baoxiangsi, Guangshan County, Henan Province
Excavated 1983
Xinyang District Cultural Relics Administration

No. 62 Rock Crystal and Agate Necklace
Eastern Zhou (6th c. B.C.)
Tomb 1 at Langjiazhuang
Linzi City, Shandong Province
Excavated 1971
Shandong Provincial Museum

Jade and other hardstones were highly prized in ancient China, perhaps as much for the exacting labor and endless patience their working required as for the beauty of the stone itself. The peoples of ancient China found delight, aesthetic satisfaction, and potent magic in the many hardstones that are lumped in the category "jade." In Chinese usage, the term is generic, while in modern Western parlance jade refers either to the mineral nephrite, one of many stones used, or the even harder mineral jadeite, which was not worked in China in early times.

Until recently, the history of jade carvings was full of ambiguities. If they have not been scientifically excavated, these prized objects rarely offer clear clues to their date and point of origin. With recent discoveries, the problem now is not a scarcity of excavated materials with which to make comparisons, but rather the inability of scholars to keep up with the flood of new evidence.

Several of the most important excavations of the last decade have been extraordinarily rich in jade carvings. The 25 tombs at Xiasi in southern Henan Province (Nos. **6-10**), for example, held more than 3,000 carvings, while the two tombs of the kings of Zhongshan (Nos. **63-65**) yielded even more. The two tombs of the State of Huang contained about 185 jade carvings, of which we include 6 (Nos. **58-61**). The accompanying burials of Tomb 1 at Langjiazhuang in Shandong Province contained thousands of stone carvings, including 700 rock crystal rings (No. **62**). With materials from dated contexts available in such abundance, the history of the art of jade during the Eastern Zhou can now be reconstructed.

Jade working flourished in the pre-imperial centuries but had reached a high state of aesthetic refinement and technical virtuosity far earlier. The Neolithic peoples of the East Coast, especially the Liangzhu Culture centered around modern Shanghai, Nanjing, and Hangzhou, and the Hongshan Culture of modern Liaoning Province and Inner Mongolia, achieved startling advances in the art and craft of jade and hardstone carving. Many objects customarily assigned to the Western and Eastern Zhou periods (11th-3rd c. B.C.) must now be reattributed, on the basis of firm archaeological data, to the 3rd millenium B.C. The objects that delighted the lords and ladies of the Eastern Zhou were part of an artistic lineage that is as old as China itself.

Personal jewelry in ancient China was dominated by jades and hardstones rather than by precious metals or gems. The necklace of rock crystal rings and agate beads (No. **62**) came from the grave of a woman in the capital of the State of Qi, a site at modern Linzi City, Shandong Province.[8] This lady, about 20 years of age, was put to death upon the demise of her lord, along with 16 others of a harem. All were buried with their personal jewelry in the pit surrounding the lord's tomb chamber. This does not mean that Linzi was itself a great center for rock crystal and agate carving. Both stones are produced in many areas of China.[9] The nearby ancient city of the State of Lu has also yielded many graves with similar necklaces, while still more examples were found in the tombs of the State of Guo in western Henan Province.[10] The love of hardstone jewelry is evident in many courts of the period, but its point of origin remains to be determined.

More elaborate forms of personal adornment were pectorals, jade carvings strung together and then worn outside the clothes. This kind of jewelry became a mark of noble status in the Bronze Age. According to early ritual texts, jade jewelry was thought to express the character and demeanor of a superior man; the sound of jades clinking together as the gentleman walked required a measured and dignified pace. The best-known example of these pectorals is now in the Freer Gallery of Art in Washington, D.C.[11] Related examples are also known from the ancient city of Qufu,[12] and it is likely that many excavated jade plaques were originally a part of such jewelry.

The plaques from the Huang tomb (Nos. **58-60**) have small perforations for suspension and many are paired.[13] It is possible that they were part of such pectorals. The intaglio double outlines on the pair of tigers heighten their sense of relief. Both sides of the human-headed snakes are carved, but a close inspection reveals subtle differences. The fish has rigid, highly conventionalized outlines carved in a different style. The most engaging of these carvings is the human head; its stylized features could represent a shaman or priest.[14] Whether it was incorporated into a pectoral of flat carvings or worn in some other way is uncertain. Both tigers and fish were associated with abstract qualities. The tiger symbolized ferocity, while the ancient Chinese word for "fish" sounded like the word for "abundance." Such punning allusions may have motivated the inclusion of these animals in the jade pectorals.

61. Human Head, jade
H: 1.5 in. (3.8 cm.); W: 1 in. (2.5 cm.)
Eastern Zhou (7th c. B.C., not later than 648 B.C.)
Tomb of Lady Meng Ji
Baoxiangsi, Guangshan County, Henan Province
Excavated 1983
Xinyang District Cultural Relics Administration

Nos. 63-65 Bronze Sculpture
Eastern Zhou (late 4th c. B.C.)
Tombs of the Kings of Zhongshan
Sanji Commune, Pingshan County, Hebei
Province
Excavated 1977
Hebei Cultural Relics Research Institute

64. Cylindrical Vessel Supported by Three Rhinoceros, bronze
H: 23 in. (58.8 cm.); Wt: 87.3 lbs. (39.6 kgs.)
Eastern Zhou (late 4th c. B.C.)
Tombs of the Kings of Zhongshan
Sanji Commune, Pingshan County, Hebei Province
Excavated 1977
Hebei Cultural Relics Research Institute

The Zhongshan Royal Tombs

Archaeology can reclaim lost history. The discovery between 1974 and 1978 of the tombs of the Warring States period Kingdom of Zhongshan is one of the most dramatic examples. Archaeologists were brought to the site in Pingshan County, Hebei Province, because of a large water conservation project.[15] They identified the last capital of the Zhongshan kingdom, the ancient city of Shouling,[16] and unearthed large tombs that can now be attributed to the kings of this state. Although each burial had been looted, enough treasure remained to allow scholars to bring to life an important episode in late Bronze Age history.

The State of Zhongshan (not to be confused with the Western Han kingdom of the same name) was ruled by a non-Han people, descendants of the White Di, "barbarians" who had gradually moved into North China during the Spring and Autumn Period (8th-5th c. B.C.).[17] By the late 6th century B.C., the White Di had established a permanent capital near modern Ding Xian, Hebei Province. A century later, in 409 B.C., Zhongshan was conquered by the state of Wei and ruled by a Wei prince. The spread of Chinese cultural influences must have started gradually from the earliest contacts with the Han-Chinese states. It accelerated at this time so that Zhongshan court culture, at least, became thoroughly familiar with the values of the Chinese states of the Central Plains. The Marquis of Wei was schooled by a disciple of Confucius, and the administrator of the Zhongshan area during its occupation by Wei is known as a proponent of the *Classic of Poetry,* a text often quoted by the Master. After 378 B.C., Zhongshan was again independent and built its last capital at Shouling, the archaeological site explored in recent years. Five generations of Zhongshan rulers reigned and were buried there. (It is ironic that Zhongshan fell in 296 B.C. to Zhao, a Han-Chinese state that had adopted "barbarian" ways in warfare, including horseback combat.)

The tombs of the Zhongshan kings were located both inside and outside the walls of the capital. The earlier rulers and their consorts were buried in the northwest corner of the city. Tomb 6 excavated in 1976 at this site has been attributed to the second ruler, Duke Cheng (r. ca. 340-320 B.C.). King Cuo, the third ruler at Lingshou (r. ca. 320-308 B.C.), moved the royal tombs about a mile (1.5 km.) further west and planned a grand funerary precinct for himself and his consorts. That design was never completed. Archaeologists found only two tombs here, that of the king (Tomb 1) and another for his consort, but not the other three called for in the "Burial District Plan" which the king had commissioned. This plan is a drawing cast onto a bronze plate recording the measurements and design of a necropolis for five tombs to be surrounded by a double wall. It is the earliest architectural site plan in East Asia and a valuable document of the history of Chinese science and technology. In this as in so much else, the Zhongshan kings were profoundly influenced by Chinese culture. The burial district envisioned for the Zhongshan kings is a forerunner of the Qin First Emperor's Lishan funerary park.

Both royal tombs had large vertical shafts approached by lengthy ramps at north and south. The base of the central shaft was surrounded by stone walls, with the wooden burial chamber within. On each side were treasuries *(Fig. 22)* holding a great portion of the wealth of each king. The burial chambers were pillaged and poorly preserved, but these treasuries were intact. Both tombs were surmounted by large pounded-earth mounds that served in turn as earth cores for offering shrines. These shrines were built atop the mounds, but encircling galleries at the base and mid-level created the illusion that the shrines were actually pyramidal, three-story structures. Near the tombs were a number of trenches for chariots, sacrificial animals and, in Tomb 1, even one for boats. This custom of interring the retinue of a lord continued into imperial times. The terra cotta army of the Qin First Emperor (Nos. **103-108**) was an imaginative alternative solution to what, for the retinue, was a regrettable practice.

A pre-imperial lord had at his command the resources of his own state as well as access to the products of trade or tribute from other states. The Kings of Zhongshan evidently carried objects both domestic and foreign with them to the grave to ensure that they were well cared for in the afterlife. A set of nine tripods (compare Nos. **6-8**) and the five trident-shaped standards from the tomb of King Cuo are royal symbols that appealed to

Fig. 22 Tomb 1 during excavation, Pingshan County, Hebei Province.

Fig. 23 Rubbing of inscriptions on winged animals (No. **63**).

Han-Chinese and White Di rituals and values, respectively.[18] The king's many bronze vessels are normal ritual equipment, but the lengthy incised inscriptions on these vessels distinguish them from comparable tripods found in the Central Plains. Their inscriptions extol the "Confucian" virtues of the Zhongshan king and use such texts as the *Classic of Poetry*.[19] On the other hand, the tombs also held many artifacts necessary for a life on the steppe: hardware for tents and chariots, collars for hunting dogs, and weapons. The tomb of King Cuo yielded an axe bearing an inscription commemorating the bestowal of the title of marquis by the Zhou king, evidence of an attempt to honor, at least in spirit, the Zhou king's sovereignty.[20]

Small Sculpture in the Late Zhou Period. All three of these exhibits are examples of the taste for small-scale sculpture in the late Zhou centuries.[21] Until the discovery of the Qin terra cotta warriors, such small examples were the best evidence for the early evolution of figural sculpture in ancient China. Although the Zhongshan sculptures pre-date the Qin army, they could reflect more ambitious, now lost or undiscovered projects of sculptors of the Warring States period (5th-3rd c. B.C.) period. The First Emperor of Qin is known to have commissioned larger-than-life metal figures for his capital. Both these small pieces and the army of life-sized warriors bear witness to a vital sculptural tradition that almost escaped notice until recent years.

The pair of winged animals (No. **63**) were possessions of King Cuo of Zhongshan. Inlaid with silver across their bodies, these powerful and aggressive beasts glare at one another, wings held up and chests thrust forward. They resemble the lions and magical beasts that came to guard tomb approaches (see No. **116**) in later periods. An inscription incised on the belly of each animal records the names of the artisan and foundry supervisor responsible for these creations (Fig. 23).

Although the two winged animals seem to be purely ornamental, most small sculpture now known from this period also served a utilitarian function. The male figure (No. **65**) is the central support for a three-dish lamp, holding serpents that bear the lamp dishes.[22] It was a common artistic conceit to create kneeling servants or animals as stands for lamps or supports for low tables or other furnishings. Many figures holding lamps are in non-Chinese costume, but this lamp's figure is wearing an elegant Chinese court robe. In creating this lamp, the artisan mixed differing materials. Black and red lacquer were applied

Detail of Winged Animal, No. **63** (see p. 134)

to the bronze body, which in turn set off the silver head with its inlaid black stone eyes.

It is less clear what practical purpose the large cylinder (No. **64**) might have served. It has rhino-like animals kneeling at its base to carry the vessel. The cylindrical form of the object may be uninspired, but its surface is enlivened with a mass of coiled and interlaced dragon designs which were stamped in the clay casting molds. The placid beasts below are as staid as the interlaced dragons are frenetic.

Proper chairs were not yet in use in China, so these furnishings were scaled for persons kneeling on a mat, rather as the Japanese still kneel on tatami. The phoenix lamp from the Mancheng tombs of the Western Han (No. **111**) was designed with the same consideration in mind. Life in a pre-imperial palace must have been stimulating as different kinds of designs, many animal and figural, attracted the eye. When the brilliant colors of architectural decor, lacquerware, and silk (see below) combined with the richly inlaid bronzes and jades, the total effect must have been one of sensory overload.

Detail of Lamp with Male Figure, No. **65** (see p. 135)

63. One of a Pair of Winged Animals, bronze
with silver inlay
L: 16 in. (40.5 cm.); H: 9.5 in. (24.6 cm.);
Wt: 48.5 lbs. (22 kgs.)
Eastern Zhou (late 4th c. B.C.)
Tombs of the Kings of Zhongshan
Sanji Commune, Pingshan County, Hebei Province
Excavated 1977
Hebei Cultural Relics Research Institute

65. Lamp with Male Figure, bronze with silver head
H: 26 in. (66.4 cm.); Wt: 25.5 lbs. (11.6 kgs.)
Eastern Zhou (late 4th c. B.C.)
Tombs of the Kings of Zhongshan
Sanji Commune, Pingshan County, Hebei Province
Excavated 1977
Hebei Cultural Relics Research Institute

67. Zhong Vessel, lacquer
H: 17 in. (43.6 cm.)
Western Han (ca. 186-168 B.C.)
Tombs of the Family of the Marquis of Dai
Mawangdui, Changsha, Hunan Province
Excavated 1972-1973
Hunan Provincial Museum

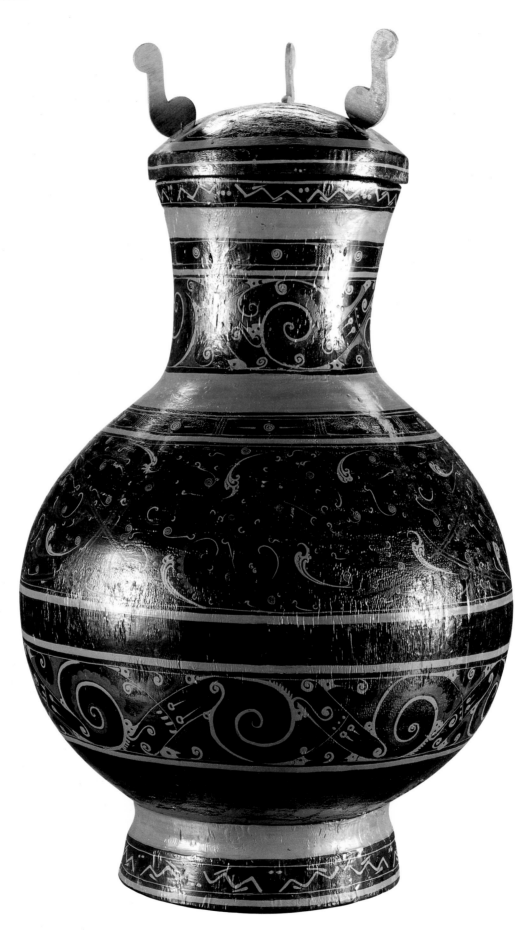

**Nos. 66-71 Lacquerware and
Silk Textiles**
Western Han (ca. 186-168 B.C.)
Tombs of the Family of the Marquis of Dai
Mawangdui, Changsha, Hunan Province
Excavated 1972-1973
Hunan Provincial Museum

The Tombs of the Marquis of Dai

When the Marquis of Dai, a man named Li
Cang, died in 186 B.C., he was Chancellor to
the Kingdom of Changsha (in modern Hunan
Province). His own fief, from which the Marquis
derived his income, was located well to the
north in modern Hubei. The wife and son of the
Marquis, however, apparently continued to live
in Linxiang, the ancient city that lies under
modern Changsha. The son, Li Xi, probably
succeeded to his father's post and passed
away in the summer of 168 B.C. He was followed soon after by his mother, the Lady Xin.
Their three tombs were constructed together
in a double mound located a few miles to the
east of the city at a site that came to be known
as Mawangdui (King Ma's Mound). Li Cang's
burial was plundered at some later time, but
the other two, the best preserved and most
richly furnished tombs of their period ever
excavated, remained undisturbed until 1972-
1973, when digging for hospital construction
began next to the mound.

*Fig. 24 Side compartment of Tomb 1 with lacquerware
Mawangdui, Hunan Province.*

Archaeologists from the nearby Hunan
Museum were called to the scene and took
over the excavation. As at Guangshan, Henan
Province (Nos. **1-5, 58-61**), the accidental
discovery of one tomb led to the scientific
excavation of others, in this case the family
cemetery of the Marquis of Dai.[23] The clay
surrounding the wooden chambers of Tomb 1
(that of Lady Xin) and Tomb 3 (that of the
Marquis' son) had never been broken, so little
decay had taken place inside their air-tight
environments. In fact, even the bacteria in the
corpse and foodstuffs of Tomb 1 soon died,
halting the decomposition of all grave goods
placed inside the chamber.

The preserved corpse of Lady Xin captured the imagination of writers and readers
everywhere,[24] but it was the tomb furnishings
that make the discovery of the Mawangdui
tombs important for all future studies of early
China. Both tombs were stocked with the
personal possessions of the two deceased:
fine silk garments and bolts of silk cloth
(Nos. **70-71**); precious lacquerware for ritual
and table use (Nos. **66-69**); musical instruments including zithers and pipes; foodstuffs,
flavorings, and alcoholic spirits; personal
accessories such as toiletries; and manu-
scripts, maps, and illustrated texts in the case
of Tomb 3. These finds were of revolutionary
importance, and even now, after other important recent discoveries, they are pre-eminent
in any accounting of the culture of the
Han period.

The Mawangdui tombs are essential for
understanding the burial culture of early
imperial times. The system of multiple chambers and of coffins within coffins represents
the culmination of the burial system of the
later Zhou centuries. Two of the coffins are
themselves great works of lacquer painting,
and inventory slips recording the burial gifts
help document the conduct of an elite funeral
of this time. Both tombs also had well-preserved painted funeral banners draped over
the innermost coffins. These banners, along
with the maps and illustrated texts of Tomb 3,
are the fundamental body of early Chinese
painting on silk.

Tomb 3 also contained a fascinating
message addressed to the underworld:

*On the 24th day, second month, the twelfth
year of Emperor Wen's reign, Household
Assistant Fen to the Gentleman in Charge of
the Dead: A list of mortuary objects is herewith
forwarded to you. Upon receiving this document please memorialize without delay to the
Lord of the Dead.*[25]

This note, written on a wooden tablet among the grave goods, suggests that the household servants of the deceased son of the Marquis prepared their master for burial and then turned him over to the care of an underworld bureaucracy. References to this underworld are scant in most literary sources because orthodox thinkers generally avoided detailed discussions of death. The household of the deceased clearly believed that the burial goods would sustain their master in this underworld and proclaim his status within the society of the dead. Thus, social rank followed one into the afterlife.

Lacquerware. The four lacquer vessels (Nos. **66-69**) are as lustrous today as when they were first placed in the side compartments of the burial chambers *(Fig. 24)*.[26] By the time of the excavation, the vessels were water-logged from being housed in a sealed, super-saturated atmosphere for almost 2,000 years. The first task of the conservators was to carefully dry the objects to prevent flaking of the lacquer skins.

The lacquerware included furnishings such as an arm-rest, sword stand, small screen, and trays with food services consisting of small plates, drinking cups, and chopsticks. Large circular boxes held sets of smaller boxes in one or more layers. These were intended for toiletries such as mirrors, combs, tweezers, cosmetics, and the like. In addition, there was a complement of ritual vessels. In Tomb 1, this included seven tripods, four square vases, two round vases, four covered cylindrical boxes, a pouring ewer, and the necessary ladles and spoons. In this tomb, lacquer ritual vessels had totally supplanted the bronze vessels of earlier eras.

In Western Han times, lacquerware was among the most precious of all goods. One Han text records that a single lacquered cup (perhaps more intricate than our No. **69**) might require the labor of a hundred artisans and be worth ten bronze cups.[27] In spite of their cost, lacquer vessels were in high demand, and the government eventually operated several factories in regions known for their tradition of working lacquer. The quantities of lacquerware coming from excavated tombs suggest a high volume of production. Inscriptions on vessels excavated some decades ago in North Korea indicate that thousands of cups could be produced in one order. The finest wares went to the palaces in Chang'an, the capital, but some circulated among the local elite, such as the family of the Marquis of Dai. Inscriptions on these vessels, including the ewer and cup, indicate the Mawangdui lacquers were actually produced at an official factory in modern Chengdu (Sichuan Province).[28] By the middle of the Western Han, this factory had been taken over by the central government.

Lacquerware involves a labor-intensive process in which tasks were divided among many hands. The cores of these vessels are wood, either carved (as in the case of the ewer and cup) or turned on a lathe (as with the large dish and vase). Lacquer is sap from the lac tree and is a natural polymer that must be boiled and purified before application. Color, in this case carbon black or cinnabar red, was then added to the lac fluid. Typically, each coat of lacquer was applied, thoroughly dried, sanded, and then the process repeated. The coat of lacquer sealed the core and, when hardened, was extremely strong and highly resistant to decay. Lacquer vessels are therefore light-weight and durable. The art of lacquerware is demonstrated in the fluent painting of their surface decoration, a difficult task due to the viscous quality of the medium. The vase, for example, is decorated with swirling cloud-like designs rendered in red and gray on a black ground. The sureness with which the motifs are placed around the vessel is matched by the aplomb with which the artisan wielded his brush through the obdurate lacquer. Both the ewer and cup are painted red on the interior and black on their outer surface, a convention that unifies all the Mawangdui vessels. Many of the Mawangdui vessels carry painted inscriptions. Some name the family of the Marquis, while others convey good wishes for the owners *(Fig. 25)*.

Fig. 25   Inscriptions on Western Han lacquer vessels.

68. Yi Vessel, lacquer
H: 3.25 in. (8.2 cm.); L: 13.5 in. (34.1 cm.);
W: 9.75 in. (25 cm.)
Western Han (ca. 186-168 B.C.)
Tombs of the Family of the Marquis of Dai
Mawangdui, Changsha, Hunan Province
Excavated 1972-1973
Hunan Provincial Museum

69. Wine Cup, lacquer
H: 1.75 in. (4.8 cm.); L: 6.75 in. (17.2 cm.);
W: 5 in. (13 cm.)
Western Han (ca. 186-168 B.C.)
Tombs of the Family of the Marquis of Dai
Mawangdui, Changsha, Hunan Province
Excavated 1972-1973
Hunan Provincial Museum

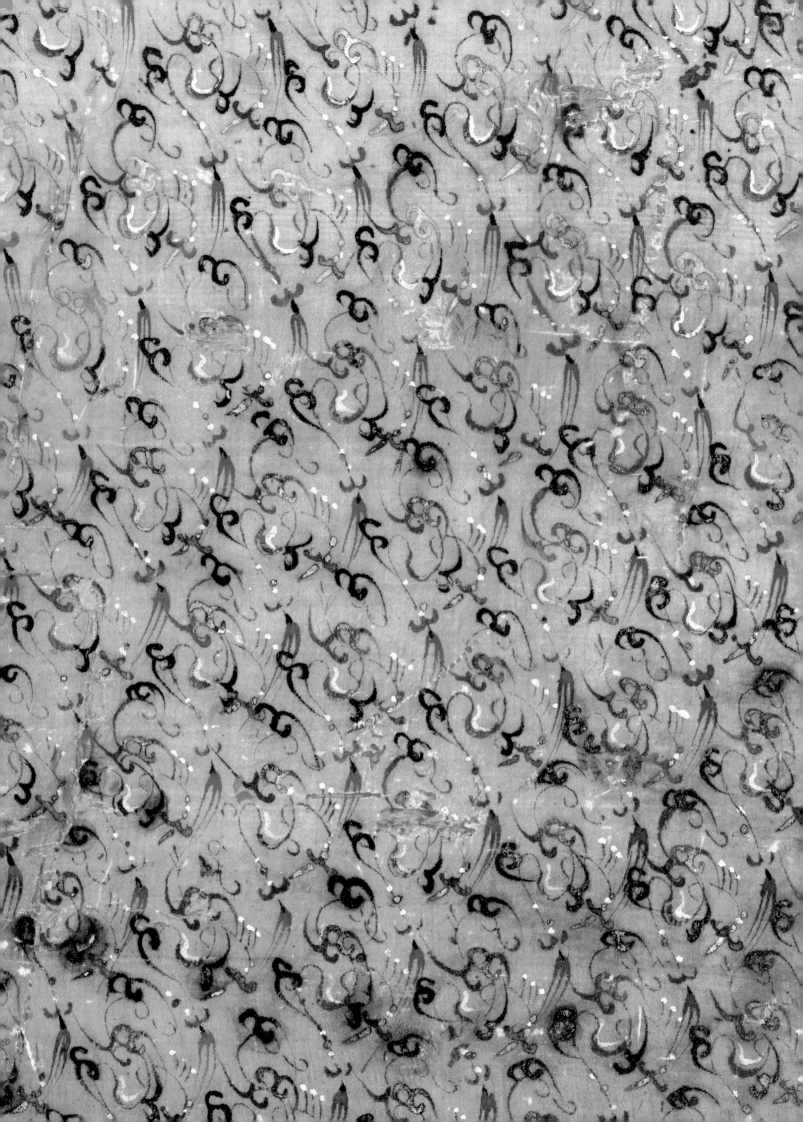

Silk Textiles. The textiles from the Mawangdui tombs included complete garments, whole bolts of cloth, and other fragments used as shrouds.[29] Two materials are represented, hemp cloth and silk. This discovery was unprecedented for the early date of the textiles, their quantities, varieties, colors, and techniques.[30] The most amazing of the garments were the single layer silk gauze robes, as "thin as a locust's wing, as light as mist," weighing only about 1.6 ounces (45 g.) each. No small selection of exhibits can do justice to a find as rich as this one.

The silk gauze (No. **70**) is the oldest example of this technique known. Designs in five colors were both printed and painted onto the fabric. The extremely small scale of the motifs, 20 units to one width of cloth, resulted in 800 motifs per meter (about 39 inches). If these motifs were printed in units of four, as seems to be the case, each meter would have required 200 impressions from the printing block. The addition of the painted pigments required six separate steps. The other piece of silk (No. **71**) is a variety of chain-stitch embroidery using colored silk thread on fabric with a woven design of paired birds and diamond figures. Three different patterns are named in the inventory of tomb furnishings. This type apparently corresponds to one called "scudding clouds." A single unit of this design measures about 6.5 by 5.5 inches (17x14.5 cm.). Red, brown, olive, and yellow threads were used to embroider its graceful designs.

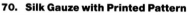

70. Silk Gauze with Printed Pattern
L: 22.5 in. (57.4 cm.); W: 16.25 in. (41.3 cm.)
Western Han (ca. 186-168 B.C.)
Tombs of the Family of the Marquis of Dai
Mawangdui, Changsha, Hunan Province
Excavated 1972-1973
Hunan Provincial Museum

71. Silk Embroidery with "Eye" Pattern
L: 7.75 in. (20 cm.); W: 6.69 in. (17 cm.)
Western Han (ca. 186-168 B.C.)
Tombs of the Family of the Marquis of Dai
Mawangdui, Changsha, Hunan Province
Excavated 1972-1973
Hunan Provincial Museum

The Inner Court

77. Lotus-leaf Lid, silver
H: 1.5 in. (4 cm.); D: 10 in. (25.6 cm.)
Tang (8th c.)
Dingmao Bridge, Dantu County, Jiangsu Province
Excavated 1982
Zhenjiang City Museum

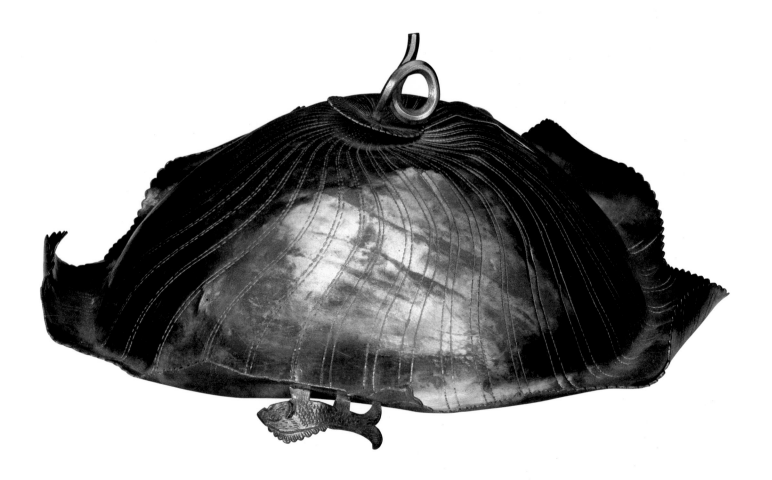

Nos. 72-77 Silver
Tang (8th c.)
Dingmao Bridge
Dantu County, Jiangsu Province
Excavated 1982
Zhenjiang City Museum

Precious objects made of gold and silver, which have always been readily convertible to cash, were among the first things looted from tombs. As a result, in spite of the many thousands of burials excavated in recent decades, few have held valuable gold and silver artifacts except for small objects such as cups, saucers, and jewelry. (The unmolested tombs at Mancheng are a rare exception to this rule.) Better knowledge of these arts, therefore, was not available until several caches of valuables were discovered accidentally at construction sites.

The most famous example of such a cache is that found in 1970 in Xi'an at Hejia Village when two crocks buried just below ground level yielded over 200 pieces of gold and silver.[31] This is the most bountiful of many discoveries made in and around Xi'an, the Western Capital of the Tang Dynasty, usually at residential sites. Evidently, in times of trouble, affluent citizens buried their most valuable possessions and all too often were unable to reclaim them after peace was restored.

Dingmao Bridge
The largest find of silver objects ever reported is from a site at the Dingmao Bridge near the Grand Canal southeast of Zhenjiang City.[32] The crock containing these objects was unearthed by workmen on New Year's Day 1982. The silver wine crock and a few vessels beside it were a little over three feet (1 m.) below ground level in an area that must have been a residential district in the Tang. (Only a year earlier, not more than 65 feet, or 20 m., away, other workers had dug up a collection of 20 Tang silver ingots weighing almost 90 pounds, or 40 kgs.) The 956 silver objects found at Dingmao Bridge constitute a second important sample of Tang silver that, together with the pieces from Hejia Village, tells us a great deal about the art of working silver in this period.

Most of the six objects chosen for the exhibition were intended for banquet use. An elegant silver dinner service might include bowls (No. **72**), covered boxes (Nos. **73-74**), stands, cups, dishes (No. **75**), saucers, trays, pitchers, lids (No. **77**), spoons, and chopsticks. These would complement larger ceramic serving platters. Another significant part of the cache consisted of hairpins (760 pieces), bracelets, and other accessories that would have adorned the women servants of a large estate. Finally, a gilt tortoise carrying a cylinder with drinking tallies on its back to count up the number of toasts *(Fig. 26),* a unique object, could have been the centerpiece for a festive drinking party.

The bowl (No. **72**) is a masterpiece of chased (hammered and incised) work, with a design of two *makara* (hybrid sea creatures from Buddhist lore) in pursuit of flaming jewels.[33] The bowl is formed as five lobes and every surface within its rim is fully decorated: ocean waves and lotuses surround the *makara,* vine tendrils are entwined with birds in flight, and flower garlands are strewn among auspicious deer. The two round covered boxes (Nos. **73-74**) are decorated with *repousse* (raised) designs, which required hammering from the back side. Sitting on a ring foot, one box and lid (No. **74**) are shaped as four-pointed lotus petals. The lid features a pair of parrots in flight encircled by a loose flower garland. More floral motifs fill the narrow bands on the lid and body. All the cut surfaces are also gilded. Similar motifs cover the surfaces of the other box (No. **73**), but here a punched design of small circles cloaks the ground areas. The four-lobed dish (No. **75**) features chased and gilded long-tailed phoenixes, with *repousse* lotus scrolls around the margins. The diminutive vase (No. **76**) once stood on three legs, now lost. Here the decoration is figural, depicting dancing, sitting, or singing children who might be compared to the playful children on the three-color pillow (No. **79**). The lid is in the shape of a lotus leaf (No. **77**) and may have been used to cover a delicacy on a serving platter. Its curling edges suggest a plant that is at or just past its prime.

*Fig. 27   Rubbing of inscription on silver lid (No. **77**).*

Scholars see Tang silver in three chronological segments. An early phase extended to the late 7th century when Sassanian shapes and motifs from Persia were common and honeysuckle designs current in many decorative arts. During the middle phase dominating the first half of the 8th century, decor became more complex and dense, and foreign elements were either assimilated or shed. In the late phase, after the military upheavals of the mid-8th century, bird and flower motifs loosely composed on simpler shapes were in vogue.[34] The dating of these stages must depend largely on external evidence because, with the exception of the late phase, most excavated silver objects do not bear inscribed dates.

Fig. 26   Gilt silver tortoise, Dingmao Bridge, Dantu County, Jiangsu Province.

For the Dingmao Bridge cache we can reconstruct an unusually complete set of historical circumstances in the best tradition of Sherlock Holmes. This cache seems to fit into the middle phase of Tang silver production. None of the shapes resembles a Sassanian prototype, nor are such "foreign" motifs as hunting scenes to be found. At the same time, the extremely dense treatment of the surfaces, where virtually every available part of the bowl and boxes is covered with plaited vines and flowers, is typical of the 8th century in a variety of decorative arts, including textiles and stone engravings. It seems likely that these objects were crafted during the reign of Tang Xuanzong (r. 712-756).

Why Were They Buried? Most of these objects bear the inscription *"Lishi" (Fig. 27)* which implies that they are part of a common set or perhaps were produced by a single workshop or for a single owner.[35] But a number of objects lack lids or are represented by odd numbers of examples. This seems to be merely part of a larger silver service that was buried in some haste. Moreover, none of the objects shows a trace of actually having been used, although the small vase is damaged. From this one may infer that they were buried shortly after their manufacture and perhaps even before they reached their intended user.

The military disturbances of the mid-8th century reached Jiangsu Province, but only one episode had a profound impact on the peace of the region. In 760, the rebel Liu Zhan raised arms in the areas surrounding modern Zhenjiang City, and fighting between his forces and those loyal to the Tang court ensued for almost two years. When the Tang general Tian Shengong entered the region, the histories tell us, several thousand families of wealthy merchants were slaughtered, and "there were caches dug everywhere within the city walls" by residents hoping to save their wealth. Although the evidence is circumstantial, this is a plausible explanation for why and when the Dingmao Bridge silver was buried.

The Imperial Connection. Runzhou, which included the Zhenjiang area, was a major source of silver production in the latter half of the Tang. Large gifts of silver were presented at court in 825 by the official Li Deyu, and other excavated finds attest to the important role of the Southeast.[36] Although the Privy Treasurer (Shaofu jian) controlled large gold and silver workshops at the capital, it is clear from both historical records and recent finds that many gifts of precious metals were presented to the imperial court by local officials. It is likely, therefore, that the silver banquet service found at Dingmao Bridge was actually made nearby and possibly intended as a gift to the court from a local official or commissioned on order from the court.

As stated above, almost all the objects that comprised the banquet service bear the two-characer inscription *"Lishi."* This term literally means "strong man" and could be interpreted as the name of the artisan who crafted the objects, the name of their owner, or a shortened form of some other meaning. The latter two explanations are the most likely because terse artisan's signatures were not common in the Tang. Two well-known men named Lishi lived in this area during the Tang. One, Gao Lishi, was active at the time these objects were made and had palace connections and great wealth. As a result, he could have been the owner of the objects and perhaps could have intended them for presentation at court. However, Tang writings use the phrase *"Lishi weng yin qi,"* translated as "a Lishi's crock of drinking vessels," apparently a colloquial expression for a well-stocked drinking service. Although the full phrase does not appear on any of the Dingmao Bridge pieces, the shortened form Lishi may be an allusion to it.

75. Lobed Dish with Phoenix Design, gilt silver
H: 1.75 in. (4.8 cm.); L: 8.25 in. (21 cm.);
W: 6 in. (15.3 cm.)
Tang (8th c.)
Dingmao Bridge, Dantu County, Jiangsu Province
Excavated 1982
Zhenjiang City Museum

76. Vase with Figural Design, gilt silver
H: 2.75 in. (7 cm.); D: 2.5 in. (6.6 cm.)
Tang (8th c.)
Dingmao Bridge, Dantu County, Jiangsu Province
Excavated 1982
Zhenjiang City Museum

73. Round Box with Parrot Design, gilt silver
H: 3.25 in. (8.5 cm.); D: 4.25 in. (11 cm.)
Tang (8th c.)
Dingmao Bridge, Dantu County, Jiangsu Province
Excavated 1982
Zhenjiang City Museum

72. Bowl with Makara Design, gilt silver
H: 2.75 in. (7.3 m.); D: 13.5 in. (34.5 cm.)
Tang (8th c.)
Dingmao Bridge, Dantu County, Jiangsu Province
Excavated 1982
Zhenjiang City Museum

80. Ewer with Dragon Head, Ding ware
porcelain
H: 10 in. (25.5 cm.); D: 2.5 in. (6.6 cm.)
Song (10th c.)
Jingzhi Temple Pagoda, Dingzhou City, Hebei
Province
Excavated 1969
Dingzhou City Museum

81. Long-neck Bottle, Ding ware porcelain
H: 7 in. (17.7 cm.); D: 3.25 in. (8.5 cm.)
Song (10th c.)
Jingzhi Temple Pagoda, Dingzhou City, Hebei
Province
Excavated 1969
Dingzhou City Museum

Nos. 78-86 Ceramics
Song and Yuan (10th-14th c.)
Hebei, Henan and Jiangsu Provinces
Dingzhou City Museum, Hebei
Provincial Museum, Henan
Cultural Relics Research
Institute, Henan Provincial
Museum, Zhenjiang City Museum

The Song and Yuan periods were undoubtedly the great age of Chinese ceramics. Measured by any criterion of technical refinement, aesthetics, quantity or quality of production, the wares manufactured from the 10th through the 14th centuries set a new standard. This is not to deny the creativity and accomplishments of earlier eras; in Chinese art history, every age produced great ceramic ware. But the Song and Yuan mark the final maturity of the potter's art in China. This was an age when nearly anything was possible, and a dazzling array of ceramic types, glazes, and decorations flourished.

Ceramics are fundamentally practical objects made with a specific utilitarian purpose in mind. The great wares of the Song and Yuan that we treasure today were made for such everyday uses as serving food, storing wine, arranging flowers, sleeping, and even spitting. The practical use of the objects determined their shapes and sizes and influenced the volume of production and care taken with glazing and decoration. These wares were manufactured at large potteries located over a wide area in both North and South China, from Hebei to Henan to Jiangxi provinces in the case of those objects included in this exhibition. The level of technology available to the potters and masters of the kilns was probably comparable in each case, and each production center was a part of a national distribution and marketing network. Products of the famous kilns at Jingde Zhen in Jiangxi Province, which made the Yingqing ware pillow (No. **78**) and the two blue-and-white vases (Nos. **85-86**), are found all over China, in the northeast and southwest as well as in such urbanized centers as the two Song capitals. The imperial court was the foremost customer for fine stoneware and porcelain and could demand and control the output of the best products from large kilns such as those making Ding and Jun ware.

Pillows. A ceramic pillow seems at first an impractical device to a culture such as ours that is accustomed to soft feathers or foam. In the warm months of summer, however, a cool pottery resting-place for the neck was a welcome relief. Ceramic pillows became popular during the Tang (7th-9th c.) and were a common product at a number of important kilns in Song and Yuan times, ranging from the Cizhou potteries of the north that supplied a popular market to the rarefied Ding and Yingqing ware intended for a more discriminating customer.

The pillows exhibited here represent two ends of the spectrum. The large three-color example from Jiyuan County, Henan Province (No. **79**), was dug up at the site of an ancient temple near sherds and a kiln that suggest a pottery was once located in the area.[37] It was made with molds from a clay that burned to a light-red bisque and then decorated by incised lines and painting. The three colors, as usual, are actually only part of a wider palette, and there is only a loose relationship with the dipped or dripped glazes on Tang figurines (Nos. **126-137**). The decoration of the central panel, reminiscent of folk painting, depicts two gentlemen enjoying a lute performance flanked by rosettes of playful children. Both the genre of garden scenes and of children at play enjoyed great popularity in Song and later times in a variety of decorative arts, including paintings of academic and scholar artists (see Nos. **92** and **98**).

On the other hand, the pillow in the shape of a sleeping child holding a lotus leaf is a relatively rare figural Yingqing ware design.[38] The term Yingqing (or Qingbai, which is the preferred contemporary usage) refers to the hue of the glaze, a tone between blue and white. The kiln that made this pillow was probably located at Jingde Zhen in Jiangxi Province, the porcelain capital of later imperial China. The origin of this pillow is not documented, but it is related to several other excavated examples from Song period tombs in the Zhenjiang area. This pillow is an art object that is both sculptural and utilitarian, an example of the enduring synthesis of form and function so prevalent in the arts of China.

Ding Porcelain. The exhibition features two of the "Five Great Wares of the Song," an appellation coined to distinguish the finest stoneware and porcelain of that great age. Ding ware, produced at several sites in North China but named after ancient Dingzhou, the region of Quyang County, Hebei Province, is the only white porcelain among the group of five. The Ding ware potteries, however,

produced other glazes as well, such as the so-called brown and black Ding. Kiln sites near Quyang investigated in recent decades confirm that these wares were produced from the late Tang into the Jin and Yuan eras (13th c.).[39] Ding ware is known for purity and fineness of body and for milk-white to ivory glazes. The potting is sleek and thin, with a variety of incised, carved, and molded decoration. Both the ewer and vase (Nos. **80-81**) have carved lotus-leaf patterns on their bodies, while the vase also carries a band of impressed floral decor on the shoulder.

The Ding potteries pioneered the technique of upside-down firing, eliminating the need for individual saggers, small firing boxes, for each vessel in the kiln (see No. **84**). This required leaving the top edges unglazed so that the vessels did not stick to the kiln during the firing as they sat on their rims. This in turn led to binding the rims of many Ding bowls and dishes with metal. According to legend, the Song palace stopped using Ding ware because of the emperor's distaste for such rims.

The most important discovery of Ding ware porcelain was made in 1969 with the opening of two pagoda foundations near Ding County, Hebei Province *(Fig. 28).*[40] These foundations were repositories for many Buddhist relics and other donations at temples rebuilt in the 10th century. Pagoda No. 5 contained more than 700 objects and 27,000 coins in a space barely 6.5 feet (2 m.) square, including 115 porcelains. Among these were both the ewer and long-neck vase and another vessel dated by inscription to 977. The cache at Ding County demonstrates the early maturity of Ding production and suggests that upside-down firing came into use after the 10th century because there are no vessels with unglazed rims in the cache. Although the ewer was made for use on Buddhist altars, the bottle could have served either in a temple or in a domestic setting.

The Ding potteries had strong ties to the court. Many examples of Ding vessels bear the inscriptions "Guan" or "Xin Guan" (Official or New Official); other inscriptions name an office of the palace kitchen (Shang Shi Ju) and an office of the court physician (Shang Yao Ju).[41] These texts were scratched in before firing and presumably indicate the intended users. Other Ding vessels have inscriptions cut in after firing which name palace halls of the Northern Song court where the objects were used. Similar inscriptions are known on Ru and Jun ware as well.[42]

Jun Stoneware. Another of the "Five Great Wares" was Jun celadon, a thickly potted stoneware with a relatively thick, even milky, glaze that varies from sky blue to greener shades, often with a blush of contrasting crimson or dark purple (aubergine). These potteries were centered in Yu County, Henan Province, during the Song, but expanded greatly during the following Jin and Yuan periods (12th-14th c.).[43] The early history of this ware is still unclear, and the name Jun was not used during Song times. Jun ware was one of two major Northern celadon traditions that served a broad market; the other is glassy, sea-green Yaozhou ware from Shaanxi Province. Because the body is gray and not translucent, Jun is not classified as a porcelain in the Western sense of this term. The most distinctive feature of Jun ware is the blushes, splotches of pale reddish color induced by copper in the glaze.

As with Ding ware, Jun products were enjoyed at the Northern Song court. Examples with incised names of Song palaces, the same halls named in Ding and Ru ware inscriptions, attest to court patronage. Many examples of large Jun ware pots have numerals scratched on their bases that scholars now believe denote sizes, from the largest (1) to smallest (10). At court Jun ware was used in the garden, as well as on the banquet table. The bowl and dish (Nos. **82-83**) were intended for culinary use. They are two of six vessels unearthed in flawless condition from a cache in Changge County, Henan Province.[44] Why they were buried in an iron crock only about three feet below ground level or by whom are unanswered questions. The bowl with sagger attached (No. **84**) shows how each vessel was placed within a protective housing for firing in the kiln. In this particular case, the bowl became affixed to its housing.

Blue-and-White Ware. Among the most widely admired and recognized porcelain of later imperial China are the blue-and-white wares. This kind of underglaze painted decoration flourished during the Ming, and today a Ming vase is a cultural icon of China. The origins of the technique and the early history of its production have engaged Chinese scholars in recent years. Since the discovery of blue-and-white vases dating to the mid-14th century, an expanding body of material has demonstrated the successful use of this technique prior to the Ming.[45] It is now recognized that some experiments with cobalt blue began as early as the Tang, but the status of the technique during the Song is not well understood. The first flowering of blue-and-white seems to coincide with the Yuan period (13th-14th c.), especially at the Jingde Zhen potteries.

The technique requires a white body, cobalt for painting, and a clear glaze. Although the ingredients were available as early as the Tang, the results were at first undependable. The earliest examples can be distinguished visually from the mature vessels of late Yuan and Ming, especially by the gray caste to the underglaze blue painting and the blue tinge to the glaze. Many examples of 13th- and 14th-century blue-and-white vessels are now known from excavations and tombs. One of the earliest important discoveries was a cache of 11 objects found in Baoding City, Hebei Province, in 1964.[46] The octagonal vase with lid and the octagonal bottle (Nos. **85-86**) are among the finest pieces from this find. The shape is ambitious, eight sides being more challenging to the potter than a circular vase, and the surfaces are enriched with gracefully painted designs in cobalt blue fading to gray. In addition, the tall vase has mold-impressed dragons on four sides of the body, a textural surface that contrasts with the blue graphic designs.

Fig. 28 Contents of pagoda foundation No. 5, Jingzhi Temple, Ding County, Hebei Province.

Detail of Pillow with "Playing the Lute" Design, No. **79**.

78. Pillow in Shape of Child, Yingqing ware porcelain
H: 6 in. (15 cm.); L: 8 in. (20.5 cm.); W: 6 in. (15.5 cm.)
Song (10th–13th c.)
Zhenjiang City Museum

79. Pillow with "Playing the Lute" Design,
three-color glazed earthenware
H: 6.25 in. (16 cm.); L: 24.75 in. (63 cm.);
W: 9.75 in. (25 cm.)
Song (10th–13th c.)
Jiyuan County, Henan Province
Excavated 1976
Henan Provincial Museum

82. Wan Bowl, Jun stoneware
H: 4.75 in. (12 cm.); D: 9.75 in. (24.8 cm.)
Song (10th-13th c.)
Changge County, Henan Province
Excavated 1978
Henan Cultural Relics Research Institute

83. Pan Dish, Jun stoneware
H: 2.5 in. (6.4 cm.); D: 10.75 in. (27.2 cm.)
Song (10th-13th c.)
Changge County, Henan Province
Excavated 1978
Henan Cultural Relics Research Institute

84. Bowl with Sagger, Jun stoneware
H: 6.5 in. (16.5 cm.); D (sagger): 10.75 in. (27 cm.)
Yuan (13th–14th c.)
Henan Provincial Museum

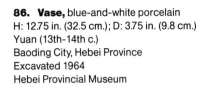

86. Vase, blue-and-white porcelain
H: 12.75 in. (32.5 cm.); D: 3.75 in. (9.8 cm.)
Yuan (13th–14th c.)
Baoding City, Hebei Province
Excavated 1964
Hebei Provincial Museum

88. Phoenix Hairpins, gold
a. L: 3.5 in. (8.6 cm.); W: 2 in. (5.3 cm.)
b. L: 3 in. (7.8 cm.); W: 2.25 in. (5.6 cm.)
Ming (14th c.)
East flank of Xiaoling, Nanjing, Jiangsu Province
Excavated 1981
Nanjing City Museum

Nos. 87-89 Later Jade, Gold and Silver Jewelry
Ming and Qing (14th and 17th c.)
Jiangsu Province
Nanjing City Museum and Zhenjiang City Museum

Personal adornment was in fashion from early times, but jades and hardstones were favored in China rather than precious metals. Few examples of gold and silver jewelry are known from the pre-imperial centuries or the early imperial era. The first flourishing of gold and silver in China was in the Tang period (7th-9th c.) when a cosmopolitan society gained access to precious metals and exotic stuffs from all over the Asian world (Nos. **72-77**).[47] Traditional love for jade and other hardstones led to a brilliant marriage of opposites: adamantine jade stones joined to precious metals.

The Ming (1368-1644) established its first capital at modern Nanjing but shifted the seat of imperial government to Beijing early in the 15th century. Nanjing remained a secondary capital and many families who had risen to prominence during the founding of the Ming maintained clan cemeteries at that city. Since 1949, the Nanjing City Museum has been entrusted with excavating the many tombs that lie all around the modern city as construction work goes forward. The greatest harvests from these excavations have been from tombs of those two epochs when Nanjing was an imperial capital: the Six Dynasties (3rd-6th c.) and the Ming.

The jade belt and gold filigree hairpins come from the tombs of persons from the early Ming. The Marquis of Dongsheng, Wang Xingzu, was the adopted son of general Zhang Desheng who served with the Ming founder. A native of Anhui, Wang was born in 1338 and died in 1371, only three years after the proclamation of the new dynasty. A veteran of more than ten years of military campaigns against the Mongols and the other Chinese claimants for the throne, Wang was heaped with honorific titles upon his death. His tomb contained both fine porcelain and gold jewelry, in addition to his 14-piece gold and jade belt.[48]

The hairpins were recovered from an anonymous tomb located on the eastern flank of the Xiaoling, the tomb of the first Ming emperor, Zhu Yuanzhang (r. 1368-1398). From the location, it is likely that the hairpins belonged to a palace lady, perhaps one of the consorts of the emperor himself.

Jade Belts. Leather belts appeared in China in ancient times and were indispensable for suspending the jade ornaments and swords that came into fashion during the late Bronze Age.[49] In later imperial times, leather belts with jade plaques became an emblem of rank and, like other articles of clothing, were prescribed for court officials. Jade plaques from such belts have often been found in burials, the most famous early example being the tomb of Wang Jian (d. 918), the King of Former Shu during the 10th century.[50] According to the official regulations of the Ming promulgated in 1393, officials of the First Rank were to wear a cap with seven ridges, a leather belt with jade plaques, and a sash of four-colored silk embroidery with their red robes (Fig. 29). Second-Rank court officials had belts with rhinoceros horn plaques, while lower ranks wore belts with gold, silver, or horn ornaments.

Ming belts are well-known from recent excavations. At one clan cemetery in Liaoning Province, several generations of Ming officials were buried, each with elaborate belt plaques.[51] Some of these belts had been worn in life, but others were apparently made only for burial, as if to confer prestige in the afterlife. Reticulate jade plaques for a belt from the tomb of a Lady Wang (d. 1634), the second consort of a Ming prince buried at Nancheng, Jiangxi, are remarkable for their intricate design, and are among the finest of their kind.[52] As the wife of a prince, she, too, was allowed to wear such a belt on formal court occasions. Few jade belts have the gold mounts of the example displayed here and few can match the quality of its multiple layers of cloud motifs, some with dragons in their midst. Such a high-quality jade belt may very well have emanated from a workshop serving the imperial court, because such accessories were not infrequently given by the Son of Heaven to high-ranking officials and other worthies. The belt in Wang Xingzu's tomb could be such an imperial gift, especially since some of the porcelains recovered from his burial were produced for exclusive imperial use, and his close personal connections to the emperor are well documented.[53]

Under the Ming system, an emperor's belt had 22 plaques; officials were entitled to 20. Five different shapes of plaques made up a belt, but this belt from Wang Xingzu's tomb is missing six of these pieces.[54] The plaques were found in a stack among sherds of a lacquered box; perhaps the set was incomplete even at the time of its burial.

Gold Hairpins. The hairpins (No. **88**) from the court lady's tomb at the Xiaoling were made by coiling gold wire. They depict phoenixes, mythical birds of good fortune according to Chinese belief. The pins were part of a woman's crown and are frequently found among the personal belongings of high-ranking ladies. There is little doubt that the finest pins came from the court. A pair of pins very similar to these found in a Ming prince's tomb in Jiangxi bear an inscription that details their date (Yongle 22nd year, 1424), the quantity of gold used (2 oz.), and their place of manufacture (the Silver Bureau of the palace).[55] Because crowns were a perquisite of the exalted rank of the lady, they were manufactured to the rigid specifications of the court and may even have been a monopoly product of the court Silver Bureau.

Gilt Silver Crown. The Qing (1644-1911) gilt silver phoenix crown (No. **89**) unearthed from a burial in Jurong County of Jiangsu Province is a kind worn in life by women who had received an honorific rank through imperial decree. During the Ming and Qing periods, officials of grades one through five customarily received such decrees for their meritorious service. The four-character phrase, *"Feng tian gao ming,"* on this crown alludes to the bestowal, probably one which established a fief. Two dragons and seven phoenixes make up the crown proper, with strands of jewels suspended from the mouths of the latter. The number of dragons and phoenixes and the quantities of jewels are indexes of the rank of the recipient.

*Fig. 29 Diagram of Ming jade belt as worn (see No. **87**).*

87. Jade Belt, 14 jade and gold plaques
Each plaque 1-3.5 x 1.5-3 in. (3-8.9 x 4.4-7.8 cm.)
Ming (before 1371)
Tomb of Wang Xingzu, Marquis of Dongsheng
Zhongyang Men, Nanjing, Jiangsu Province
Excavated 1970
Nanjing City Museum

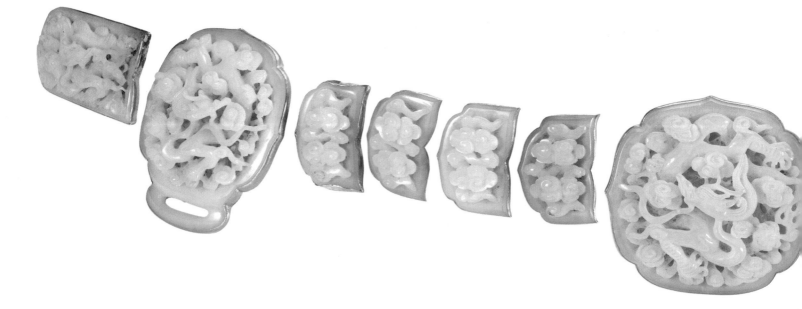

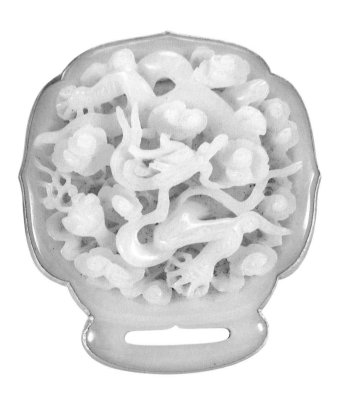

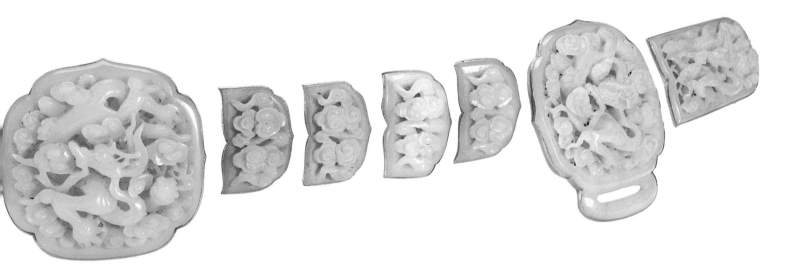

97. "Mynas on a Pine Tree," by Emperor Wuzong (r. 1506-1521), hanging scroll
H: 41.75 in. (106 cm.); W: 22.5 in. (57 cm.)
Ming (16th c.)
Shenyang, Liaoning Province
Liaoning Provincial Museum

Two mynas, as if in animated conversation, perch on the branches of this pine tree. The emperor's self-inscription dates the work to his own reign but does not specify the year. Less well known than Xuanzong (No. **90**), Wuzong shows a light and well-practiced hand in this painting.

Nos. 90-102 Paintings from Palace Collections
Ming and Qing (15th-18th c.)
Shenyang, Liaoning Province
Liaoning Provincial Museum

There has always been a strong symbiotic relationship between the greatest of Chinese painters and the imperial court. As the center of cultural life, it was only natural that the court and capital should attract painters to meet the needs of imperial patrons. In modern Western cultures painters have often been disdainful of the establishment, keeping a distance between themselves and the state, but in imperial China the state played a major role in the recruitment and training of artists. In some periods, the finest (or at least most esteemed) painters were also ranking members of court society both because of their artistic talents and other expertise. Art academies, both formal and informal, were generally maintained at court, and their artists were responsible for all manner of painting: from palace murals, portraits, and documentary paintings (Nos. **25** and **96**) to decorative screens and scrolls for imperial enjoyment. In a world without modern printing and photography, court artists frequently reproduced ancient works through faithful copies, a practice that "saved" many early scrolls. Imperial enthusiasm for the art, especially from the Song period (10th-13th c.) onward, led to the formation of enormous collections of paintings at court, an activity that often also led to the destruction of countless paintings at the fall of a dynasty. A few emperors even played with the brush themselves and achieved a modest reputation as artists.

These multiple relationships frame the history of Chinese painting in all periods. Even when scholar-amateurs (known in Western writings as literati) outside the court represented the vanguard of creativity, court influence continued through collecting, patronage, and the activities of academic artists. The history of Chinese painting is far broader than the insular activities of select circles of scholar painters, although 20th-century painting studies have been slow to admit this. If we focus exclusively on scholar-amateurs, we neglect a wider range of painting styles and subjects that surround and give meaning to the achievements of the literati.

The Ming Emperors as Painters
Both of the works by Ming emperors exhibited here are competent exercises in conventional subjects, a judgment no member of their entourage would have had the temerity to voice. The hand scroll of a gnarled pine tree (No. **90**) by Emperor Xuanzong (r. 1426-1435), painted as a gift to his mother, is one of several dozen works attributed to the ruler, whose short reign saw a brilliant flowering of court patronage in such arts as blue-and-white porcelain and carved lacquerware. Xuanzong succeeded the activist Yongle Emperor, who had relocated the capital to Beijing, and trusted advisors of the deceased emperor shouldered some of the burden of rulership, allowing the young man to dabble with brush and ink. Xuanzong's finest works are well-observed studies of dogs and other animals rendered in monochrome or very light colors. In a genre such as old trees, however, the emperor's competence is unremarkable. Although he was trained by talented court artists, the young ruler was truly only an amateur, earnest and striving, when he painted works such as this scroll.

The hanging scroll by Emperor Wuzong (r. 1506-1521) is less well known, as are the emperor's achievements as a painter. Some historians question his abilities altogether. "Mynas on a Pine Tree" (No. **97**) is another conventional subject, meant as a felicitous wish for the long life and health in old age of its recipient and as such is a social act as much as an artistic creation. This work on silk posed more technical challenges than Xuanzong's paper ground, but the rendering is no less accomplished. The large seal and inscription imply the emperor's authorship but do not prove it.

With any work attributed to a Son of Heaven, one must raise the question of authorship. It was not unusual for the emperor to sign and affix his seal to documents produced by others, and paintings may have been similarly treated. In some cases, an imperial signature may mean only that the work in question was copied or produced under the emperor's aegis. In the case of Xuanzong, we have a reasonably large and consistent body of work, and the attributions are probably valid. With so few works or other external documentation, the case of Wuzong remains open to speculation.

Artists at Court
The status of artists at court defies easy generalizations. At all times there were artists whose jobs were akin to those of modern house painters, paper-hangers, and interior decorators. There was a constant need for highly skilled portraitists and painters who could record important events such as the Qianlong Emperor's banquet on an island in the pleasure parks west of the Forbidden City (No. **96**). Such paintings were often assembled by a committee and it is here that the question becomes complicated. Such a committee in the Qing period (17th c. and after) would include a few artists formally enrolled in and paid by the court academy, but it might be chaired by a well-known scholar who had an entirely different court rank and ostensible range of duties (such as Wang Hui, No. **95**).[56] That some court officials were as highly skilled with their brushes at such demanding subjects as the "academicians" reveals what had become of so-called amateur painting among Qing scholars.

The official who combined high rank and formal responsibilities as a court official with an elevated reputation as an excellent painter (as with Wang Yuanqi, No. **101**, or Dong Bangda, No. **102**) predates the Qing by many dynasties. Yan Liben (d. 673) of the Tang disliked being at the Son of Heaven's beck and call for his brush skills. As one of the two highest court ministers, he felt that rushing to the palace garden to paint a rare bird was so demeaning that he is quoted as advising his sons not to learn the art. The dilemma was a matter of long standing.

Whether or not a formal structure was officially established at court, an informal academy existed in almost every period. Its members included connoisseurs, highly skilled painters of screens and scrolls, amateurs whose principal activities really were outside the realm of art, and many anonymous copyists, portraitists, etc. In some periods, it became fashionable for many members of the court, including imperial princes and high officials, to present paintings to the emperor as a way of currying favor. Imperial excursions could be commemorated or imperial poetry rendered in pictorial art (No. **102**). Like much occasional verse, such paintings may be slight in their artistic achievements.

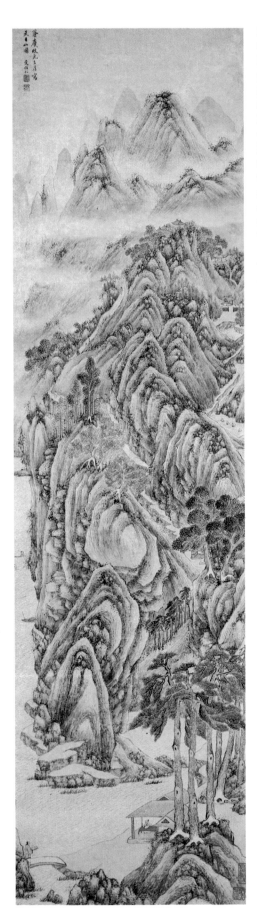

Imperial Collecting and the Modern Study of Painting

In many respects, the later history of Chinese painting has become the history of scholar's painting. This selective way of looking at the subject began in China and was well underway by the Qing period. Influential painters at court were often scholars adept at styles established by earlier scholars (see No. **95** by Wang Hui and No. **101** by Wang Yuanqi). The emperors themselves practiced such scholarly subjects as bamboo or the "Three Friends of Winter," and collected works by the great amateurs of earlier periods. Works by Shen Zhou and Wen Zhengming (Nos. **98** and **92**), the two patriarchs of the Wu School, became essential to the imperial collection, as did the calligraphic and painterly exploits of the scholarly ideal in art, Dong Qichang (No. **99**).

Imperial collecting of such works, in turn, created the "five-foot shelf" of approved masterpieces for students of Chinese painting in this century, many of them native sons of cities that had sustained the scholarly tradition in the Song, Yuan, and Ming. Because the imperial collection also became the basic inventory of both the Beijing Palace Museum and the National Palace Museum on Taiwan, the modern conception of "major monuments" has itself been strongly affected by tastes established at the end of the Ming and beginning of the Qing (17th c.).

93. "Mount Tianmu," by Wen Boren (1502-1575), hanging scroll
H: 5 ft. (151 cm.); W: 16.5 in. (41.8 cm.)
Ming (dated 1567)
Shenyang, Liaoning Province
Liaoning Provincial Museum

The nephew of Wen Zhengming, Wen Boren carried on the Wen-family style in this tall, narrow hanging scroll that is typical of many 16th-century Suzhou artists. It is both an art historical homage to such great Yuan artists as Wang Meng and a topographical painting. The composition therefore straddles the worlds of painting and reality.

1. See Wang Zhongshu, *Han Civilization,* New Haven, 1982, Ch. 1, and Robert L. Thorp, "Architectural Principles in Early Imperial China: Structural Problems and Their Solution," *The Art Bulletin* 58(1986):360-378.

2. On Ye, see Liu Dunzhen, ed., *Zhongguo gudai jianzhu shi* [History of Ancient Chinese Architecture], Beijing, 1980, pp. 46-48.

3. The bibliography on Chang'an is enormous. In addition to Liu cited above, see *Zhongguo gudai jianzhu jishu shi* [A History of Ancient Chinese Architectural Technology], Beijing, 1985, pp. 416-419. A good introduction in English is Arthur Wright, "Reflections on Ch'ang-an and Other Great Cities," *Journal of Asian Studies* 24(1965):667-679.

4. *Tang Chang'an Da Ming Gong* [The Tang Da Ming Palace], Beijing, 1959.

5. Nancy S. Steinhardt, "The Plan of Khubilai Khan's Imperial City," *Artibus Asiae* 44(1983):137-158.

6. Yu Zhuoyun, ed., *Palaces of the Forbidden City,* New York, 1984, pp. 72-119.

7. See Preston M. Torbert, *The Ch'ing Imperial Household Department,* Cambridge, Mass., 1977, and Wan Yi et al., *Qingdai gongting shenghuo* [Life in the Qing Palaces], Hong Kong, 1985.

8. "Eastern Zhou Tomb No. 1 with Human Victims at Langjiazhuang, Linzi" (in Chinese), *Kaogu Xuebao* 1977.1:73-104.

9. Luan Bing'ao, *Zenyang jianding gu yuqi* [How to Identify Ancient Jades], Beijing, 1984, pp. 23-26 and 39-40. Agate sources are recorded in Jilin, Hebei, Gansu, Shaanxi, Henan, Guangxi, and Jiangsu Provinces.

10. *Qufu Lu guo gu cheng* [The Ancient City of the State of Lu at Qufu], Jinan, 1982, p. 181 and Pl. 118, and *Shangcunling Guo guo mudi* [The Cemetery of the State of Guo at Shangcunling], Beijing, 1959, pp. 23-25.

11. Thomas Lawton, *Chinese Art of the Warring States Period: Change and Continuity, 480-222 B.C.,* Washington, D.C., 1982, pp. 132-134.

12. *Qufu Lu guo gu cheng,* Pl. 106.

13. "Excavation Report of the Tombs of Lord Meng of Huang and His Consort of the Early Spring and Autumn Period" (in Chinese), *Kaogu* 1984.4:302-332. Published in *Zhongguo meishu quanji* [Encyclopedia of Chinese Arts], *Gongyi meishu bian* [Arts and Crafts], Vol. 9, *Yuqi* [Jades], ed. Yang Boda, Beijing, 1986, Nos. 98-100.

14. For discussions of images of this kind, see Doris J. Dohrenwend, "Jade Demonic Images from Early China," *Ars Orientalis* 10(1975):55-78, and Zhang Changshou, "Notes on an Animal Mask Jade Ornament Newly Discovered at the Feng Xi Site," *Kaogu* 1987.5:470-473, 469.

15. "Brief Excavation Report of the Warring States Period Tombs of the State of Zhongshan at Pingshan, Hebei" (in Chinese), *Wenwu* 1979.1-31.

16. Chen Yingqi, "A Brief Discussion of Several Questions about the Zhongshan State as Reflected by the Ancient Shouling City Site" (in Chinese), *Zhongguo kaogu xuehui disanci nianhui lunwenji 1981* [Collected Papers from the Third Annual Meeting of the Chinese Archaeology Association for 1981], Beijing, 1982, pp. 230-237.

17. For a different view, see Huang Shengzhang, "A Further Discussion of Several Questions Concerning the Zhongshan State Tombs at Pingshan" (in Chinese), *Kaogu* 1980.5:444-447, 435.

18. For the tridents, see *The Great Bronze Age of China*, New York, 1980, No. 92.

19. On these inscriptions, see Li Xueqin and Li Ling, "The Three Pingshan Vessels and Several Questions About the History of the State of Zhongshan" (in Chinese), *Kaogu Xuebao* 1979.1:147-170. There is already a voluminous bibliography about these inscriptions.

20. Huang ("Several Questions Concerning the Zhongshan State Tombs," p. 446) regards this axe and its inscription as evidence that the later kings of Zhongshan were relatives of the Zhou house enfeoffed by the Zhou king, rather than descendants of the non-Chinese White Di.

21. Well-illustrated in *Chuzan okoku bunbutsuten* [Exhibition of Cultural Relics of the Kingdom of Zhongshan], Tokyo, 1981.

22. Wu Hong, "A Discussion of the Form and Decoration of Several Zhongshan State Objects" (in Chinese), *Wenwu* 1979.5:46-50.

23. *Changsha Mawangdui Yi-hao Han mu* [Han Tomb No. 1 at Mawangdui, Changsha], Beijing, 1973; "Brief Excavation Report of Han Tombs Nos. 2 and 3 at Mawangdui, Changsha" (in Chinese), *Wenwu* 1974.7:39-48, 63. See also David D. Buck, "Three Han Dynasty Tombs at Ma-wang-tui," *World Archaeology* 7 (1975):30-45..

24. Alice J. Hall, "A Lady from China's Past," *National Geographic* May, 1974, pp. 660-681.

25. Translation (here modified) by Yu Ying-shih, "New Evidence on the Early Chinese Conception of the Afterlife," *Journal of Asian Studies* 41 (1981):82.

26. Well-illustrated in *Hunan sheng bowuguan* [The Hunan Provincial Museum], Zhongguo bowuguan [Museums of China], Vol. 2, Beijing, 1983.

27. Wang, *Han Civilization,* p. 83, quoting *Yan tie lun* [Debates on Iron and Salt].

28. Yu Weichao and Li Jiahao, "Questions Concerning the Place of Manufacture of the Lacquerware from Han Tomb No. 1 at Mawangdui" (in Chinese), *Kaogu* 1975.6:344-348.

29. *Changsha Mawangdui Yi-hao Han mu chutu fangzhipin de yanjiu* [Research on Textiles Unearthed from Han Tomb No. 1 at Mawangdui, Changsha], Beijing, 1980, and Xia Nai, trans. Chu-tsing Li, *Jade and Silk of Han China,* Franklin D. Murphy Lectures III, Lawrence, Kansas, 1983.

30. A more recent discovery extends the history of silk textiles back to the late 4th or early 3rd centuries B.C. See *Jiangling Mashan yihao Chu mu* [Chu Tomb No. 1 at Mashan, Jiangling], Beijing, 1985.

31. "Cultural Relics from a Tang Cache Discovered at Hejiacun in the South Suburbs of Xi'an" (in Chinese), *Wenwu* 1972.1:30-42. A good selection of these objects was included in *The Chinese Exhibition,* Washington, D.C., 1974, Nos. 305-328.

32. "A Cache of Tang Period Silver Unearthed at Dingmao Bridge, Dantu, Jiangsu" (in Chinese), *Wenwu* 1982.11:15-27.

33. Another example of this motif is a silver bowl in the Nelson Gallery, Kansas City; see Jan Fontein and Wu Tung, *Unearthing China's Past,* Boston, 1973, pp. 176-185.

34. Duan Pengqi, "A Modest Proposal Concerning the Tang Gold and Silver Vessels from Hejiacun in the South Suburbs of Xi'an" (in Chinese), *Kaogu* 1980.6:536-541, 543. Duan divides Tang silver into early and late phases, each with sub-phases.

35. Lu Jiugao and Liu Jianguo, "A Preliminary Analysis of Tang Silver Unearthed at Dingmao Bridge, Dantu" (in Chinese), *Wenwu* 1982.11:28-33.

36. "A Group of Tang Silver Objects Unearthed at Beiyincun, Liulin, Yao Xian, Shaanxi" (in Chinese), *Wenwu* 1966:1. These objects also came from Runzhou and were presented by the Salt and Iron Intendant Jing Mei to the Xuanhui Drinking Hall at Chang'an. See also "Tang Gilt Silver Objects Found at Karachin Banner, Jouda League, Liaoning" (in Chinese), *Kaogu* 1977.5:327-334. These objects are identified by inscription as emanating from Xuanzhou (modern Anhui Province).

37. Wei Pingfu, "Two Three-color Song Pillows" (in Chinese), *Wenwu* 1982.1:81-82.

38. Xiao Menglong, "Yingqing Porcelain Pillows in the Zhenjiang City Museum" (in Chinese), *Wenwu* 1978.11:92-93.

39. "Investigation and Trial Excavations at the Ding Ware Kilns at Jianci Village, Quyang, Hebei" (in Chinese), *Kaogu* 1965.8.

40. "Two Song Period Pagoda Foundations Discovered at Ding County, Hebei" (in Chinese), *Wenwu* 1972.8:39-51. Published in *Ding Yao* [Ding Wares], Zhongguo Taoci [Chinese Pottery and Porcelains], Shanghai, 1983, Nos. 24 and 50.

41. Li Huibing, "An Investigation of the Place of Production of White Porcelains with the Inscriptions 'Guan' and 'Xin Guan'" (in Chinese), *Wenwu* 1984.12:58-63, 90.

42. Li Zhiyan, "A General Discussion of Ancient Chinese Pottery and Porcelains" (in Chinese), Shi Hua, ed., *Zhongguo Taoci* [Pottery and Porcelain of China], Beijing, 1985, p. 234.

43. "Excavation of the Juntai Kilns in Yu Xian, Henan" (in Chinese), *Wenwu* 1975.6:57-63.

44. "Jun Wares Discovered in a Cache at Shigu, Changge County" (in Chinese), *Zhongyuan wenwu* 1983.4:109-110.

45. *Zhongguo taoci shi* [History of Chinese Pottery and Porcelains], Beijing, 1982, pp. 338-343. The pioneering investigations of J. A. Pope mark the beginning of serious research after World War II. See *Chinese Porcelains from the Ardebil Shrine,* Washington, D.C., 1956, and *Fourteenth-Century Blue-and-White,* Washington, D.C., 1952.

46. "A Group of Yuan Period Porcelains Discovered in Baoding" (in Chinese), *Kaogu* 1965.2:17-18, 22. Also published in *Hebei sheng chutu wenwu xuanji* [A Selection of Cultural Relics From Hebei Province], Beijing, 1980, Nos. 404-405.

47. Edward J. Schafer, *The Golden Peaches of Samarkand,* Berkeley, 1963.

48. "Brief Report of Clearing the Tomb of Wang Xingzu of the Ming at Nanjing" (in Chinese), *Kaogu* 1972.4:31-33, 23. Illustrated in *Zhongguo meishu quanji, Gongyi meishu bian,* Vol. 9, *Yuqi,* No. 279.

49. Sun Ji, "Ancient Chinese Leather Belts" (in Chinese), in *Wenwu yu kaogu lunji* [Essays on Cultural Relics and Archaeology], Beijing, 1986, pp. 297-321.

50. Feng Hanyi, "Wang Jian mu nei chutu 'dadai' kao" [A Study of the 'Great Belt' Unearthed from the Tomb of Wang Jian], in *Feng Hanyi kaoguxue lunwenji* [Collected Archaeological Essays of Feng Hanyi], Beijing, 1985, pp. 114-118.

51. "Excavation of the Tombs of the Clan of Cui Yuan of the Ming at Nijiatai, Anshan" (in Chinese), *Wenwu* 1978.11:11-34.

52. "Brief Excavation Report of the Tomb of Zhu Youmu, the Yiding Prince of the Ming at Nancheng, Jiangxi" (in Chinese), *Wenwu* 1983.2:56-64.

53. Li Weiran, "A Preliminary Discussion of the Date of Blue-and-White Porcelains Unearthed from Early Ming Tombs in the Nanjing Region" (in Chinese), *Wenwu* 1977.9:76-79, 39.

54. Sun, "Ancient Chinese Leather Belts," p. 317.

55. "Excavation Report of the Tomb of the Ming Yi Prince, Zhu Youbin, at Nancheng, Jiangxi" (in Chinese), *Wenwu* 1973.3:33-45. Another burial of the same fief contained pins produced by the same Bureau in 1547. See "The Joint Burial of the Ming Yixuan Prince, Zhu Yiyin and His Consorts at Nancheng, Jiangxi" (in Chinese), *Wenwu* 1982.8:16-28.

56. For excellent discussions of the Qing court painting establishment, see Ju-hsi Chou and Claudia Brown, *The Elegant Brush: Chinese Painting Under the Qianlong Emperor, 1735-1795,* Phoenix, 1985, especially the essays by Howard Rogers, She Ch'eng, and Yang Xin.

91. "The Eight Immortals of Drinking, after Li Gonglin," by Tang Yin (1470-1523), hand scroll (section)
H: 12.5 in. (31.9 cm.); L: 20 ft. 9 in. (632.8 cm.)
Ming (dated 1517)
Shenyang, Liaoning Province
Liaoning Provincial Museum

94. "Palace Beauty," Anonymous,
hanging scroll
H: 5 ft. 3 in. (161 cm.); W: 32.5 in. (83 cm.)
Ming (17th c.?)
Shenyang, Liaoning Province
Liaoning Provincial Museum

A court lady fixes her coiffure amid a palace garden while an attendant looks on. This kind of highly detailed and fully colored painting was always prominent at court. Although the style suggests a late Ming date (17th c.?), there is a spurious signature of the early Yuan master Zhao Mengfu in the lower left corner.

95. "Thatched Cottage at Nanshan," by Wang Hui (1632-1717), hanging scroll
H: 3 ft. (95 cm.); W: 13.5 in. (34.7 cm.)
Qing (dated 1703)
Shenyang, Liaoning Province
Liaoning Provincial Museum

This painting was created in the artist's 72nd year, 1703. This depiction places a retreat amid nature rather than within the artificially defined world of the garden, as with Wen Zhengming's "Thatched Hut at Huqi" (No. **92**). One of the most influential artists of his day, Wang Hui was a great advocate of reworking the styles and compositions of past masters to achieve a personal style.

This long hand scroll depicts the so-called "Eight Immortals of Drinking" as they progress from convivial sobriety to profound inebriation. The artist uses a crisp monochrome outline for his figures and defines their setting through loose ink washes. An inscription by the great calligrapher Zhu Yunming praises the work, comparing it favorably to past masters: "When I first looked at this scroll, I thought it was unquestionably from the hand of a Song master. Upon closer inspection, I realized it was a copy from Tang Yin's brush." The artist has written out the text of Du Fu's poem on this same subject, noting that he made the painting after viewing the original work by Li Gonglin of the Northern Song.

92. "Thatched Hut at Huqi," by Wen Zhengming (1470-1559), hand scroll (section)
H: 10.5 in. (26.7 cm.); L: 4 ft. 8 in. (142.5 cm.)
Ming (16th c.)
Shenyang, Liaoning Province
Liaoning Provincial Museum

This colorful rendering of scholars amid the pleasures of their garden retreat is one of many works by the artist that evokes the joys of a life of retirement from civil service duties. A placid composition in mild colors is enlivened by the fine dottings in rich black ink. The title and signature of the artist at the end of this scroll are followed by numerous inscriptions written by contemporaries in Suzhou and later Qing admirers.

96. "Banquet at Yingtai," by Zhang Hao (fl. 1736-1795?), hand scroll (section)
H: 4.5 in. (36.7 cm.); L: 6 ft. 10 in. (207.7 cm.)
Qing (18th c.)
Shenyang, Liaoning Province
Liaoning Provincial Museum

Few works of the court artist Zhang Hao are known, but he was a master of finely drawn architectural compositions and the documentary paintings frequently patronized by the Qing court. The scene is a banquet given by the Qianlong Emperor on an island in the Western Garden outside the Forbidden City.

98. "Enjoying Chrysanthemums," by Shen Zhou (1420-1509), hand scroll (section)
H: 9.25 in. (23.4 cm.); L: 33.75 in. (86 cm.)
Ming (15th-16th c.)
Shenyang, Liaoning Province
Liaoning Provincial Museum

The scholars in this garden retreat can enjoy the magnificent autumn display of chrysanthemums, a theme echoed in the artist's poem written after the scroll and in the appreciative comments of three later poetic inscriptions. Shen Zhou is now regarded as the patriarch of the Wu School, a tradition that continued with his proteges Wen Zhengming (No. **92**) and Tang Yin (No. **91**).

102. "Sixteen Views of Panshan," by Dong Bangda (1699-1769), hand scroll (section)
H: 16.5 in. (41.9 cm.); L: 18 ft. 8 in. (569.8 cm.)
Qing (18th c.)
Shenyang, Liaoning Province
Liaoning Provincial Museum

This is another example of the contribution of high-ranking court officials to the art of painting during the Qing. Dong Bangda, like Wang Yuanqi, served as a minister and was also a skilled painter serving the Son of Heaven. Dong's assignment here was to describe the imperial retreats east of Beijing at Panshan, scenery that inspired the Qianlong Emperor's own poetry. Each major site is labeled for the viewer's reference, while another courtier, Liang Shizheng, transcribed the sovereign's poems on the colophon paper following.

Section of "Grasses and Insects"

100. "Grasses and Insects," by Du Dacheng, and "Lofty Scholars of the Bamboo Grove," by Du Jin (fl. 1465-1487), hand scroll (sections)
H: 11.25 in. (28.7 cm.); L: 4 ft. 10 in. (149.1 cm.)
Ming (15th c.)
Shenyang, Liaoning Province
Liaoning Provincial Museum

This scroll combines the work of two Ming artists. Each painting is a masterful composition. In the "Grasses and Insects," Du Dacheng uses meticulous, controlled brush work and wash to open up the world beneath our gaze. "Seven Lofty Scholars" by Du Jin is an essay in the monochrome drawing style first seen in Tang Yin's "The Eight Immortals of Drinking."

Section of "Lofty Scholars of the Bamboo Grove"

99. "White Clouds Over the Xiao and Xiang Rivers," by Dong Qichang (1555-1636), hand scroll (section)
H: 11 in. (28.2 cm.); L: 46.75 in. (119 cm.)
Ming (dated 1627)
Shenyang, Liaoning Province
Liaoning Provincial Museum

The date inscribed by the artist is 1627 and he proclaims his debt to Dong Yuan, a 10th-century master active in the Nanjing area, and Mi Fu, a Northern Song scholar of the 11th century who championed Dong Yuan's works. The subject is the fabulous land of clouds and mists drained by the Xiao and Xiang Rivers of modern Hunan Province. Dong's calligraphy is a poetic essay on the wall paintings of the great Tang master Wu Daozi. The artist's absorption in the history of Chinese painting is apparent everywhere in this scroll.

101. "Clouds and Mist at Xiling," by Wang Yuanqi (1642-1715), hand scroll (section)
H: 15.25 in. (38.8 cm.); L: 11 ft. 4 in. (344.6 cm.)
Qing (dated 1710)
Shenyang, Liaoning Province
Liaoning Provincial Museum

This work dated 1710 is a tribute to the styles of antiquity by a high-ranking Qing court official who was an accomplished painter. Wang Yuanqi passed the Jinshi examination in 1670 and became Minister of the Board of Revenue. At the same time, as the grandson of Wang Shimin, one of the most famous painters of the early Qing period, Wang Yuanqi was learned in the art and dextrous in the kind of self-consciously art historical painting then in vogue. In his inscription, Wang acknowledges the great masters of the 10th century and especially their noble successor, Huang Gongwang, one of the Four Great Masters of the Yuan.

5 THE TOMB
Imperial Burials

Few imperial tombs have yet been opened by archaeologists in China. In spite of the discovery of the "underground army," the tomb of the Qin First Emperor is still sealed, although a thorough program of surveys and trial excavations has progressed for the last decade. None of the Han imperial tombs nor the necropolises of the Tang and Song have been excavated. For these early periods of the imperial institution, we have direct knowledge of some of the royal and imperial burials of the Six Dynasties (3rd-6th c.) located outside modern Nanjing, of a single imperial tomb of the Northern Wei (from the 5th c.) near modern Datong, Shanxi Province, and of several tombs from the 10th-century period of disunity known as the Five Dynasties. These include the burial of Wang Jian, the emperor of the state of Former Shu (d. 942) at Chengdu and two burials from the Southern Tang state (dated 943 and 961, respectively), again at Nanjing. Imperial tombs of the later unified regimes are known through excavations from the late Ming (the Dingling tomb of the Wanli Emperor, d. 1620) and the Qing (the Yuling of the Qianlong Emperor, d. 1799).

The locations of other imperial burials are not unknown. On the contrary, monuments like Tang Gaozong's Qianling *(Fig. 30)* have been known to Chinese scholars and the Chinese people since the time of their construction. Burial sites intended as eternal resting places have been physical symbols of fleeting glory or of lost grandeur to scholars and peasants alike. On visiting the former site of the Eastern Han capital, Luoyang, a poet wrote in the 3rd century:

At Beimang how they rise to Heaven,
Those high mounds, four or five in the fields!
What men lie buried under these tombs?
All of them were lords of the Han world.
The Gongling and the Wenling gaze across at each other:
The Yuanling is all grown over with weeds.
When the dynasty was falling, tumult and disorder arose,
Thieves and robbers roamed like wild beasts.
Of earth they have carried away more than one handful,
They have gone into vaults and opened the secret doors.
Jewelled scabbards lie twisted and defaced:
The stones that were set in them, thieves have carried away.
The ancestral temples are hummocks in the ground:
The walls that went round them are all leveled flat.
Over everything the tangled thorns are growing:
A herd-boy pushes through them up the path.
Down in the thorns rabbits have made their burrows:
The weeds and thistles will never be cleared away.
Over the tombs the ploughshares will be driven
And peasants will have their fields and orchards there.
They that were once lords of a thousand hosts
Are now become the dust of the hills and ridges.
I think of what Yunmen said
And am sorely grieved at the thought of "then" and "now."[1]

Although the tombs of the emperors were subjected to looting and neglect, they have endured as symbols of times now past.

Notes to Chapter 5 are on p. 206.

103. Officer, terra cotta
H: 6 ft. 4 in. (192 cm.)
Qin (ca. 210 B.C.)
Tomb of the First Emperor
Lishan, Lintong County, Shaanxi Province
Excavated 1974-1979
Museum of Qin Figures

Especially in the late imperial period, Chinese scholars devoted themselves to historical geography and antiquarian pursuits. Visiting ancient tomb sites became an avocation that could lead to a learned footnote correcting the standard histories or to erecting a stone monument identifying a historic site. Modern archaeologists build on these earlier studies as they begin the gargantuan task of taking inventory of China's cultural properties. Frequently modern scholars are able to amend the researches of their predecessors. We now know the correct identities of the nine Western Han tombs located north and west of Xi'an, for example, and must reattribute other putative Zhou and Qin tombs in that region.[2] The task is formidable: the Tang imperial tombs alone stretch over a distance of about 60 miles (100 k.) in the foothills of the mountains north of the Wei River above Xi'an. At present most of the imperial tombs have been designated as "Important Cultural Sites" and are protected by the national and provincial governments. Many imperial tombs have been surveyed, but the only excavations attempted have been of random finds in areas surrounding the mounds.

Mortuary Culture

The burials of the emperors were only a part of a larger social edifice: a system of mourning and burial that embraced all of elite society. The tombs of lesser-ranking members of the imperial family were scaled-down renderings of those of the Son of Heaven. Burials for other members of the aristocracy or gentry in turn mimicked imperial fashions, albeit at a much reduced scale. The imperial tombs served as a model for each generation, and even as ideas about death and the afterlife evolved, the tombs of the elite perpetuated plans and furnishings first created for imperial patrons in the early and middle imperial periods (the Han through Tang). Thus, in later periods, although the ideas that first motivated burial customs had lost their power, the forms of mourning and burial perpetuated ancient precedents.

The impetus for elaborate imperial burials lay in a complex of ideas and ingrained social customs. Throughout the Bronze Age, the kings and lords of Shang and Zhou had been sent to the afterlife with a conspicuous array of personal servants and possessions.[3] In the Shang (the latter half of the second millenium B.C.), human sacrifice was common for the elite, and in the Zhou period (ca. 1050-250 B.C.) for many centuries the custom endured of "following in death" whereby servants and concubines were put to death when their lord passed away. The Qin First Emperor (d. 210

B.C.) seems to have followed that custom. The ritual specialists who created the rites of mourning and burial for the first emperors of Qin and Western Han were intimately familiar with such customs and their symbolic and social significance. Death was viewed in many ways as another chapter of the life cycle rather than as a final demise. The care accorded the deceased assured a status and a lifestyle in the other world comparable to that enjoyed among the living. Above all, status had to be observed, and no one ranked higher than the Son of Heaven.

At the same time, more "rational" ideas motivated burial customs. Confucius professed not to understand death, but his followers, most notably Xun Zi (Hsün Tzu), developed a symbolic view of mourning and burial rituals that emphasized their utility as expressions of grief and love and their function of carrying human customs across the threshold of death.

The rites of the dead can be performed only once for each individual, and never again. They are the last occasion upon which the subject may fully express respect for his ruler, the son express respect for his parents… In the funeral rites, one adorns the dead as though they were still living, and sends them to the grave with forms symbolic of life. They are treated as though dead, and yet as still alive, as though gone, and yet as still present….[4]

The virtue explicit in this rationalization of burial customs is filial piety, the proper respect that a child shows his parent in life and after death. As with romantic love in the West, filial piety gave rise to a literature of its own with tales of filial devotion, and also to filial abuse when sons and daughters honored the letter but not the spirit of this concept.[5]

Burial Furnishings

In imperial times the pendulum swung back and forth between poles of extreme extravagance (houzang) and (by imperial standards) more modest burials. The First Emperor clearly spared no expense and created for himself a mausoleum of unprecedented size and grandeur. The Han emperors largely followed Qin precedent but could not accept the more extreme forms of self-expression, such as the First Emperor's "underground army." Even in Han times, however, there were contrary views. Emperor Wen (r. 180-157 B.C.) issued an edict that only ceramic grave goods need be placed in his tomb and that no man-made tumulus, or burial mound, should be constructed within his necropolis. What such edicts meant for this Son of Heaven's tomb will not be known until his vault is opened. It is clear from other princely burials of the same century, however, that it was more common to consign many precious possessions to the tomb chamber, as shown by the artifacts from the tombs of the Prince and Princess of Zhongshan (Nos. **109-114**).

Many of the tomb artifacts in "Son of Heaven" were discovered in recent decades. The superlative lacquerware and silks from Mawangdui (Nos. **66-71**) survived only because they were sealed within an air-tight, unspoiled tomb in the 2nd century B.C. Other artifacts removed by archaeologists are the ritual bronzes and bells of Guangshan and Xiasi, Henan Province (Nos. **1-10**), the jade disk from Ding Xian, Hebei Province (No. **11**), the jades and hardstones (Nos. **58-62**), bronze sculpture (Nos. **63-65**), and the Ming jade belt and gold hairpins (Nos. **87-88**). None of these objects was created expressly for use in the rites of mourning and burial. None had a prescribed place within the complement of grave goods manufactured as tomb accessories. Instead, all are testimony to the universal human attachment to beautiful things and to the desire of the deceased or the bereaved to send those special objects along to the grave. Had this custom not flourished throughout Chinese history, we would be immeasurably poorer in our knowledge of Chinese art.

The Tomb

Exhibits for this unit were selected to explain the kinds of arts that were created for an imperial burial. By selecting above-ground sculpture as well as the better-known ceramic figurines placed within or nearby the tomb, the role of this art within an imperial necropolis can be traced from Qin through Tang, arguably the great age of Chinese sculpture. We chose the jade burial shroud and personal possessions from Mancheng, Hebei Province, to illustrate what the custom of extravagant burial might mean and at the same time to describe the sumptuary regulations that affected members of the imperial family. These and other burial objects of the Han princes give the best clues to the rites accorded a Son of Heaven in early imperial times.

Many of the objects displayed were crafted in imperial workshops, even though the tomb where they were placed was not that of an emperor. It was common for the Son of Heaven to bestow gifts on a worthy minister or other notable.

Huo Guang passed away, and the emperor and empress dowager came in person to perform lamentations beside his corpse. The palace counselor Ren Xuan, along with five secretaries of the censorate, was presented with the imperial credentials and ordered to take charge of the funeral, while officials of the middle two thousand picul class prepared the tents to be erected on the grave mound. The emperor provided gifts of gold, cash, silk fabrics, a hundred embroidered coverlets, fifty boxes of clothing, jade disks, various kinds of pearls, a shroud made of pieces of jade sewn together, an inner coffin of catalpa wood, an outer coffin of camphor wood, an outer chamber made of the yellow core of cypress, fifteen coffins of fir wood for the outer burial chamber, and a "warm bright," all supplied by the Eastern Garden Office, all the same as those used in the burial of an emperor.[6]

Thus, the figurines from the tomb of Lou Rui (Nos. **117-125**) and An Pu (Nos. **126-137**), produced by the imperial workshop for mortuary accessories, are probably gifts from the imperial court to the deceased. At the great imperial tomb sites, there are hundreds of accompanying burials of princes and princesses, distaff relatives, and meritorious officials, many of whom would have been honored in death with such gifts.

The selection of exhibits emphasizes two phases in Chinese history: the early empire of Qin and Han and the "second" empire, the Tang and its immediate predecessors. For the mortuary arts, these were the two great ages of artistic production. The grandest schemes and most creative solutions were realized in the service of imperial burials. As evident from the vast amount of freshly excavated materials now available, any selection is at best only a glimpse of the possibilities that lay before an imperial patron.

Fig. 30 *Spirit Path of Qianling, tomb of Tang Gaozong, Qianling County, Shaanxi Province.*

105. Armored Warrior, terra cotta
H: 5 ft. 10 in. (178 cm.)
Qin (ca. 210 B.C.)
Tomb of the First Emperor
Lishan, Lintong County, Shaanxi Province
Excavated 1974-1979
Museum of Qin Figures

Nos. 103-108 Terra Cotta Warriors and Horses
Qin (ca. 210 B.C.)
Tomb of the First Emperor
Lishan, Lintong County, Shaanxi Province
Excavated 1974-1979
Museum of Qin Figures

Because of a succession of truly unprecedented discoveries, the archaeology of the Qin dynasty (ca. 221-210 B.C.) has exploded in recent years. Some aspects of the legacy of the Qin unification have long been known. Stone inscriptions and weights and measures with edicts issued by the Qin First Emperor have been collected by antiquarian scholars since the Song period (10th-12th c.). The burial mound of the First Emperor's tomb near Lintong County east of Xi'an in Shaanxi Province was a well-known, potent reminder of the transience of his regime. But it was not until the early 1970s that modern archaeology began to take the measure of the Qin Empire. Even then, as so often happens, the impetus was not a carefully thought-out, pre-planned archaeological reconnaissance, but rather a chance discovery by peasants digging amid an orchard.

The discovery at Yanzhai Commune in March 1974 was both unexpected and revolutionary.[7] Several yards below ground in the shaft of a well being dug by peasants, large fragments of gray terra cotta figures began to appear. Responsible authorities were called in from the county and province, and the well shaft was expanded until a pit about 50 by 200 feet (15x60 m.) lay exposed. The 500 life-sized figures and 24 horses found in this pit were, however, merely the beginning of the story. Probings revealed that this pit was the east end of a much larger underground trench measuring about 700 feet (210 m.) east to west and 200 feet (60 m.) across, populated with an estimated 6,000 life-sized warriors (Fig. 31). The archaeologists made two further discoveries. A second smaller trench was located in May 1976 about 65 feet (20 m.) north of the east end of Trench 1. It is estimated to contain about 90 chariots, with 350 horses and 260 warriors, plus some 115 cavalry riders and horses, and 560 foot soldiers. The next month a third still smaller trench was located at the west end of Trench 1.

About 70 to 80 figures are estimated to lie in Trench 3, which represented a headquarters unit. Neither Trench 2 nor Trench 3 has yet been thoroughly excavated. Both were refilled after they were probed and a number of their figures removed. Excavations at Trench 1, which has been roofed over to create a great indoor site museum, have continued periodically and are now once again underway.

The three Qin trenches probably contain about 7,000 life-sized warriors, 100 chariots, and 400 chariot horses.[8] This military formation constituted a sentinel army guarding both the eastern flank of the First Emperor's tomb, less than a mile (about 1,200 m.) behind it to the west, and the approach to the imperial capital. Probings indicate a fourth trench was begun but never completed, while a large, ramped tomb has been located almost 1,000 feet (300 m.) west of Trench 3. Chinese archaeologists suggest this was the burial of the general commanding the army. It, too, has not yet been opened.

The excitement generated by these discoveries led to further investigations throughout the area of the First Emperor's tomb and to renewed attention to the palace district of the First Emperor's capital at Xianyang. Fresh excavations have also begun in the area of the earlier Qin capital at Yong in modern Fengxiang County. Each of these efforts has repaid archaeologists with yet more rewards. We now know that the First Emperor's necropolis, called Lishan after the mountains south of the site, was but one component of a megalomaniac's grand designs. The scale and complexity of the funerary park and its capital district set a new standard that would serve as a model, good or bad, for all later imperial rulers.

The Lishan Necropolis
The First Emperor's necropolis is now better explored than ever before, but many tantalizing prospects await further excavation.[9] Several workshop sites used during the construction of the tomb have been found on the periphery. Lesser burials, probably of low-ranking members of the First Emperor's court, are reported from a tract east of the outer wall near Shangjia Village. Several tracts of sacrificial pits containing actual horses and half-life-sized terra cotta stable attendants are now known. A graveyard for the convict laborers who built the necropolis has also been reported. Within the double walls there are recent discoveries of pounded-earth architectural foundations and artifacts bearing inscriptions naming the site. Probing around the tumulus itself has located the position of

the two original access ramps to the central underground burial shaft. This same probing uncovered pits on the mound's west flank containing at least two half-life-sized bronze chariots. A survey by geologists suggests heavy concentrations of mercury in the area covered by the earthen mound. This evidence supports literary accounts that the First Emperor's tomb chamber contained a topographical map with bodies of water represented by mercury. All these discoveries indicate that the true scope of the Lishan necropolis is still to be fully appreciated.

Making the Terra Cotta Warriors
The creation of the warriors and horses was no less ambitious. To manufacture approximately 7,000 life-sized human figures and more than 400 horses at one time required an organizational genius and the administrative machinery to orchestrate a great many tasks in a timely and effective manner. Workers and artisans of every kind had to be brought to the site to dig and carry earth, cut wood, fire brick, quarry stone, cast metal, and, last but not least, model the warriors and horses. Those workers, however strict the Qin regime, had to be housed, clothed, and fed. Raw materials were brought to the site and then processed. To provide the artisans with fine, smooth-textured clay and to furnish the kilns with charcoal to fire the figures, there must have been a transportation and supply system that reached outside the capital district itself. The production line had to be carefully coordinated so that the moist clay could be worked or finished by each skilled artisan in the assembly-line process. Traditional histories report that the First Emperor had a force of 700,000 convict laborers on hand in the capital district during much of the time the Lishan necropolis was under construction.

The production process was a combination of hand work and mold techniques.[10] The plinths that the warriors stand on were formed in a draw mold, sometimes in one piece with the feet. Their solid shoes were usually modeled by hand, often in two parts (top and bottom, or front and back), and then joined to the legs, which might be either solid or hollow. Leggings were rendered by molds, while the body trunk was created by a combination of hand and mold techniques. Thick strips of coarse clay were coiled by hand, and then pressed into outer molds that gave the torsos their shape. Much of the armor was created by molds impressed against the still pliable outer coating of clay. Arms, both hollow and solid, seem to have been created entirely by hand-modeling and

106. Armored Warrior, terra cotta
H: 6 ft. (183 cm.)
Qin (ca. 210 B.C.)
Tomb of the First Emperor
Lishan, Lintong County, Shaanxi Province
Excavated 1974-1979
Museum of Qin Figures

then bent to the appropriate gesture. Hands, which were inserted into the hollow ends of the arms, were both modeled by hand and pressed from molds, with fingers joined to separately rendered palms. The heads were created in two steps. First, the two parts of the head were pressed into two molds shaped like half-melons. Then, by applying finer clay and modeling it with fingers and stylus, the facial features were realized. Among the warriors that have been restored to date, there are at least 24 different styles of facial hair with varied combinations of moustaches, chin whiskers, and so on. Each step was a blend of techniques that facilitated rapid, high-volume production and permitted the artisans to capitalize on their individual skills.

The figures are a gray terra cotta, but that was not their original appearance. They were first placed in the ground as brightly painted figures. After being removed from the soil, however, the pigments crumbled away. Figures from Trench 2 originally had brown shoes with red laces; green or purple leggings; brown armor with red ties; green, red or purple tunics;and yellow, red or purple straps for their brown or white hats. The horses were a reddish brown with pink nostrils, ears, and gums. As seen today, the terra cotta warriors are only shadows of their original selves.

The discovery of the Qin army has upset the previous conventional notion of early Chinese sculpture. Until this find, it was reasonable, if shortsighted, to claim that large-scale sculpture was not important in ancient China (compare Nos. **63** and **65**). The true inception of naturalistic, figural sculpture was linked to the development of Buddhist stone and bronze images after the Han (see Nos. **42-46**). Crude, small-scale clay figurines were known from Bronze Age tombs, as were somewhat larger wooden figurines, but the early history of the tomb figurine was dominated by Han examples produced in two-part molds on a modest scale. The Lishan army demonstrates a mature figural style in China by the end of the Bronze Age, a style that surely did not arise from the crude clay tomb figurines of the previous two centuries. It also places the achievements of the Han in a new perspective. Many Han ceramic figurines are best seen as a reflection of Qin models. In fact, some of the best Han figurines and small-scale sculpture reveal first-hand knowledge of the Qin army. They could have been created by artisans from the same families.

108. Chariot Horse, terra cotta
H: 5 ft. 8 in. (172 cm.); L: 6 ft. 9 in. (205 cm.)
Qin (ca. 210 B.C.)
Tomb of the First Emperor
Lishan, Lintong County, Shaanxi Province
Excavated 1974-1979
Museum of Qin Figures

107. Chariot Horse, terra cotta
H: 5 ft. 8 in. (172 cm.); L: 6 ft. 9 in. (205 cm.)
Qin (ca. 210 B.C.)
Tomb of the First Emperor
Lishan, Lintong County, Shaanxi Province
Excavated 1974-1979
Museum of Qin Figures

109. Burial Suit and Accessories, jade with
gold thread
L: 5 ft. 8 in. (172 cm.)
Western Han (2nd c. B.C., not later than 104 B.C.)
Tomb of Dou Wan, Princess of Zhongshan
Lingshan, Mancheng County, Hebei Province
Excavated 1968
Hebei Cultural Relics Research Institute

Nos. 109-114 Jade Burial Suit and Metalwork
Western Han (2nd c. B.C., not later than 113-104 B.C.)
Tombs of the Prince and Princess of Zhongshan
Lingshan, Mancheng County, Hebei Province
Excavated 1968
Hebei Cultural Relics Research Institute

Even during the chaos of the Cultural
Revolution in the 1960s, archaeological
discoveries were made and controlled
excavations carried out. In May 1968, a
detachment of the People's Liberation Army
(PLA) working on Lingshan, a low rock
mountain in Mancheng County, Hebei
Province, stumbled upon an underground
passageway. This led to a side-chamber of an
immense tomb carved from the living rock of
the mountain. Archaeologists from Hebei
Province and the Institute of Archaeology in
Beijing were dispatched upon the orders of
Premier Zhou Enlai. During the excavation
of Tomb 1, another substantial rock-cut
excavation was also detected about 330 feet
(100 m.) away. By the end of the summer, two
large tombs of the Western Han Prince and
Princess of Zhongshan had been cleared.[11]

The Western Han emperors perpetuated
the Qin system of dividing the realm into
large territorial units called commanderies.
However, Liu Bang, the founder of the Han,
assigned some territories to his trusted
colleagues and others to imperial princes.
These "kingdoms" were in a sense a reversion
to the decentralized, feudal, pre-Qin system.
During most of the Han, kingdoms were
governed by imperial princes who had little
power but did gain income from the taxes of
their fief. The Kingdom of Zhongshan was
established in 154 B.C. and was made the fief
of Liu Sheng, son of the Han emperor Jingdi
(r. 157-141 B.C.). Zhongshan was the second
most populous and third largest of the Han
kingdoms, and the taxes and other wealth
available to Liu Sheng (d. 113 B.C.). and his
consort, Lady Dou Wan, supported them in
great style:

*Liu Sheng loved to drink and was very fond
of women so that with all of his offspring and
their families, his household numbered over
120 persons. He was always criticizing his
older brother, the Prince of Zhao, saying,
"Although my brother is a Prince, he spends all
of his time doing the work of his own clerks and
officials. A true Prince should pass his days
listening to music and delighting himself with
beautiful sights and sounds." The Prince of
Zhao replied with criticism of his own, saying,
"The Prince of Zhongshan fritters away his days
in sensual gratification instead of assisting the
Son of Heaven to bring order to the common
people..."*[12]

This argument between brothers was not
just a debate over lifestyle. The issue was
rulership. Liu Sheng favored the "non-action"
(wu wei) much in vogue among some political
thinkers, a theory in which the ruler did little
but still achieved his goals. The Prince of Zhao,
on the other hand, favored a more activist
and pragmatic manner of rule.

Although no Qin or Han imperial tombs
have been excavated, there is considerable
evidence now for the burials of the Han
imperial princes.[13] Because the princes were
merely one step below the Son of Heaven in
social rank, their tombs closely approximated
imperial burials. The greatest difference was
probably scale or, in some cases, in the quality
and quantity of the grave goods. In the case
of the two burials at Mancheng, it is likely
that most of the components had their
counterparts in an imperial mausoleum. The
Western Han was a great age of lavish burials
(houzang) in which no expense was spared on
the construction of the tomb, the preparation
of burial goods, and furnishings from the
deceased's own palace apartments. This was

one age in China in which the dead, at least of
a certain social rank, truly took much of their
wealth with them.

The two Mancheng tombs were cut into
the rock of a mountain. Long approach
tunnels from the east led to immense caverns
that served as the central tomb chamber
(Fig. 32). In the case of Tomb 1, that of Prince
Liu Sheng, the cavern was almost 23 feet
(7 m.) high and about 43 by 50 feet (13x15 m.)
in size. This cavern housed a wooden-frame
structure with tile roof that transformed the
cave-like environment into a simulation of the
Prince's own palace chambers. Additional
side-chambers were cut at right angles to the
main axis, while a chamber for the Prince's
coffin was dug at the rear, with a stone
house constructed within it. The maximum
dimensions of the "underground palace" were
170 feet (52 m.) (from front door to rear wall)
by 125 feet (38 m.) (from the end of one side-
chamber to the end of the other). Chinese
archaeologists have estimated that 100
artisans laboring for a year were required to
hollow out this rock-cut burial. Tomb 2 of Lady
Dou was even larger and more sophisticated
in its design.

In addition, elaborate measures were
taken to protect the contents of these tombs
from looting and to insure the eternal repose
of the two deceased. Each approach passage
was filled with rubble from its excavation and
then blocked with a pair of brick walls. Molten
iron was poured into the space between these
walls, creating a sturdy seal that permanently
closed the entrance. In addition, the stone
burial chamber of Tomb 1 had a self-locking
device in the floor. Once its two doors were
closed, they could not be reopened. Needless
to say, neither of the tombs had ever been
robbed.

*Fig. 33   Jade suit of Liu Sheng at time of excavation,
Lingshan, Mancheng County, Hebei Province.*

The Tomb

114. Coffin Handle, gilt bronze
L: 4.75 in. (12.2 cm.); W: 2.75 in. (7.3 cm.)
Western Han (2nd c. B.C., not later than 113 B.C.)
Tomb of Liu Sheng, Prince of Zhongshan
Lingshan, Mancheng County, Hebei Province
Excavated 1968
Hebei Cultural Relics Research Institute

Fig. 32 View of central chamber of Tomb 1, Mancheng County, Hebei Province.

Jade Burial Suits

Most important to insure the safety of the deceased in the afterlife was a jade burial suit (No. **109**). Belief in the magical properties of jade has ancient roots in China, and during the Qin and Han periods many persons at court believed a shroud of jade could protect the mortal remains from decay to achieve what Joseph Needham has called "terminal incorruptibility."[14] The Han emperors had jade suits sewn with gold thread made by the Artisan of the Eastern Garden Workshop, the palace office charged with producing all mortuary accessories. Han princes were entitled to a similar jade suit, but in theory, and in keeping with their lesser status, their shrouds were sewn with silver thread. For unknown reasons, however, those of Liu Sheng and Dou Wan were sewn together with gold thread, requiring 39 and 25 ounces (1,100 and 700 g.) of gold respectively. Over 2,000 plaques of jade were needed for these body suits, which were in 12 parts: face mask, stocking cap, chest cover, back cover, two sleeves, two legs, two gloves, and two boots. The plaques were backed and edged with fabric, but in spite of their estimable workmanship they did nothing to preserve the mortal remains. Only fragments of eight teeth survived in the case of Dou Wan, while no traces of Liu Sheng endured *(Fig. 33)*. Perhaps this was due to improper dressing of the corpse; in the case of Liu Sheng, the two legs and the chest and back covers of the jade suit were reversed in what appears to have been a hasty preparation of the corpse.

The jade suits were placed within lacquered coffins. That of Dou Wan was especially fine. Square and rectangular sheets of jade, 192 pieces altogether, were used as an interior lining for her coffin, while 26 *bi* disks (compare No. **11**) were mounted on the exterior. Liu Sheng's two coffins were less elaborate, but were equipped with 30 escutcheons and handles, mostly made of gilt bronze. The best were placed on the west, or head end of each coffin. The escutcheon and handle from the inner coffin (No. **114**) combine a beaked animal mask with climbing dragons and an ogre. The weight of the two coffins and jade shroud made them too unwieldy to carry into the burial chamber so small wheels were mounted to the base of the outer coffin. The deceased Liu Sheng was thus pulled to his final resting place.

Fig. 34 Rubbing of inscription on hu *vessel (No. 112).*

Luxury Goods

In addition to burial furnishings, the prince and princess were accompanied in death by some of their finest possessions. The prince had a complement of bronze wine vessels placed in his rear burial chamber, of which four *hu* were the most beautiful. Two of these *hu* had inlaid gold "bird script" decor extolling the medicinal properties of their contents, while a third was inset with gold dragons. The fourth (No. **112**) was gilt bronze decorated with diamond-shaped glass plaques. A similar vessel is reported to have come from the extremely rich graves at Jincun near Luoyang.[15] Glass was a rare material in ancient China, and it is most often encountered not as small vessels but rather as colored beads and plaques used for inlay. This particular *hu* bears an inscription *(Fig. 34)* naming an official of the food office of the empress' residence, the Palace of Everlasting Joy (Changle Gong). The grandmother of Liu Sheng was the Empress Dou, and it is very likely that this object was a gift from the empress's family. Liu Sheng's tomb had many other fine luxury items, including a set of five bronze drinking cups (Nos. **113**). These cups are similar in shape to the lacquered cup from Tomb 3 at Mawangdui (No. **69**), but lack "ears," the small curved handles for cradling the cup between the hands. Liu Sheng's bronze cups are meant to be lifted instead by the gilt phoenix ring at one end.

Dou Wan also carried rich objects to her grave. One of the most unusual, and as yet unique, is a bronze lamp in the shape of a phoenix perching on a dragon (No. **111**). The dish, phoenix, and dragon base were all cast separately and then soldered together. This lamp is similar to that found in the tomb of a Warring States king of the state of Zhongshan (No. **65**). Grease or tallow tapers were stuck onto the prongs in the lamp dishes. Although the three dishes of the Warring States example bathed a considerable area in soft light, the single, low dish of Dou Wan's lamp would have produced rather little illumination.

Detail of Jade Burial Suit, No. **109** (see p. 178)

111. Phoenix Lamp, bronze
H: 11.75 in. (30 cm.)
Western Han (2nd c. B.C., not later than 104 B.C.)
Tomb of Dou Wan, Princess of Zhongshan
Lingshan, Mancheng County, Hebei Province
Excavated 1968
Hebei Cultural Relics Research Institute

110. Pillow, gilt bronze and jade
H: 8 in. (20.2 cm.); L: 16 in. (41 cm.); W: 4.25 - 4.75 in. (11.1 - 11.8 cm.)
Western Han (2nd c. B.C., not later than 104 B.C.)
Tomb of Dou Wan, Princess of Zhongshan
Lingshan, Mancheng County, Hebei Province
Excavated 1968
Hebei Cultural Relics Research Institute

113. Oval Cups, bronze with silver handles
a. L: 8.25 in. (20.9 cm.); D: 7 x 4 in. (18 x 10.5 cm.);
   H: 2.25 in. (6 cm.)
b. L: 11.25 in. (29.2 cm.);
   D: 10.25 x 7 in. (25.9 x 18.2 cm.); H: 3.5 in. (9 cm.)
Western Han (2nd c. B.C., not later than 113 B.C.)
Tomb of Liu Sheng, Prince of Zhongshan
Lingshan, Mancheng County, Hebei Province
Excavated 1968
Hebei Cultural Relics Research Institute

112. Hu Vessel, gilt bronze with glass-paste
decor
H: 17.75 in. (45 cm.)
Western Han (2nd c. B.C., not later than 113 B.C.)
Tomb of Liu Sheng, Prince of Zhongshan
Lingshan, Mancheng County, Hebei Province
Excavated 1968
Hebei Cultural Relics Research Institute

No. 115 Bronze Horse
Eastern Han (2nd-3rd c.)
Tomb 2 at Fangling
Xushui, Baoding District, Hebei Province
Excavated 1981
Baoding District Cultural Relics Administration

115. Bronze Horse
H: 45.5 in. (116 cm.); L: 27.5 in. (70 cm.)
Eastern Han (2nd-3rd c.)
Tomb 2 at Fangling
Xushui, Baoding District, Hebei Province
Excavated 1981
Baoding District Cultural Relics Administration

The Han Chinese fell in love with fine horses. The passion was all the more intense because the Han empire itself had only limited access to good breeding stock. Horses were vital to Han military strength, especially to keep the Xiongnu armies at bay. Word came to the capital of amazing steeds in far Western Asia, horses that were fleet and indefatigable, horses that "sweated blood."[16] A mythology grew up around the finest horses, equating their spirit and strength to dragons. On a more mundane level, Han officials of any stature or pretension required an entourage of horsemen and chariots, a scene frequently depicted on Han tomb walls. The finest horses were styled "Heavenly Horses," or "bayards" *(jun),* and became a subject for imperial artists.[17]

It is not surprising, therefore, that figurines of horses in a variety of materials— pottery, wood, and bronze—are found among grave goods in Han tombs. The most renowned is perhaps the "Flying Horse of Gansu," one of a large ensemble of mounted warriors, carts, and chariots in bronze from a late Eastern Han tomb near Wuwei.[18] The idea of providing the deceased with fine horses was equally well satisfied by either mural decoration or three-dimensional figurines. The Gansu examples stand at the end of a long line of worthy predecessors in Chinese art, commencing with the magnificent life-size chariot steeds of the First Emperor (Nos. **107-108**) and continuing with the standing and kneeling stone horses arrayed around the tomb mound of the Han general Huo Qubing.

Bronze horses, such as the fine miniature pair of steppe ponies in the Nelson Gallery, Kansas City, are known from the late Zhou centuries.[19] The First Emperor's bronze chariot is drawn by a team of four, half-life-size horses, a stockier breed than his full-size terra cotta mounts. The finest of the Western Han bronze horses is the gilded stallion found in a burial pit near a tomb at the Maoling, the burial of Han Wudi. This pit may have been designed to house the accessories buried at the death of the great statesman Huo Guang (see above) or another member of his family.[20] The golden stallion recalls the story of the model cast by the Han general Ma Yuan (14 B.C.-A.D. 49), an image "designed to make clear the points to be observed in judging horses." The model bore the inscription: "Horses are the foundation of military might, the great resource of the state."[21]

Less costly examples of bronze horses are known from Western and Eastern Han tombs in both North and South China. A fine example is the striding, perhaps dancing, horse from a Western Han tomb at Gui Xian in the Guangxi Autonomous Region, assembled from nine pre-cast parts.[22] More fantastic steeds are the two-horned animals from a tomb in Hengyang, Hunan Province, dated to the latter Eastern Han.[23] Our horse from Baoding in Hebei Province is a cousin of these other specimens, one of a pair found in an Eastern Han tomb.[24] Like the example from Guangxi, this horse is animated, with flaring nostrils and an attentive pose. It too was assembled from several parts. From the neck up, however, the Hebei horses are markedly stylized. The planes of the face are flattened and meet at sharp angles, while the nostrils, ears, and mane are reduced to abbreviated forms.

No. 116 Stone Chimera
Eastern Han (2nd-3rd c.)
Sunqitun, Luoyang, Henan Province
Unearthed 1954
Luoyang Guanlin Stone Sculpture Museum

The late development of monumental stone sculpture in China is not easily understood and a technical explanation will not suffice. The working of stone, even of soft varieties like limestone, requires good cutting tools which the Chinese had in abundance, especially from the late Zhou period onward when iron became widely available. The feat of carving the rock chambers for the tombs of Liu Sheng and Dou Wan is adequate testimony that good chisels existed. From the earliest times, hard jade stones had been crafted with consummate skill. But the beginnings of large stone carvings can at present be traced only to the Han dynasties, a period of considerable foreign intercourse and the height of activity on the Silk Road to the Roman West. Possible knowledge of non-Chinese traditions, however, is not in itself sufficient to explain the inception of this art form. The question must remain unanswered for now, but should not be ignored.

This beast (No. **116**) and its mate *(Fig. 35, now in the Historical Museum, Beijing)* were unearthed in 1954 near Sunqitun, a village in the suburbs of Luoyang.[25] Both animals are felines, but from their bodies emerge wings at the shoulders, feathery tails, and horns growing from their heads. Clearly these are no ordinary creatures. This two-horned beast is in arrested motion, but its powerful rear haunches are tense with great strength and the potential energy to spring into action. Its stance is alert, with head raised and eyes wide open. The jaws pull apart in a bellowing roar. (The nose and part of the jaw have been restored.)

The sculptor was a master of his craft. A large limestone block has become a fully rounded, convincing beast of true-life proportions. Unlike the earliest large stone images, the granite carvings of about 116 B.C. at the Western Han tomb of General Huo Qubing, this creature's belly and legs are completely released from the stone.[?]The only concession to the practical problems of weight and strength is the stone plinth to which each leg is attached. An inscription *(Fig. 36)* on the back of the neck gives credit to the accomplished artisan responsible. He was a native of Gaoju Village in Houshi, a district near Luoyang.

What was the nature of such a fantastic beast? The term "chimera," now conventional in Western usage, while not accurate in relation to Classical precedents (a fire-breathing she-monster having a lion's head, a goat's body, and a serpent's tail), has been widely adopted since the writings of Victor Segalen and Osvald Siren. The most frequent choices in Chinese are *tianlu* for one-horned animals, and *bixie* for two-horned ones, according to a commentary to the *History of Han's* "Treatise on the Western Regions."[27] The meaning of the first name, "Heavenly Emolument," suggests a creature that brings good fortune, one of the many fantastic animals that, according to Chinese belief, appear when a worthy sovereign is on the throne. The sense of the second name, "Averter of Evil," offers a complementary role to the other: one that repels misfortune or noxious influences. Both played a role in Chinese architectural sites such as palaces and tombs, and it is very likely that this creature was once installed near the entrance to a tomb precinct.

Based on the stone images that survive near Nanjing, the capital of the six Southern Dynasties during the era of division from the 3rd to 6th centuries, some scholars believe that these winged and horned beasts were reserved as imperial prerogatives, while winged lions without horns were standard for the tombs of royal princes and nobles. If this distinction prevailed during the Eastern Han, it is possible that this chimera was a part of an imperial tomb at Luoyang, the Han capital.

116. Stone Chimera

H: 42.5 in. (108 cm.); L: 66 in. (168 cm.);
W: 17 in. (43 cm.)
Eastern Han (2nd-3rd c.)
Sunqitun, Luoyang, Henan Province
Excavated 1954
Luoyang Guanlin Stone Sculpture Museum

Fig. 36   Rubbing of inscription on stone chimera (No. **116**).

Stone Animals at Han Tombs. Unlike the well-documented Western Han tombs outside Xi'an, the Eastern Han tombs located near Luoyang are not yet clearly identified, and none has been properly surveyed.[28] Perhaps five Eastern Han imperial tombs have been isolated with some certainty among the many mounds and ruins in the high ground north of the city, an area also favored for burials by later sovereigns of the Cao Wei (ca. 220-265), Western Jin (ca. 265-316) and Northern Wei (ca. 494-535) dynasties. Unfortunately stone carvings of any kind are infrequent at these sites. This paucity of physical evidence for stone animals at the capital stands in contrast to a record in the *History of Later Han* (the Eastern Han) that Emperor Guangwu (r. 25-57) had stone beasts installed in front of his tomb.

A number of tomb sites dedicated to local worthies in areas outside the capital do have stone animals, and several of these are dated by inscriptions or other evidence to the late Eastern Han. Stone beasts are known from Sishui, Linzi, Qufu, and Jiaxiang in Shandong Province, from Lushan and Ya'an in Sichuan Province, and from Nanyang, Yichuan, and Yanshi in Henan Province. The earliest of these are dated 147 and 167, the latest to 209 and 215. In addition, on stylistic grounds, a number of undocumented stone images in Western museum collections can be attributed to much the same time.[29] There is little doubt that stone creatures became a feature at later Eastern Han tomb sites. The cost of such impressive fixtures can be judged from the inscription at the Wu family cemetery in Jiaxiang County, Shandong Province. The artisan in charge of carving the lions, one Sun Zong, was paid no less than 40,000 pieces of Han cash, a princely sum.[30]

Because of their winged appearance, early Western scholars imagined foreign precedents prompted these stones. Chinese scholars linked the appearance of such strange animals to exotic animals imported as tribute from the Western Regions during the Han. However, recent discoveries challenge such notions. The royal Zhongshan tombs at Pingshan County, Hebei Province, of the late 3rd century B.C. contained several related fantastic animals. One pair of winged beasts, more dragon-like than feline, is exhibited here (No. **63**). These creatures are a plausible and proximate precedent for the later, Han and post-Han tradition of stone chimeras.

Fig. 35   Stone chimera, Sunqitun, Luoyang, Henan Province.

123. Bullock, painted earthenware
H: 13.75 in. (35 cm.)
Northern Qi (ca. 570)
Tomb of Lou Rui, Prince of Dong'an Commandery
Wangguo Village, Taiyuan, Shanxi Province
Excavated 1981
Shanxi Archaeology Institute

Nos. 117-125 Tomb Figurines and Vessels
Northern Qi (ca. 570)
Tomb of Lou Rui, Prince of Dong'an Commandery
Wangguo Village, Taiyuan, Shanxi Province
Excavated 1981
Shanxi Archaeology Institute

China entered an aristocratic age after the dissolution of the Han empire. The aristocrats of this period of disunion (ca. 220-581) were both families of Chinese ancestry and elites of various non-Chinese peoples settled in the north. The latter were descended from the many peoples who originally occupied steppe territories north and west of the settled farming communities of North China. During the Northern Dynasties, these peoples often adopted Chinese surnames, learned the Chinese language, wore Chinese costume rather than their own, and followed Chinese etiquette.

The imperial families of many of the Northern Dynasties were closely related by marriage alliances which continued into the Sui (581-618) and Tang (618-906). A relatively small number of aristocratic families thus dominated the politics and court life of much of China from the 6th century through the Tang. Their tastes, fashions, and habits became powerful influences on the growth of Chinese culture during these centuries. The strong patronage of Buddhism during this period owes much to the devotion of these non-Chinese aristocrats. Equally important were the varieties of interaction with peoples and cultures west of China that were linked to the capitals by trade routes, religious pilgrimages, and military campaigns. The vogue for foreign styles in dress, coiffures, music, dance, and the decorative arts that so epitomized the Tang was the final expression of a fascination with exotica that began in the 6th century.

During the Northern Qi Dynasty (550-577), the imperial family maintained two capitals: one near Anyang, Henan Province (then called Ye), and the other at modern Taiyuan, Shanxi Province (known as Jinyang). Palace establishments and temples were constructed on a magnificent scale in both areas (the Xiangtang Shan and Tianlong Shan cave chapels are well known), and each capital had its aristocratic estates and their cemeteries. The founder of Northern Qi, Gao Huan, took as his empress a woman of the Xianbi (a Turkish tribe) Lou family, natives by this time of the capital at Taiyuan. Lou Rui, whose tomb yielded the figurines and vessels exhibited here, was a nephew of Empress Lou and, as a distaff relative, was repeatedly honored with impressive-sounding noble ranks and official sinecures. At his death in 570, Lou Rui enjoyed the status of Prince of Dong'an Commandery and was buried in great style south of the capital. When the tomb was excavated in 1979-1981, it enriched our knowledge of the Northern aristocrats and specifically of the habits of the imperial court.[31]

Furnishings for a "Proper First-Rank Noble." Burials were constructed and furnished in accordance with restrictive sumptuary regulations that dictated the kind of tomb and the quality and quantity of grave goods. The aristocracy enjoyed both noble rank and official positions on a scale with as many as nine grades. Lou Rui was honored as an official of the "Proper First Rank," but he also benefited from his family ties to the reigning empress. His tomb was a single large brick chamber almost 20 feet (6 m.) square with a four-part vaulted ceiling. Entry was gained by a sloping ramp 69 feet (21 m.) long that descended from ground level to a brick corridor about 26 feet (8 m.) long before the stone doors of the chamber. All the wall surfaces, both within the chamber and along the ramp and corridor, were decorated with extremely well-painted murals. A stone epitaph recorded the biography and official titles of the deceased. About 600 tomb figurines comprised the principal furnishings.

Compared to other excavated Northern Qi tombs, it is obvious that Lou Rui was buried in high style. Perhaps the only tomb that surpasses Lou's is that of Gao Run in Ci Xian County, Hebei Province, the area of the other Northern Qi capital.[32] Gao, as his surname suggests, was the fourteenth son of the Emperor Gao Huan (husband of the Empress Lou, Rui's aunt). As a member of the imperial line, albeit not a likely successor to the throne, Gao Huan was buried with slightly more attention and generosity than Lou Rui. Gao's tomb was larger, both in the size of its chamber and in the length of its ramp, and his tomb furnishings may have been somewhat more impressive (the tomb was robbed prior to excavation).

Fig. 37 Diagram of wall paintings in tomb of Lou Rui, Wangguo Village, Taiyuan, Shanxi Province.

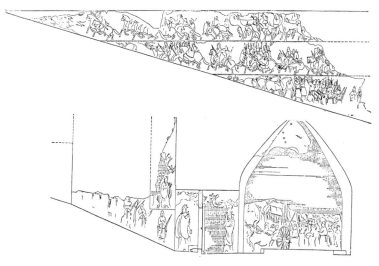

Other Northern Qi tombs of First-Rank nobles and officials, however, are less impressive than the two burials described above. Without ties to the imperial house, even a very high-ranking person was accorded less honor.[33] Such tombs lacked the wall paintings and fine furnishings of Lou Rui's burial. However, all these tombs contained figurines made in the workshops at their capitals. Several of the Lou Rui figurines have close parallels in the tombs of Gao Run and Han Yi, for example. The Lou Rui examples are remarkable for their well-preserved, original colors.

Northern Qi Stoneware. The Lou Rui tomb is also notable for its selection of glazed stoneware (Nos. **124-125**), which is much larger and of higher quality than most previously known. Both the ewer and vase have hard gray bodies covered with a yellow glaze. In each case, their shapes are augmented by appliqued ornaments, especially lotus and honeysuckle motifs combined with monster masks. These ornamental motifs are pervasive in the arts of the Northern Qi period and reflect the artistic interaction of Buddhist and non-Buddhist media.[34] Similar designs can be found amid the cave chapels at Xiangtang Shan and on metalwork. The lead glaze used for these vessels was sometimes colored by adding a mineral such as iron or copper. Further experimentation of this kind would yield the three-color wares of the Tang about a century later. It appears that these stonewares were made at both of the Northern Qi capitals, but the kiln sites have yet to be located.

Wall Paintings. The murals that covered every wall surface within the tomb comprise the largest find of late 6th-century painting *(Fig. 37)*.[35] The ramp walls were divided into three superimposed registers, the west illustrating a procession leaving and the east a similar entourage returning. Guardians and celestial imagery covered the corridor and lightwell above, while within the chamber were the deceased's portrait, his household, various immortals, and another complement of cosmological motifs, including the earliest pictorial representation of the 12 animals of the native Chinese zodiac. Remarking on the high quality of these paintings, Professor Su Bai of Beijing University has suggested that a court or palace artist may have been employed for the decoration of Lou Rui's tomb. In view of Lou's family ties to the court, this suggestion must be taken seriously.

121. Male Servant, painted earthenware
H: 7.5 in. (19 cm.)
Northern Qi (ca. 570)
Tomb of Lou Rui, Prince of Dong'an Commandery
Wangguo Village, Taiyuan, Shanxi Province
Excavated 1981
Shanxi Archaeology Institute

120. Female Servants, painted earthenware
Left, Kneeling, H: 4.75 in. (12 cm.)
Right, Standing, H: 7.75 in. (19.5 cm.)
Northern Qi (ca. 570)
Tomb of Lou Rui, Prince of Dong'an Commandery
Wangguo Village, Taiyuan, Shanxi Province
Excavated 1981
Shanxi Archaeology Institute

119. Male Riders, painted earthenware
Right, Rider with helmet, H: 13 in. (33.1 cm.)
Left, Rider with hat, H: 12.5 in. (32.2 cm.)
Northern Qi (ca. 570)
Tomb of Lou Rui, Prince of Dong'an Commandery
Wangguo Village, Taiyuan, Shanxi Province
Excavated 1981
Shanxi Archaeology Institute

117. Guardian Animal, painted earthenware
H: 19.75 in. (50.2 cm.)
Northern Qi (ca. 570)
Tomb of Lou Rui, Prince of Dong'an Commandery
Wangguo Village, Taiyuan, Shanxi Province
Excavated 1981
Shanxi Archaeology Institute

122. Kneeling Camel, painted earthenware
H: 9.75 in. (24.7 cm.)
Northern Qi (ca. 570)
Tomb of Lou Rui, Prince of Dong'an Commandery
Wangguo Village, Taiyuan, Shanxi Province
Excavated 1981
Shanxi Archaeology Institute

124. Vase, glazed stoneware
H: 15.75 in. (39.8 cm.); D: 11 in. (28 cm.)
Northern Qi (ca. 570)
Tomb of Lou Rui, Prince of Dong'an Commandery
Wangguo Village, Taiyuan, Shanxi Province
Excavated 1981
Shanxi Archaeology Institute

125. Chicken-headed Ewer, glazed stoneware
H: 19 in. (48.2 cm.); D: 12.75 in. (32.5 cm.)
Northern Qi (ca. 570)
Tomb of Lou Rui, Prince of Dong'an Commandery
Wangguo Village, Taiyuan, Shanxi Province
Excavated 1981
Shanxi Archaeology Institute

129. Groom, glazed earthenware
H: 24.5 in. (62 cm.)
Tang (ca. 709)
Tomb of An Pu, Dingyuan General
Longmen, Luoyang, Henan Province
Excavated 1981
Luoyang Cultural Relics Work Team

128. Camel, glazed earthenware
H: 32 in. (81.5 cm.); L: 27.5 in. (70 cm.)
Tang (ca. 709)
Tomb of An Pu, Dingyuan General
Longmen, Luoyang, Henan Province
Excavated 1981
Luoyang Cultural Relics Work Team

Nos. 126-137 Three-color Tomb Figurines
Tang (ca. 709)
Tomb of An Pu, the Dingyuan General
Longmen, Luoyang, Henan Province
Excavated 1981
Luoyang Cultural Relics Work Team

Few artifacts from ancient China are as well-known as three-color figurines of the Tang. They are superb examples of both the ceramic and sculptural arts that matured in the late 7th century, virtually vanishing by the latter half of the 8th century. Their rapid development and high achievements are evidence of a society that placed great demands on the artisans who crafted these works and rewarded them for their creativity. The florescence of three-color figurines corresponds to a great age in the artistic culture of the Tang Dynasty, while their disappearance coincided with the havoc of mid-8th century rebellions and invasions.

Three-color figurines are a low-fired pottery covered with a lead glaze to which various minerals have been added to create colorful effects. The bodies were modeled from a high-quality white *kaolin* clay using a variety of molds, and then covered with a white slip before their initial firing. Those areas needing color were covered with glazes containing iron (for brown and yellow), copper (for green), cobalt (for blue), and other appropriate minerals. After another firing at 800 to 900 degrees centigrade, the figurines emerged from the kiln with lustrous, richly colored surfaces. The critical lead flux, which allows the silica of the glaze recipe to melt and combine with the other ingredients, itself contributed to the brilliant results.[36] Some figurines then were painted with mineral pigments on unglazed surfaces such as faces. The term "three-color" is misleading as there are figurines with monochrome, two-color, and polychrome decoration all in this category. The potter's palette was not limited to three hues.

The An Pu Tomb
During the Tang, Luoyang served as the Eastern Capital and, in certain periods such as the reign of Empress Wu (684-704), the imperial court actually spent more time here than in the primary Western Capital of Chang'an (modern Xi'an). A large court establishment of resident noble families and officials had to be maintained at Luoyang. Since 1949, construction in and around Luoyang has revealed many Tang sites, and hundreds of Tang graves have been cleared by archaeologists of the Luoyang Cultural Relics Work Team. The An Pu tomb was excavated by this team in spring 1981 prior to a construction project.[37] The location is unusual, on the east bank of the Yi River at Longmen, most famous for its cave chapels, and near the grave of one of the greatest Tang poets, Bo Juyi (known in English translations as Po Chu-yi). The An Pu tomb had never been disturbed by robbers, and its figurines represent, by all accounts,

one of the finest and most complete set of three-color tomb furnishings ever excavated in Luoyang.

The single tomb chamber was filled by two coffins placed on stone and earth beds along the sides *(Fig. 38)*. Within the short entry corridor there were three pairs of figurines: two civil officials (No. **132**), two "Heavenly King" guardians (No. **131**), and two guardian beasts (No. **130**). Such a complement became standard in the latter 7th century, and is attested in undisturbed tombs in Xi'an as well.[38] Between the two coffin beds stood four horses and two camels, each with their grooms (Nos. **126-129**). On the east coffin bed, presumably that of An Pu himself, were placed the riders (No. **134-135**), other male servants, and an attendant wearing a tall cap (No. **133**). Opposite, on the coffin couch of Lady He, were female servant figurines (Nos. **136-137**). The selection on exhibit is a small representation of the 124 pieces of pottery placed in the chamber.

It is likely that three-color ware and figurines were an innovation of a workshop serving the imperial court. The earliest datable tomb with true three-color furnishings is in the burial of Li Feng, Prince of Guo, fifteenth son of the Tang founder Gaozu, who was interred in an accompanying burial at his father's necropolis, the Xianling, in 675[39] The technique became an important feature among the burial objects of imperial princes, clansmen, and other Tang aristocrats. The volume of surviving three-color vessels and figurines attests to a flourishing industry both at Chang'an and Luoyang. Hundreds of three-color figurines were looted from tombs before 1949, and controlled excavations since then have yielded thousands more. Only a limited percentage of the figurines, however, can truly be identified as suitable for an imperial burial.

The An Pu figurines are among the largest, best-sculpted, and best-painted examples excavated at Luoyang. Some are sufficiently tall (about 39 inches, 100 cm.) (Nos. **130-132**) to compare favorably with examples taken from the imperial tombs outside of Xi'an. The tomb guardian beast and Heavenly King guardian from the An Pu tomb are about the same size as comparable pieces from the tomb of Prince Zhanghuai, one of three imperial offspring buried with great honors after the demise of Empress Wu in 706.[40] Comparable pieces from Luoyang excavations can also be found, including furnishings from several tombs in the Guanlin cemeteries south of Luoyang on the way to Longmen.[41] Unfortunately, only the An Pu ensemble can be dated, and only in An Pu's case is the identity of the deceased known.

The production of three-color ware must have been centered at both of the Tang capitals, but only traces of this output have been discovered at kiln sites. The best explored kiln near Luoyang is in Gong Xian County, 25 miles (40 km.) east of the city. Evidence for three-color production is also noted at other neighboring sites, and all these wares could have been transported to the capital by boat. There is still no good evidence for the molds used in the manufacture of figurines.[42]

The Retinue

The stylish and upscale assortment of figurines found in the An Pu tomb is appropriate for a man and woman who enjoyed some rank in Tang capital society. The civil official (No. **132**) represents the household bureaucracy of the deceased, remaining in charge in the afterlife as he was during life and the funeral. The armored guardian is part of the ensemble of "four spirits" named in Tang ritual texts as responsible for the security of the tomb. By the middle of the 7th century, "Heavenly Kings" *(tian wang)* had begun to replace armored generals in such sets, and by the time of Empress Wu these guardians were often of two types: one trampling an earth spirit, the other surmounting a recumbent animal, such as an ox (No. **131**). Although the representation of these guardians clearly corresponds to warrior deities in Buddhism, their Chinese names reflect their mortuary roles: "Protector of the Burial Vault" and "Protector of the Burial Ground."[43] Likewise, the guardian beast (No. **130**) is one of a pair known as "Ancestral Intelligence" and "Earth Axis," also charged with protecting the tomb.

The wealth of the deceased is epitomized by his horses and camels, with their Central Asian grooms (Nos. **126-129**). Both the lad attending the horse and the old man with the camel have facial features (broad noses, chin whiskers) that are distinctly non-Chinese. The horse is caparisoned with fittings on both front and rear flanks with a carpet-like blanket over the saddle. The camel, braying as it arches its neck, carries a saddlebag with a gross monster mask on each pouch. The status of the family is also indicated by the presence of household servants. One servant poses an enigma: is it a woman dressed as a man wearing the tall hat (No. **133**), or is it a man? In any case, the tall hat itself is another fashionable bit of exotica.

An Pu

The tomb contained a lengthy epitaph carved on a large slab of limestone *(Fig. 39).*[44] Its text informs us of the family and life of An Pu and his wife. An Pu was descended from the nobility of the Kingdom of Anxi (identified with the Arsacid Persians); his grandfather and father had been in the service of the Turks who were defeated by the army of the Tang founder in 630. Some of the Turks' followers surrendered to the Tang and some of those, including An Pu's family, took up residence in Chang'an. There they enjoyed the privileges of middle-rank capital officials. An Pu himself may well have participated in a great victory of 646, and this might have been the rationale for his honorific rank, Dingyuan ("Surpressing the Distant") General. An died in Chang'an in 664 at age 63. His wife, who was also of Central Asian ancestry, died many years later in 704, also in Chang'an. Their son, An Jinzang, whose biography is included in the official histories, was a man of great filial piety. He had his mother interred at the Eastern Capital near the great Jingshan temple at Longmen. Five years later in 709, by now an official of the music office of the bureau of court ceremonial, An Jinzang arranged the joint reburial of both his father and mother.

One can infer imperial connections between An Jinzang and the Tang court that facilitated this filial gesture. The Tang histories record an incident in which, during the nightmare reign of Empress Wu, young An was accused of plotting against the heir-apparent. To prove his innocence, An stabbed himself with a knife, but his life was saved when the Empress dispatched the court physician. Some 25 years later, while serving in the court bureau of ceremonial, An somehow procured high quality furnishings for his parents' joint burial. These included not only the figurines discussed above, but also a deluxe suite of engraved limestone doors and the epitaph summarized above. Such outfittings are uncommon in Luoyang and demonstrate connections in high places.

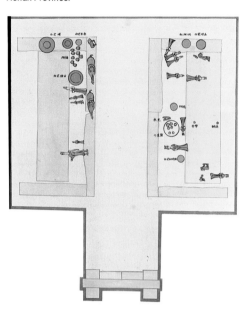

Fig. 38 Plan of An Pu's tomb chamber, Longmen, Luoyang, Henan Province.

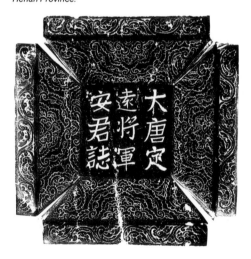

Fig. 39 Rubbing of epitaph of An Pu, Longmen, Luoyang, Henan Province.

131. **"Heavenly King,"** glazed earthenware
H: 43.25 in. (110 cm.)
Tang (ca. 709)
Tomb of An Pu, Dingyuan General
Longmen, Luoyang, Henan Province
Excavated 1981
Luoyang Cultural Relics Work Team

127. Groom, glazed earthenware
H: 24.5 in. (62 cm.)
Tang (ca. 709)
Tomb of An Pu, Dingyuan General
Longmen, Luoyang, Henan Province
Excavated 1981
Luoyang Cultural Relics Work Team

126. Horse, glazed earthenware
H: 28.75 in. (73 cm.); L: 33.5 in. (85 cm.)
Tang (ca. 709)
Tomb of An Pu, Dingyuan General
Longmen, Luoyang, Henan Province
Excavated 1981
Luoyang Cultural Relics Work Team

The Tomb

135. Woman Rider, glazed earthenware
H: 16.75 in. (42.5 cm.)
Tang (ca. 709)
Tomb of An Pu, Dingyuan General
Longmen, Luoyang, Henan Province
Excavated 1981
Luoyang Cultural Relics Work Team

134. Woman Rider, glazed earthenware
H: 16.25 in. (41.5 cm.)
Tang (ca. 709)
Tomb of An Pu, Dingyuan General
Longmen, Luoyang, Henan Province
Excavated 1981
Luoyang Cultural Relics Work Team

132. Civil Official, glazed earthenware
H: 43.5 in. (110.5 cm.)
Tang (ca. 709)
Tomb of An Pu, Dingyuan General
Longmen, Luoyang, Henan Province
Excavated 1981
Luoyang Cultural Relics Work Team

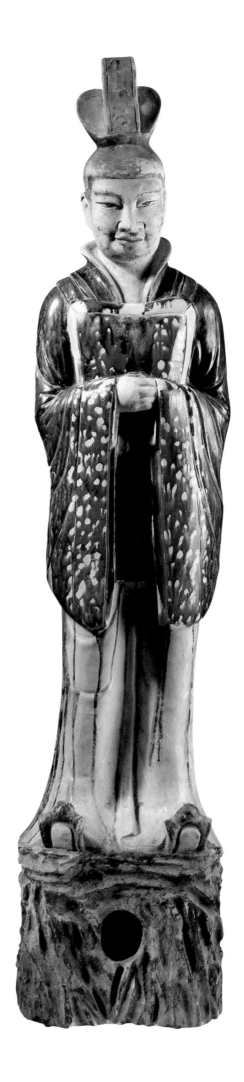

133. Male Attendant with Tall Cap, glazed earthenware
H: 14.75 in. (37.5 cm.)
Tang (ca. 709)
Tomb of An Pu, Dingyuan General
Longmen, Luoyang, Henan Province
Excavated 1981
Luoyang Cultural Relics Work Team

136. Female Attendant, glazed earthenware
H: 15.25 in. (39 cm.)
Tang (ca. 709)
Tomb of An Pu, Dingyuan General
Longmen, Luoyang, Henan Province
Excavated 1981
Luoyang Cultural Relics Work Team

137. Female Attendant, glazed earthenware
H: 11 in. (28 cm.)
Tang (ca. 709)
Tomb of An Pu, Dingyuan General
Longmen, Luoyang, Henan Province
Excavated 1981
Luoyang Cultural Relics Work Team

1. Translation by Arthur Waley (modified), *A Hundred and Seventy Chinese Poems,* New York, 1919, pp. 97-98.

2. Liu Qingzhu and Li Yufang, "Investigations and Research on the Western Han Imperial Tombs," (in Chinese), *Wenwu ziliao congkan* [Data on Cultural Relics], No. 6, 1982, pp. 1-15.

3. Robert L. Thorp, "Burial Practices of Bronze Age China," in *The Great Bronze Age of China,* ed. W. Fong, New York, 1980, pp. 51-64.

4. Translation by Burton Watson, *Hsün Tzu: Basic Writings,* New York, 1963, pp. 97-105.

5. Martin J. Powers, "Pictorial Art and Its Public in Early Imperial China," *Art History* 7.2 (June 1984):135-163.

6. Translation by Burton Watson (modified), *Courtier and Commoner in Ancient China,"* New York, 1974, p. 139.

7. "First Brief Report of Trial Excavations at the Qin Trench with Figurines at Lintong County" (in Chinese), *Wenwu* 1975.11:1-18; "Brief Report of Probings and Trial Excavations at Trench No. 2 with Figurines of Warriors and Horses on the East Flank of the Tomb of the Qin First Emperor" (in Chinese), *Wenwu* 1978.5:1-16; "Brief Report of Clearing Pit No. 3 with Figurines of Warriors and Horses on the East Flank of the Tomb of the Qin First Emperor" (in Chinese), *Wenwu* 1979.12:1-12. The finds have been well-published in *Qin shihuang ling bingma yong* [Warrior and Horse Figurines from the Tomb of the Qin First Emperor], Beijing, 1983. This volume contains a useful English summary of the finds.

8. Among the numerous publications of the warriors are *The Great Bronze Age of China,* New York, 1980, Nos. 98-105, and *The Quest for Eternity,* Los Angeles, 1987, Nos. 6-9.

9. Robert L. Thorp, "An Archaeological Reconstruction of the Lishan Necropolis," in *The Great Bronze Age of China: A Symposium,* Los Angeles, 1983, pp. 72-83, and *Idem.,* "The Qin and Han Imperial Tombs and the Development of Mortuary Architecture," in *The Quest for Eternity,* pp. 17-37.

10. The best account is "The Manufacturing Techniques of the Ceramic Warriors and Ceramic Horses Unearthed from the Trenches with Warriors and Horses of the Qin First Emperor" (in Chinese), *Kaogu yu wenwu* [Archaeology and Cultural Relics] 1980.3:108-24.

11. *Mancheng Han mu fajue baogao* [Excavation Report of the Han Tombs at Mancheng], 2 Vols., Beijing, 1980.

12. Translation by Burton Watson (modified), *Records of the Grand Historian of China,* Vol. 1, New York, 1961, p. 456.

13. See Thorp, "The Qin and Han Imperial Tombs," pp. 26-28

14. *Science and Civilization in China,* Cambridge (England), 1974, Vol. 5, Part 2, p. 298.

15. Umehara Sueji, *Rakuyo Kinson kobo shuei* [Collected Treasures from the Ancient Tombs at Jincun, Luoyang], Kyoto, 1937, p. 22, Pl. 18.

16. Herrlee G. Creel, "The Role of the Horse in Chinese History," in *What Is Taoism and Other Studies in Chinese Cultural History,* Chicago, 1970, pp. 160-186.

17. Edward H. Schafer, *The Golden Peaches of Samarkand: A Study of T'ang Exotics,* Berkeley, 1963, pp. 58-70.

18. "The Han Tomb at Leitai, Wuwei" (in Chinese), *Kaogu Xuebao* 1974.2: 87-110. Best known through *The Chinese Exhibition,* Washington, D.C., 1974, No. 222.

19. *Handbook of the Collections,* Kansas City, 1973, p. 16 (Acc. Nos. 33-185/7).

20. Mou Anzhi, "Excavation of Accompanying Pit 1 at Anonymous Burial Mound 1 at the Maoling, Shaanxi" (in Chinese), *Wenwu* 1982.9:1-17. Recently published in *Koga bunmei ten* [The Civilization of the Yellow River], Tokyo, 1986, No. 72.

21. Creel, "The Role of the Horse," p. 173.

22. "Brief Report of Clearing Western Han Tomb No. 31 at Fengliuling, Gui Xian, Guangxi" (in Chinese), *Kaogu* 1984.1:59-62, 68.

23. "Brief Excavation Report of the Eastern Han Tomb at Daoziping, Hengyang County, Hunan" (in Chinese), *Wenwu* 1981.12:35-37. Illustrated in *Hunan sheng bowuguan* [The Hunan Provincial Museum], Zhongguo bowuguan [Chinese Museums], Beijing, 1983, No. 190.

24. "Han Tomb No. 2 at Fanglingcun, Xushui County, Hebei Province" (in Chinese), *Wenwu* 1984.4:45-46. Illustrated in *Zhongguo meishu chuanji* [Compendium of Chinese Art], Diaosuo bian [Sculpture], Vol. 2, *Qin Han diaosuo* [Qin and Han Sculpture], Beijing, 1985, No. 144.

25. "Introduction to the Luoyang Ancient Art Museum" (in Chinese), *Zhongyuan wenwu* 1982.3:55-60. Published in *Zhongguo meishu chuanji, Diaosuo bian,* Vol. 2, *Qin Han diaosuo,* No. 93. The mate is illustrated in *Lishi bowuguan* [The Museum of Chinese History], Zhongguo bowuguan [Chinese Museums], Beijing, 1983, No. 119.

26. Shaanxi Museum, *Huo Qubing mu shike* [Stone Sculptures at the Huo Qubing Tomb], Xi'an, 1984, and Shi Yan, *Zhongguo diaosuo shi tulu* [Pictorial Treasury of the History of Chinese Sculpture], Shanghai, 1983, Vol. 1, Nos. 220-231.

27. Yao Qian, *Liuchao yishu* [Arts of the Six Dynasties], Beijing, 1981, p. 3.

28. Chen Chang'an, "Preliminary Investigation of the Eastern Han Tombs at Mangshan, Luoyang" (in Chinese), *Zhongyuan wenwu* 1982.3:31-36.

29. Barry Till, "Some Observations on Stone Winged Chimeras at Ancient Chinese Tomb Sites," *Artibus Asiae* 42 (1980):261-81. Till establishes two "categories" of such beasts. Examples in the Nelson Gallery in Kansas City, Asian Art Museum in San Francisco, and Stockholm Museum of Far Eastern Antiquities are most closely related to the Luoyang chimera.

30. Yang Shuda, "The Funeral and Burial System of the Han Period" (in Chinese), *Qinghua Xuebao* [The Qinghua Journal], 8(1932):73 citing *Jinshi lu,* 14. The two artisans in charge of the stone gate towers *(que)* were rewarded with a payment of 150,000 cash.

31. "Brief Excavation Report of the Northern Qi Tomb of Lou Rui at Taiyuan" (in Chinese), *Wenwu* 1983.10:1-23. Published in Han Zhongmin and Hubert Delahaye, *A Journey Through Ancient China,* New York, 1985, pp. 196-203.

32. "The Tomb of Gao Run of the Northern Qi at Ci Xian, Hebei" (in Chinese), *Kaogu* 1979.3:235-243, 234. A wall painting from this tomb is illustrated in *Koga bunmei ten,* No. 103.

33. See, for example, the tombs of Kudi Huiluo (d. 562) and Han Yi (d. 567): "The Northern Qi Tomb of Kudi Huiluo" (in Chinese), *Kaogu Xuebao* 1979.3:377-401, and "The Northern Qi Tomb of Han Yi at Baigui, Qi County, Shanxi" (in Chinese), *Wenwu* 1975.9:64-73. Some figurines from the latter are included in *Koga bunmei ten,* Nos. 104-105.

34. See Hin-cheung Lovell, "Some Northern Chinese Ceramic Wares of the Sixth and Seventh Centuries," *Oriental Art* 21 (1975), pp. 328-343.

35. "Notes from a Discussion of the Luo Rui Tomb at Taiyuan" (in Chinese), *Wenwu* 1983.10:24-39. See also Wang Tianxiu *et al.,* "A Brief Introduction to the Murals in the Tomb of Lou Rui," *Chinese Arts* 1 (1986):5-29.

36. For general discussions of three-color wares, see Feng Xianming, *Zhongguo taoci shi* [History of Chinese Pottery and Porcelains], Beijing, 1982, pp. 214-219, and Li Zhiyan, "A General Account of Ancient Chinese Pottery and Porcelains" (in Chinese) in *Zhongguo Taoci* [Chinese Pottery and Porcelains], Beijing, 1985, pp. 101-105. A good English-language treatment is Suzanne G. Valenstein, *A Handbook of Chinese Ceramics,* New York, 1975.

37. "The Tang Tomb of An Pu and His Spouse at Longmen, Luoyang" (in Chinese), *Zhongyuan wenwu* 1982.3:21-26, 14.

38. *Tang Chang'an chengjiao Sui Tang mu* [Sui and Tang Tombs in the Suburbs of Tang Chang'an], Beijing, 1980, Pls. 29-30 (tomb of Dugu Sizhen, died 697).

39. "Brief Report of the Excavation of the Tomb of Li Feng of the Tang" (in Chinese), *Kaogu* 1977.5:313-326.

40. "Brief Report of the Excavation of the Tomb of the Heir-Apparent Zhanghuai of the Tang" (in Chinese), *Wenwu* 1972.7:13-25. Well-illustrated in *The Quest for Eternity,* Nos. 63-64.

41. *Luoyang Tang sancai* [Tang Three-color Pottery from Luoyang], Beijing, 1980.

42. Feng Xianming, "Summary of an Investigation of the Ancient Kiln Sites in Gong Xian, Henan" (in Chinese), *Wenwu* 1959.3:56-58; Liu Jianzhou, "Investigation of the Tang Three-color Kiln Site at Gong Xian" (in Chinese), *Zhongyuan wenwu* 1981.3:16-22.

43. Tentative translations by Virginia Bower, in Robert L. Thorp and Virginia L. Bower, *Spirit and Ritual: The Morse Collection of Ancient Chinese Art,* New York, 1982, pp. 51-52.

44. Zhao Zhenhua and Zhu Liang, "Preliminary Investigation of the Epitaph of An Pu" (in Chinese), *Zhongyuan wenwu* 1982.3:37-40.

Afterword

In the best of all possible worlds, the audience for this exhibition would be taken to China to visit the sites where the objects were first made and used. Even though most former palaces lie hidden underground, there is still much to see in any tour that includes the capitals of the major dynasties. Xi'an, Luoyang, Nanjing, Kaifeng, Hangzhou, and Beijing all have much to offer the visitor in search of China's imperial legacy in the arts. A visit brings home what no exhibition can hope to accomplish: a sense of the physical scale of imperial sites and the volume of artistic production.

In "Son of Heaven," a single object, plucked from its original setting amid other objects, must often stand both for a class of things and for its original environment. Several groups of objects selected for their common significance must invoke a far more complex historical situation involving human actors, sights, sounds and smells. The reality of a sacrifice at an ancestral shrine or the Temple of Heaven can only be vaguely grasped from a display of ritual vessels (Nos. **1-5**) and bells (No. **9**). The pomp of a morning court is merely hinted at by the costumes (Nos. **12-14**) and throne (No. **26**) of the Son of Heaven.

In an ideal exhibition, one would assemble objects from all over China and the world, without regard for mere practical realities. Every trip to China brings fresh discoveries of previously unknown or little-noticed objects. Every curatorial choice summons up images of related pieces from other provinces, periods or collections outside of China. While many of the objects in this exhibition are unique, they all belong to categories that are represented by other works, some of equal quality or historical significance, in collections elsewhere. Both the curator and the visitor to the exhibition would profit from the juxtaposition of all relevant objects on an occasion like "Son of Heaven." This would require an even more ambitious exhibition and the cooperation of many governments and dozens of museums and collectors. It may, however, be possible in the future to examine specific aspects of the imperial arts of China with international loan exhibitions that concentrate on a single period, medium or theme.

What are the self-imposed limitations and rewards of an exhibition like "Son of Heaven?"

The first limitation of this exhibition was chronological. While we have attempted to present aspects of the arts from the entire Imperial period (ca. 221 B.C.—A.D. 1911), it has proven useful to focus on five "great ages" in the life of that institution. These great ages —Qin and Han, Tang, Song, Ming, and Qing —are not evenly represented in our selection of objects, largely because the kinds of art that flourished varied from one period to the next. There is less of interest in the thematic categories of Altar and Tomb from the later ages, whereas there is little extant in such areas as court costume, regalia and furnishings from the earlier periods. These five great ages, in turn, were selected both because they were periods when the imperial institution was vigorous, and because several kinds of art flowered during each of them. Nonetheless, no time period is given all the attention it deserves, and a number of "Great Age" exhibitions could be mounted in the future without repeating objects from this exhibition.

A second limitation was the decision not to follow a timeline. Rather than present all of the objects in a true historical sequence, we have chosen to divide them among five thematic environments. Thus an 8th-century Tang Buddhist sculpture rubs shoulders with the set of five 15th-century Ming paintings, and Bronze Age jades and miniature sculptures are displayed in the same gallery as much later silver, porcelains and paintings. This choice gave us the ability to tell a story about each theme and each group of objects. We can learn a good deal about the artistic forms of imperial patronage of the Three Teachings by assembling all of the relevant exhibits in one place (Nos. **42-57**). The continuity in purposes and the development of specific artistic traditions emerge more clearly by gathering together all of the objects that relate to the theme of the Tomb as the eternal resting place for the Son of Heaven (Nos. **103-137**). In each case, sorting objects by their time period would obscure their connections and actually work against a sense of the history of the arts. One role of this catalogue has been to point out chronological developments, comparing and contrasting exhibits from all portions of "Son of Heaven."

The greatest virtue of the thematic approach of "Son of Heaven" is that it allows a variety of media to be exhibited together. This is not merely an exhibition for enthusiasts of Chinese painting or Chinese archaeology. The so-called decorative arts take an important place in this kind of exhibition because they were a major aspect of the use of the arts by the emperors and their courts. Critical distinctions between "fine" and "decorative arts" are usually invidious, and nowhere is this more true than in the study of Imperial China. Almost all categories of art in traditional China were produced by anonymous artisans or craftsmen, most plying their considerable skills in a workshop setting. With the notable exceptions of calligraphy and painting (Nos. **47-50** and Nos. **90-102**), artistic personalities were virtually unknown in the arts of Imperial China. It matters little that most of the objects in the exhibition cannot be related by name to their actual makers. The objects and their historical and cultural circumstances still speak volumes about the arts of China and their role in that society.

In short, "Son of Heaven" has allowed us to take a long look at the history of the arts in China. This is not to say that all aspects of Chinese art can be equally well addressed in this way. There are several other exhibitions implicit in "Son of Heaven." Architecture, which is not easily presented in an exhibition gallery, was an important aspect of imperial patronage and life style. Religious art, while presented as one thematic group here, has more to it than our limited selection would indicate. The history of each medium offers the potential for further exhibitions, especially the early history of painting and calligraphy. Finally, the history of collecting, also suggested by several groups of objects, could easily sustain several exhibitions in the future.

We hope that "Son of Heaven" will inspire others to examine the history of Chinese art from this or similar perspectives, so that some years hence an even better exhibition can be mounted.

Robert L. Thorp

Suggested Reading

Ancient Chinese Architecture. Beijing, 1982.

Chang, Kwang-chih. *The Archaeology of Ancient China.* 4th ed. New Haven, 1987.

Ch'en, Kenneth J. *Buddhism in China: A Historical Survey.* Princeton, 1964.

The Chinese Exhibition. The National Gallery of Art. Washington, D.C., 1974.

Chou, Ju-hsi, and Claudia Brown. *The Elegant Brush: Chinese Painting under the Qianlong Emperor, 1735-1795.* Phoenix, 1985.

Creel, H. G. *Confucius and the Chinese Way.* New York, 1960.

———. *What is Taoism and Other Studies in Chinese Cultural History.* Chicago, 1970.

deBary, W. Theodore, ed. *Sources of Chinese Tradition.* 2 vols. New York, 1960.

Fong, Wen, ed. *The Great Bronze Age of China.* New York, 1980.

Fontein, Jan, and Wu Tung. *Unearthing China's Past.* Boston, 1973.

Ho, Wai-kam, et al. *Eight Dynasties of Chinese Painting.* Cleveland, 1980.

Hucker, Charles W. *China's Imperial Past: An Introduction to Chinese History and Culture.* Stanford, 1975.

Lawton, Thomas. *Chinese Art of the Warring States Period: Change and Continuity, 480-222 B.C.* Washington, D.C., 1982.

Ledderose, Lothar. *Mi Fu and the Classical Tradition in Chinese Calligraphy.* Princeton, 1979.

Li, Xueqin. *Eastern Zhou and Qin Civilizations.* New Haven, 1985.

Li, Yu-ning. *The First Emperor of China.* White Plains, New York, 1975.

Liang, Ssu-ch'eng. *A Pictorial History of Chinese Architecture.* Cambridge, Mass., 1984.

Loehr, Max, with Louisa G. Fitzgerald Huber. *Ancient Chinese Jades from the Grenville L. Winthrop Collection in the Fogg Art Museum, Harvard University.* Cambridge, Mass., 1975.

Loewe, Michael A. N. *Chinese Ideas of Life and Death.* London, 1982.

Medley, Margaret. *The Chinese Potter: A Practical History of Chinese Ceramics.* New York, 1976.

Medley, Margaret. *T'ang Pottery and Porcelain.* London, 1981.

Mote, Frederick W. *Intellectual Foundations of China.* New York, 1971.

The Quest for Eternity: Chinese Ceramics from the People's Republic of China. Los Angeles County Museum of Art. Los Angeles, 1987.

Schafer, Edward H. *The Golden Peaches of Samarkand: A Study of T'ang Exotics.* Berkeley, 1963.

Spence, Jonathan D. *Emperor of China: Self-Portrait of K'ang-hsi.* New York, 1974.

Tsien, T. H. *Written on Bamboo and Silk: The Beginnings of Chinese Books and Writing.* Chicago, 1962.

Twitchett, Denis, and John K. Fairbank, eds. *The Cambridge History of China.* Cambridge, England, 1979.

Valenstein, Suzanne G. *A Handbook of Chinese Ceramics.* New York, 1975.

Vollmer, John. *In the Presence of the Dragon Throne: Ch'ing Dynasty Costume in the Royal Ontario Museum.* Toronto, 1977.

Wang, Zhongshu. *Han Civilization.* New Haven, 1982.

Wechsler, Howard J. *Mirror to the Son of Heaven: Wei Cheng at the Court of T'ang T'ai-tsung.* New Haven, 1974.

Wechsler, Howard J. *Offerings of Jade and Silk: Ritual and Symbol in the Legitimation of the T'ang Dynasty.* New Haven, 1985.

Weinstein, Stanley. *Buddhism under the T'ang.* Cambridge, England, 1987.

Weng, Wan-go, and Yang Boda. *The Palace Museum Peking: Treasures of the Forbidden City.* New York, 1982.

Wilson, Verity. *Chinese Dress.* London, 1986.

Yu, Zhuoyun. *Palaces of the Forbidden City.* Hong Kong, 1984.